New Perspectives on Fiscal State Aid

Legitimacy and Effectiveness of Fiscal State Aid Control

EUCOTAX Series on European Taxation

VOLUME 64

Series Editors

Prof. Dr Peter H.J. Essers, Fiscal Institute Tilburg/Center for Company Law, Tilburg University
Prof. Dr Eric C.C.M. Kemmeren, Fiscal Institute Tilburg/Center for Company Law, Tilburg University
Prof. Dr Dr h.c. Michael Lang, WU (Vienna University of Economics and Business)

Introduction

EUCOTAX (European Universities Cooperating on Taxes) is a network of tax institutes currently consisting of eleven universities: WU (Vienna University of Economics and Business) in Austria, Katholieke Universiteit Leuven in Belgium, Corvinus University of Budapest, Hungary, Université Paris-I Panthéon-Sorbonne in France, Universität Osnabrück in Germany, Libera, Università Internazionale di Studi Sociali in Rome (and Università degli Studi di Bologna for the research part), in Italy, Fiscaal Instituut Tilburg at Tilburg University in the Netherlands, Universidad de Barcelona in Spain, Uppsala University in Sweden, Queen Mary and Westfield College at the University of London in the United Kingdom, and Georgetown University in Washington DC, United States of America. The network aims at initiating and coordinating both comparative education in taxation, through the organization of activities such as winter courses and guest lectures, and comparative research in the field, by means of joint research projects, international conferences and exchange of researchers between various countries.

Contents/Subjects

The EUCOTAX series covers a wide range of topics in European tax law. For example tax treaties, EC case law, tax planning, exchange of information and VAT. The series is well-known for its high-quality research and practical solutions.

Objective

The series aims to provide insights on new developments in European taxation.

Readership

Practitioners and academics dealing with European tax law.

Frequency of Publication

2-3 new volumes published each year.

The titles published in this series are listed at the end of this volume.

New Perspectives on Fiscal State Aid

Legitimacy and Effectiveness of Fiscal State Aid Control

Edited by

Carla De Pietro

Wolters Kluwer

Published by:
Kluwer Law International B.V.
PO Box 316
2400 AH Alphen aan den Rijn
The Netherlands
E-mail: international-sales@wolterskluwer.com
Website: lrus.wolterskluwer.com

Sold and distributed in North, Central and South America by:
Wolters Kluwer Legal & Regulatory U.S.
7201 McKinney Circle
Frederick, MD 21704
United States of America
Email: customer.service@wolterskluwer.com

Sold and distributed in all other countries by:
Air Business Subscriptions
Rockwood House
Haywards Heath
West Sussex
RH16 3DH
United Kingdom
Email: international-customerservice@wolterskluwer.com

ISBN 978-94-035-1415-4

e-Book: ISBN 978-94-035-1424-6
web-PDF: ISBN 978-94-035-1425-3

Editor

Carla De Pietro works as Assistant Professor at the Fiscal Institute Tilburg of Tilburg University. Her research has mainly been developed in the field of international and EU taxation. Her articles are published in some of the leading journals in this field. She has published another book in the EUCOTAX Series, entitled "Tax Treaty Override".

Contributors

Marc Fierstra is Justice of the Supreme Court of the Netherlands. From 2000 till 2009 he was judge of the Court of Appeal for Trade and Industry. Before his appointment as judge he was head of the European law division of the Ministry of Foreign Affairs. Previously he worked as a lawyer in private practice and as legal secretary at the -at that time- Court of First Instance of the EC.

Julie Leroy obtained her Master's degree in Law at Hasselt University (Belgium) in 2016. She currently prepares a PhD thesis on the recovery of fiscal State aid in Belgium, also at Hasselt University. More generally, Julie's research interests cover State aid, European and Belgian tax law. She is part of the Law, Tax & Business Unit of CORe.

Paul-John Loewenthal is a member of the European Commission's Legal Service. He has represented the Commission as an agent in over 100 cases, predominantly in the field of fiscal State aid. He previously worked as a référendaire at the European Court of Justice and as an attorney at an international law firm. He holds degrees from Harvard Law School, Oxford University, and Leiden University.

Alexandra Miladinovic received an LLM and LLB in Business Law as well as a BSc in Business Administration, from WU (Vienna University of Economics and Business). She works as a research and teaching associate at the Institute for Austrian and International Tax Law, WU. Currently, she is writing her PhD thesis on the Arm's Length Principle in EU State aid.

Bruno Peeters is full professor at the University of Antwerp (Faculty of Law), where he is director of the Master of Tax Law and director of the Antwerp Tax Academy. He is member of the executive board of the European Association of Tax Law Professors, Assessor in the Legislative Section of the Belgian Council of State and also Lawyer.

Cees Peters works as an assistant professor at the Fiscal Institute Tilburg of Tilburg University. His research focuses on global tax governance and corporate taxation, including EU fiscal state aid control. His work received recognition with the granting of the 'Jaap van den Berge Literatuurprijs' in 2019 for its contribution to the development of tax law in the Netherlands.

Daniël Smit is a professor in taxation at the Fiscal Institute Tilburg, Tilburg University, the Netherlands. He is the author of more than 100 national and international publications in the field of European and international tax law and is a frequent speaker at seminars and conferences. Daniël Smit has also been employed at EY since 2002.

Paulina Szotek obtained a Master's degree in International and European Tax Law from UM (Maastricht University), The Netherlands. She is a PhD candidate at UM, where she is currently finalising her PhD research on the topic of Group Taxation, Transfer Pricing, and State aid. Paulina also works as a teaching associate in Transfer Pricing at the Department of Tax Law, UM. She has gained a practical experience during her work as a Senior Tax Consultant at PwC Brussels, where she contributed to a wide range of the firm's tax advisory practices in the field of Transfer Pricing and EU Competition Law.

Anne Van de Vijver is Associate Professor of Tax Law at the University of Antwerp and member of the Management Committee of Antwerp Tax Academy (interfaculty institute for tax science). Her research interests include international and European tax law, legal principles, and tax ethics. In 2015, she received the Ius Commune Prize for her publication with the title "International Double (Non)-Taxation: Comparative Guidance from European Legal Principles". Before joining academia, she was a tax lawyer for more than 15 years.

Summary of Contents

Table of Contents

CHAPTER 1

Introduction: Legitimacy and Effectiveness of Fiscal State Aid Control and the Role of National Tax Judges

Carla De Pietro

This book is the result of a project co-funded by the European Commission and developed by Tilburg University, in collaboration with the University of Antwerp, the University of Bologna and the Vienna University of Economics and Business. The project was dedicated to 'Fiscal State Aid and the Role of National Judges within the European Commission's Modernization Programme'. The core of the project consisted in four seminars, four workshops and a final conference aimed at training national tax judges from the four different countries involved in the project (Austria, Belgium, Italy and the Netherlands). These meetings (including the final conference) were, however, at the same time very important occasions of discussion and reflection on EU fiscal State aid law, also together with international academics and other tax professionals who participated as speakers and/or discussants.

Within the context of the Commission's modernization program as outlined in May 2012, sustainable growth necessarily implies the effectiveness of State aid control.[1] However, it is evident that the obtainment of this effectiveness, in addition to the improvement of the quality of the Commission's assessment,[2] also requires clear and effective powers in the hands of national (tax) judges. In fact, the role of national (tax) judges is extremely important as substantially aimed at protecting the rights of individuals under Article 108(3) of the Treaty on the Functioning of the European Union (TFEU). Thus, national (tax) judges must not only guarantee full recovery in

1. *See*, European Commission, *Communication from the Commission to the European Parliament, the Council, the European Economic and Social Committee of the Regions (EU State Aid Modernization (SAM))*, COM(2012) 209 final, 2012.
2. *Ibid.*, p. 3.

case of unlawful aid, but they must also protect rights, which are at the basis of the rule of law, like – for example – legitimate expectations. Indirectly, therefore, national (tax) judges are also required to evaluate the existence of possible (fiscal) State aid under Article 107(1) TFEU. Furthermore, national (tax) judges have relevant powers in cases in which the Commission has already ordered recovery. Thus, the central role of national (tax) judges in guaranteeing an effective State aid control is undeniable.

As a consequence, it is clear that such a central role necessarily requires a substantial autonomy of national (tax) judges and, therefore, also the existence of clear rules defining their powers.

This book aims at investing to what extent national (tax) judges enjoy such autonomy and, consequently, to what extent are they actually in the position of guaranteeing such an effective enforcement of (fiscal) State aid law at national level.

Very importantly, in the framework of this book, this analysis goes beyond the examination of the powers formally granted to national (tax) judges (indeed, also in light of the interpretative positions taken by the Court of Justice). In fact, an effective enforcement of (fiscal) State aid law necessarily requires clarity on the legitimacy of (fiscal) State aid control. Most importantly, different conceptions in terms of legitimacy of (fiscal) State aid control imply the application of a broader or narrower notion of (fiscal) State aid under Article 107(1) TFEU. National (tax) judges can autonomously guarantee an effective enforcement only to the extent that the scope of the applicable notion of (fiscal) State aid is clear in advance.

At the same time, an effective enforcement of (fiscal) State aid law has the consequence of shaping the Internal Market. In fact, the application of a broader or narrower notion of (fiscal) State aid implies – indeed – a different functioning of the Internal Market. Therefore, the acknowledged concept of legitimacy of (fiscal) State aid control determines a certain functioning of the Internal Market.

The very innovative approach of this book, therefore, consists in developing an analysis that defines the connection between an effective State aid control, its legitimacy and a desirable functioning of the Internal Market.

For this reason, Chapter 2 contains an analysis of the (empirical) legitimacy of State aid control. It connects dominant legal theories about the notion of (fiscal) State aid with a political science perspective on output legitimacy and the legitimation of (fiscal) State aid control. This chapter distinguishes three different 'legitimation narratives' that relate (fiscal) State aid control to specific normative conceptions of the goals and functions of (fiscal) State aid control. Thus, with the help of these 'legitimation narratives' this chapter attempts to connect the intense legal discussion about the interpretation of the notion of (fiscal) State aid with different normative views about the goals and functions of (fiscal) State aid control. In this way, it relates the discussion about the notion of (fiscal) State aid under Article 107(1) TFEU to the (empirical) legitimacy of (fiscal) State aid control.

The analysis on the empirical legitimacy of State aid control is, consequently, connected with the concrete application of State aid law. Chapter 3, in a legal perspective, focuses on the notion of (fiscal) State aid – and mainly on the concept of selectivity – as applied in the case law of the Court of Justice. Through this chapter it will become apparent to what extent the three different State aid 'legitimation narratives' underlying the three different approaches on the legitimacy of State aid control outlined in Chapter 2 are actually reflected in the interpretative solutions offered by the Court of Justice.

Very significantly, Chapter 4 further investigates the notion of (fiscal) State aid by focusing on the most recent decisions of the European Commission concerning mismatches.

With the aim of further clarifying the scope of (fiscal) State aid law, Chapter 5 has the important function of analysing the relationship between (fiscal) State aid law and anti-tax avoidance measures. More specifically, this chapter investigates whether and to what extent (fiscal) State aid law limits EU Member States in designing anti-tax avoidance measures.

In light of the analysis underlying the first part of the book, which aims at evaluating the current status of implementation of (fiscal) State aid law and its legitimacy, the subsequent chapters verify to what extent national judges can guarantee an effective State aid control. Thus, Chapter 6 analyses to what extent the powers of national judges can be considered effective when the protection of legitimate expectations is at issue. Chapter 7 evaluates to what extent national judges are required to apply State aid rules *ex officio*. Chapter 8 outlines the powers of national judges in connection with the national obligation of guaranteeing an immediate and effective recovery on the basis of an order issued by the European Commission. Chapters 9 and 10 discuss specific pieces of legislation aimed at guaranteeing an immediate and effective recovery (in Belgium, the legislation specifically concerning the excess profit ruling regime and, in the Netherlands, the new State aid Recovery Act).

Do the powers of national (tax) judges guarantee an effective (fiscal) State aid control at national level? What is the connection between legitimacy of (fiscal) State aid law and the effectiveness of (fiscal) State aid control? To what extent are legitimacy and effectiveness functional to a certain conception of Internal Market? These are the questions dealt with in Chapter 11, where conclusive remarks are addressed.

It is in this perspective that this book connects the legitimacy of (fiscal) State aid control with the functioning of the Internal Market. As it is well known, the constitutional framework of the EU has essentially an economic character. Indeed, a broad application of (fiscal) State aid law, and mainly of the notion of (fiscal) State aid, limits the possibilities of applying non-market values within the Internal Market. However, also in light of the very deep social and political crisis that the EU has been enduring in these years, this author wonders whether the solution on the legitimacy of (fiscal) State aid control should not be built on the strengthening of non-market values within the Internal Market.

This book, therefore, represents an important and concrete contribution that analyses the dynamics characterizing (fiscal) State aid control. It emphasises the inter-dependence between the EU and the national level of application of (fiscal) State aid law in order to guarantee the effectiveness of the control. As a consequence, the book aims at stimulating solutions in terms of legitimacy of (fiscal) State aid control that also take into consideration the most desirable functioning of the Internal Market.

CHAPTER 2

The Legitimacy of EU Fiscal State Aid Control: What Is Your Legitimation Narrative?

Cees Peters

§2.01 INTRODUCTION

Any specialist of European Union (EU) state aid law would probably confirm that the application of the criteria of Article 107 of the Treaty on the Functioning of the European Union (TFEU) to the domain of direct taxation is notoriously difficult.[1] The interpretation of the legal notion of fiscal state aid is actually surrounded by many uncertainties. Especially the broad notion of material selectivity has already taken a lot of mental hassle of both advocate-generals[2] and legal scholars.[3] Merola writes about this "rebus of selectivity" and claims convincingly that there is currently no "comprehensive theoretical framework, such as to enable the Commission and the Court of Justice to solve specific cases by applying commonly accepted general principles."[4] Without a doubt this lack of a comprehensive theoretical framework also affects

1. There is obviously a substantial amount of literature about this topic. *See, e.g.*, W. Schön, Tax legislation and the notion of fiscal aid: A review of 5 years of European jurisprudence, in *State aid law and business taxation* 3, 3-26 (I. Richelle, W. Schön, and E. Traversa eds., Berlin and Heidelberg: Springer Verlag 2016) and R. Szudoczky, Selectivity, derogation, comparison: How to put together the pieces of the puzzle in the state aid review of national tax measures?, in *EU income tax law: Issues for the years ahead*, 163-196 (D. Weber ed., IBFD, Amsterdam, 2013).
2. Compare, e.g., Conclusion of A-G Wahl in case *Dirk Andres v. European Commission* (C-203/16, EU:C:2017:1017).
3. *See, e.g.*, C. Micheau, *Tax selectivity in European law of state aid: Legal assessment and alternative approaches*, 40(3) European Law Review 323-348 (2015).
4. M. Merola, *The rebus of selectivity in fiscal aid: A nonconformist view on and beyond case law*, 39(4) World Competition 539 (2016). Also compare H. López López, *General though on selectivity and consequences of a broad concept of state aid in tax matters*, 9(4) Eur. St. Aid L.Q. 807 (2010).

national tax judges who are equally part of the institutional framework of EU fiscal state aid control. For good reason, A-G Saugmandsgaard mentions explicitly that it is not opportune to saddle national tax judges with a complex and uncertain analysis of fiscal state aid.[5]

These kinds of difficulties with the definition of the notion of fiscal state aid coincide with the concerns about the legitimacy of EU fiscal state aid control. This sense of worry became an issue when the European Commission started to test seriously the limits of the autonomy of the Member States in the area of direct taxation. Nanetti and Mamelli, for example, criticized the "creeping normative role" of the European Commission.[6] They even questioned the authority of this watchdog to monitor such tax measures when they made reference to a "democratic deficit" in the European institutional framework.[7] Also the present-day developments concerning the tax ruling practices of some Member States bring about such sentiments. Almost twenty years later there are, after all, again the allegations of some legal scholars that the initiatives of the European Commission constitute a form of "stealthy tax harmonization."[8] Such concerns are actually fueled by the statements of Margrethe Vestager, the responsible European Commissioner, who claims that "she is doing this because the people are angry."[9] In this way, she directly relates the investigations into the tax ruling practices to the debate in society about the taxation of multinational companies.

The starting point of this chapter is that both described problems are intrinsically related. They constitute, as it were, the legal and the political side of the same coin. Both of them have their origin in the absence of agreement about the goals and functions of EU fiscal state aid control. There are simply different normative views about the very essence of EU fiscal state aid control.[10] It is argued that a better

5. Conclusion of A-G Saugmandsgaard in case *Finanzamt B v. A-Brauerei* (C-374/17, EU:C:2018:741).
6. F. Nanetti and G. Mameli, *The creeping normative role of the EC Commission in the twin-track struggle against State aids and harmful tax competition*, 11(4) EC Tax Review 185–191 (2002).
7. Nanetti and Mamelli, *supra* n. 6, 191. *See also* A. Fantozzi, The applicability of state aid rules to tax competition measures: a process of "de facto" harmonization in the tax field?, in *Tax competition in Europe* 121, 131 (W. Schön ed., Amsterdam: IBFD Publications BV 2003).
8. Compare, e.g., D. Kyriazis, *From soft law to soft law through hard law: The Commission's approach to the state aid assessment of tax rulings*, 15(3) Eur. St. Aid L.Q. 436 (2016).
9. https://www.theguardian.com/world/2017/sep/17/margrethe-vestager-people-feel-angry-about-tax-avoidance-european-competition-commissioner (last visited Apr. 15, 2019).
10. This debate centers *grosso modo* on: (a) the (political) economic rationales for state aid control in general, and (b) on the question whether EU state aid control constitutes a part of EU competition law or of EU internal market law.

    A good overview of the first discussion can be found in D. Spector, The economic analysis of state aid control, in *Economic analysis of state aid rules – Contributions and limits* 7–27 (M. Merola and J. Derenne eds., Berlin: Lexicon 2007); H. Hofmann, State aid review in a multi-level system: Motivations for aid, why control it, and the evolution of state aid law in the EU, in *State aid law of the European Union* 3–11 (H. Hofmann and C. Micheau eds., Oxford: Oxford University Press 2016); V. Verouden and P. Werner, Introduction – The Law and Economics of EU State Aid Control, in *EU state aid control. Law and economics* 7–62 (P. Werner and V. Verouden eds., B.V., Alphen aan den Rijn: Wolters Kluwer International, 2017).

    A useful overview of the second debate can be found in F. De Cecco, *State aid and the European economic constitution* 31–55 (Oxford and Portland: Hart Publishing 2013) and C. Micheau, *State aid, subsidy, and tax incentives under EU and WTO law*, 38–40 (Alphen Aan Den Rijn: Kluwer Law International 2014).

understanding of these different positions will spell out in an innovative way the difficulties with the notion of fiscal state aid and the concerns about the legitimacy of EU fiscal state aid control. In other words, the intense discussions about the legitimacy of the tax rulings initiatives of the European Commission are actually an indication that there are, to use the words of Beetham, "disagreements about whether the law itself is justifiable."[11]

It is therefore the purpose of this chapter to analyze both related problems on the basis of three competing normative visions of EU fiscal state aid control. Inspiration for these analytical views is found in the contribution of Kleiner who distinguished three "Ideal typen" to analyze the modernization of state aid policy (in general).[12] This chapter builds on the shoulders of his models and attempts to relate these to the current debate about the goals and functions of EU *fiscal* state aid control.[13] In this way, the chapter fits in with the debate in legal scholarship about the strengths and weaknesses of both the benchmark test and the discrimination.[14]

The three different visions effectively differ with regard to the impact of EU fiscal state aid control on the autonomy of the Member States. The chapter characterizes these three competing models on the basis of the *legitimation narrative* that drives the decision-making processes concerning the determination of fiscal state aid in these models. The tax expenditure narrative is a truly technocratic narrative that can be related to a model of EU fiscal state aid control which attempts to safeguard the autonomy of the Member States to the greatest possible extent. It counts on the premise that independent experts are able to "measure" the existence of fiscal state aid with scientific objectivity. The discrimination narrative is a truly legal narrative that can be related to a model which explicitly attaches value to the further completion of the internal market. It is based on the assumption that legal, rather formalistic, concepts are able to identify fiscal state aids in an objective way. The democracy narrative constitutes a truly political narrative that explicitly attempts to realize deeper integration between the economies of the Member States.

The research question of this chapter is therefore what the analytical establishment of three competing models of EU fiscal state aid control—as characterized by three legitimation narratives—is able to make clear about the problems with the legal definition of fiscal state aid and to what extent this analytical distinction is able to explain the "creeping normative" role of the European Commission in matters of fiscal state aid control.[15] In order to deal with these related issues this chapter makes use of

---

11. D. Beetham, *The legitimation of power. 2nd edition*, 4 (Basingstoke: Palgrave Macmillan 2013).
12. T. Kleiner, Modernization of State aid policy, in *Research handbook on European State aid law* 1-27 (E. Szyszczak ed., Cheltenham: Edward Elgar Publishing Limited, 2011). Kleiner named the models the "competition model," the "derogatory model" and the "political integration" model.
13. At the outset it should be clear that these three models do not perfectly capture the nuanced case law of the CJEU about the notion of fiscal state aid. These are real models that are used for heuristic purposes in order to illustrate the weaknesses of the various legitimation narratives. In practice, the CJEU seems to be applying a mix of the various legitimation narratives.
14. *See* ss. 3 and 4.
15. It should be made clear at the outset that it is not the objective of this chapter to find the "best" legitimation narrative for EU fiscal state aid control. Such an analysis would require an analysis

a governance perspective that has its origin in the work of political scientists. It is argued that this research methodology is a useful way to establish a connection between EU fiscal state aid *law* and EU fiscal state aid *policy*. The starting point is that the legitimacy of EU fiscal state aid control substantially depends on the "output" that it is establishing, but that there is no normative agreement about what this output is supposed to be. Consequently, the European Commission constantly needs to legitimize its initiatives in the domain of EU fiscal state aid control and for these purposes it is counting on these legitimation narratives. It is however questionable whether these legitimation narratives are able to guarantee a truly objective—i.e., more or less mechanical—assessment of fiscal state aids.

The structure of this chapter is as follows. Section 2 outlines the governance perspective that should explain the underlying "mechanics" of the legitimation of EU fiscal state aid control. It makes clear how the dynamics between "process" and "performance" are decisive for the legitimacy of EU fiscal state aid control and it introduces the three legitimation narratives. Section 3 gives an overview of the tax expenditure narrative and the related model of EU fiscal state aid control. Moreover, it outlines the difficulties of this narrative to determine the existence of fiscal state aid in an objective way. Section 4 does the same for the discrimination narrative and that particular vision of EU fiscal state aid control. On the basis of these analyses, section 5 outlines the rise of the democracy narrative and the related model of EU fiscal state aid control. This should also make clear for what reason the European Commission is able to take a creeping normative role. Section 6 concludes the chapter with some observations about the future.

§2.02 THE LEGITIMATION OF EU FISCAL STATE AID CONTROL: OUTLINE OF THE GOVERNANCE PERSPECTIVE

[A] Sources of Empirical Legitimacy

The necessity to unravel the underlying political causes for the problems with EU fiscal state aid control requires an understanding of the so-called "sources of empirical legitimacy" of EU fiscal state aid control.[16] At this point, it is useful to start with the writings of Scharpf who distinguished "input legitimacy" from "output legitimacy" in

of the desirable functions and objectives of the institution of EU fiscal state aid control within the political and legal order of the EU. Consequently, it would be necessary to derive normative criteria from political or legal philosophy to evaluate the normative legitimacy of this institution as such. Such a research would connect to the growing body of academic scholarship about the legitimacy of global tax governance. *See, e.g.*, C. Peters, *On the legitimacy of international tax law* (Amsterdam: IBFD 2014) and T. Dagan, *International tax policy. Between competition and cooperation* (Cambridge: Cambridge University Press 2018).

16. This particular term is derived from Zürn. *See* M. Zürn, *A theory of global governance: Authority, legitimacy, and contestation*, 67–70 (Oxford: Oxford University Press 2018). Also the term "institutional sources of legitimacy" is being used in this regard. *See* L. Dellmuth, J. Scholte, and J. Tallberg, *Institutional sources of legitimacy for international organizations: Beyond procedure versus performance*, Review of International Studies 1–20 (2019), doi:10.1017/S026021051900007X.

order to justify the authority of the European Union to be "governing in Europe."[17] He explained the difference between both in an exemplifying way when he characterized input legitimacy as "government by the people" and output legitimacy as "government for the people."[18] Consequently, the input legitimacy of a political institution is critically dependent on the "authentic preferences" of the citizens.[19] The output legitimacy of institutions, on the other hand, is guaranteed when "they effectively promote the common welfare of the constituency in question."[20] Scharpf forcefully argues that the institutions of the European Union should focus on "government for the people," since democratic decision-making processes (i.e., the input factors) fail to realize solutions that are in the long-term interest of the economy and/or society.[21] In his view, such effective problem-solving capacity, as he calls it, is directly related to the need to counter the undesirable effects of economic integration on the possibilities for Member States themselves to maintain their national welfare systems.[22]

Scharpf developed these two notions in order to provide *normative* reasons that should justify the governance activities of the European Union (as a political order). The concepts are therefore in the first place concerned with the *normative* legitimacy of the European Union. They are prescriptive in the sense that, as Steffek explains, "social science should tell us under which conditions governance deserves the predicate legitimate."[23] As explained at the outset, it is not the purpose of this chapter to engage in a debate about the normative legitimacy of EU fiscal state aid control. The emphasis on this chapter is on the *empirical* legitimacy of EU fiscal state aid control instead. Empirical legitimacy, as applied by political scientists, basically implies that "the subjects of the norm or institutional arrangement believe that norm or arrangement to be legitimate."[24] This requires a more descriptive rather prescriptive approach in the sense that, in the words of Steffek, "social science should tell us why the subjects to that governance accept and support it in reality."[25]

This emphasis on the empirical perspective implies a concern with the so-called sources of empirical legitimacy. On what grounds does the European Commission *factually* deserve the recognition from the EU Member States and EU citizens that it has the authority to perform EU fiscal state aid control? In order to analyze these empirical

17. *See, e.g.*, F. Scharpf, *Governing in Europe: Effective and democratic?* (Oxford: Oxford University Press, 1999).
18. *Ibid*, p. 6.
19. *Ibid*, p. 6.
20. *Ibid*, p. 6.
21. *See* B. Netelenbos, *Political legitimacy beyond Weber: An analytical framework*, 82–83 (London: Palgrave Macmillan, 2016).
22. *See, e.g.*, F. Scharpf, *Economic integration, democracy and the welfare state*, 4(1) Journal of European Public Policy 18–36 (1997) and the collection of contributions in F. Scharpf, *Community and autonomy: Institutions, policies, and legitimacy in multilevel Europe* (Frankfurt/New York: Campus Verlag, 2010).
23. J. Steffek, *The legitimation of international governance: A discourse approach*, 9(2) European Journal of International Relations 253 (2003).
24. L. Meyer and P. Sanklecha, Introduction: Legitimacy, justice and public international law. Three perspectives on the debate, in *Legitimacy, justice and public international law* 2 (L. Meyer ed., Cambridge: Cambridge University Press, 2009).
25. Steffek, *supra* n. 23, p. 253.

sources of legitimacy, political scientists build on the shoulders of the above distinction of Scharpf. Consequently, they hold that both "process" and "performance" may serve as such sources of empirical legitimacy.[26] These two concepts illustrate that an international organization, like the European Commission, may obtain empirical legitimacy from, in the words of Dellmuth, Scholte and Tallberg, "the way the institution functions, irrespective of the effects of its policies" (i.e., process) and / or "from its consequences, irrespective of how the institution formulated and executed the relevant policy" (i.e., performance).[27]

These considerations actually lead to a crucial ascertainment about the complex relationship between the empirical and the normative legitimacy of EU fiscal state aid control. At the normative level, it is clear that the legitimacy of EU fiscal state aid control should be assessed in the light of its ability to serve, in the words of Scharpf, the "common welfare" or, pace Zürn, the "shared social purpose" of the Member States and the EU citizens in an effective way.[28] The European Commission is not supposed to derive its right to exercise its authority from the democratic "input" processes of the Member States and the EU citizenry, but from the "output" performances that it is establishing on the basis of its expert knowledge. It is therefore a form of governance with clearly technocratic characteristics.[29]

Consequently, at the empirical level, the legitimacy of EU fiscal state aid control (i.e., the mere factual acceptance) depends on the ability of the European Commission—in close cooperation with the national judges—to deliver the shared social purpose that it is supposed to deliver. This *performance* can however not be assessed in isolation from the *process* of EU fiscal state aid control. The empirical legitimacy of the actions of the European Commission does not only depend on the question whether it is actually doing what it is supposed to be doing. It is equally important in this regard that it establishes this result in accordance with the relevant processes. Several procedural characteristics are important in this regard. A lawyer would confirm that adherence to the procedural rules of Article 108 TFEU contributes to the empirical legitimacy of EU fiscal state aid control. Moreover, it is fair to argue, as a political scientist would add, that another process feature is decisive in this context. This concerns the independence and the impartiality of the European Commission as the guardian of EU fiscal state aid control.[30] The allegations that the European

26. Zürn, *supra* n. 16, pp. 69-70.
27. Dellmuth, Scholte, and Tallberg, *supra* n. 16, p. 2.
28. Scharpf, *supra* n. 17, p. 6 and Zürn, *supra* n. 16, p. 67.
29. Given the scope of this contribution no attention is paid to the *normative* desirability of this form of governance. There is obviously no lack of criticism in academic literature. *See, e.g.*, J. Habermas, *The lure of technocracy* (Cambridge: Polity Press, 2015).
30. The relevance of these process features is for example very clear in the writings of Majone who is another member of the "output legitimacy school." *See*, amongst others, G. Majone, Regulatory legitimacy, in Regulating Europe 284-301 (G. Majone ed., London and New York: Routledge, 1996) and G. Majone, *Europe's "democratic deficit": The question of standards*, 4(1) European Law Journal 5-28 (1998).

Commission is selectively targeting some well-liked (American?) companies is therefore damaging the credibility of EU fiscal state aid control on the longer run.[31]

Notwithstanding the relevance of these considerations the focus of this chapter is on another element of the complex puzzle concerning the legitimacy of EU fiscal state aid control. This concerns the possibility for the European Commission and the national judges to perform the *substantive* state aid analysis (i.e., concerning the notion of fiscal state aid) in an objective—let's call it mechanical—way. Such a "legal-rational" process-based source of empirical legitimacy would imply that "governance is regarded as appropriate because properly appointed authorities follow properly formulated decision-taking processes."[32] This would seem to be an important requirement of a technocratic form of governance like EU fiscal state aid control. It basically implies that the "executives" of EU fiscal state aid control realize the objectives of this institution in an objective way. It is exactly this path that relates the discussion about the definition of fiscal state aid to the empirical legitimacy of EU fiscal state aid control. The sections 3 and 4 will therefore analyze whether and to what extent the tax expenditure narrative and the discrimination narrative are actually based on such a more or less mechanical decision-making process. In order to perform this assessment, it should however first of all be explained what is actually meant with such "legitimation narratives." This is the subject of the next two sub-sections.

[B] Legitimation of EU Fiscal State Aid Control in the Absence of Normative Consensus

The tax ruling initiatives of the European Commission are clearly illustrating that the discussions about the scope of EU fiscal state aid control cannot be seen in isolation from the political and societal sentiments about the taxation of multinational companies. An important claim of this chapter is that the European Commission is currently playing a crucial role as the "mediator" between the legal realm and the political and societal setting in this regard.[33] Consequently, it is argued that the European Commission is reverting to so-called "legitimation narratives" in order to ensure that both the Member States and the EU citizens are actually of the opinion that it has the rightful authority to perform EU fiscal state aid control.

The core of this argument is that there is a concise relationship between the legitimation efforts of the institutions of global governance and their empirical legitimacy.[34] Political scientists recognize that there is a causal relationship between the

31. Compare the views of Gunn and Vleggeert in this article in the Dutch newspaper Trouw following the decision of the European Commission to open an in-depth investigation into the tax treatment of Nike in the Netherlands. *See* https://www.trouw.nl/home/is-nike-de-zondebok-~a95a4f3e/ (last visited Apr. 15, 2019).
32. Dellmuth, Scholte, and Tallberg, *supra* n. 16, p. 17.
33. It is outside the scope of this chapter to analyze whether this is actually a desirable state of affairs. That is the subject for another study.
34. There is an increasing body of academic scholarship about this topic. Compare, e.g., Zürn, *supra* n. 16, J. Gronau and H. Schmidtke, *The quest for legitimacy in world politics – international institutions' legitimation strategies*, 42(3) Review of International Studies 535–557 (2016) and J.

mere fact that citizens actually believe that an institution of global governance has the legitimate authority to rule (i.e., empirical legitimacy) and the process that "actors *deliberately* seek to make a political institution more legitimate, by boosting beliefs that its rule is exercised appropriately" (i.e., legitimation).[35] The recognition that there is a *causal* relationship between such purposeful legitimation efforts and the empirical legitimacy of an institution of global governance is based on the assumption that this legitimacy is, in the words of Beetham, a "social construction."[36] This means that the confidence of citizens in an institution (i.e., the empirical legitimacy of the institution) is embedded in social norms and is constantly subject to change as "the result of an *interactive* political process between rulers and subjects."[37] An institution of global governance therefore needs to take for granted that the legitimacy of its authority will be challenged by its "subjects" (i.e., delegitimation processes), whereas it also has to accept that it has to take action to ensure that the "subjects" continue to support its legitimacy (i.e., legitimation processes).[38] For these reasons it is actually understandable why such institutions are "taking an increasing interest in the management of their legitimacy."[39]

Under these conditions, it is very likely that the European Commission reverts to "legitimation narratives" in order to ensure that both the Member States and the EU citizens acknowledge its authority to perform EU fiscal state aid control. Following the description of Zürn it is possible to define a legitimation narrative as a deliberate effort of an institution—like the European Commission—to convince its "constituents" that it is pursuing a shared social purpose that deserves their recognition.[40] In this way, such a narrative actually "binds the authority" of this institution to the shared "social purpose" that it is claiming to pursue in an impartial way.[41] Zürn recognizes several legitimation narratives that may be used by institutions of global governance, such as the participatory narrative, the legal narrative, the fairness narrative, the technocratic narrative, and the relative gains narrative.[42]

In order to explain this perspective it is useful to revert to the described efforts of the European Commission to legitimize its inquiries into tax rulings. As explained in the introduction, Vestager famously claimed that "she is doing this because the people are angry." This assertion is part of a legitimation narrative that directly relates the authority of the European Commission to the taxation of multinational companies in the EU. In this way, this legitimation effort clearly aligns with the current process of politicization of global tax governance and the efforts of the EU to become a dominant

Tallberg and M. Zürn, *The legitimacy and legitimation of international organizations: Introduction and framework*, The Review of International Organizations, https://doi.org/10.1007/s11558-018-9330-7. Further references can be found in these contributions.

35. *See* Tallberg and Zürn, *supra* n. 34, p. 5. *Italics* added.
36. Beetham, *supra* n. 11, chapter 4 and p. 104 in particular.
37. Gronau and Schmidtke, *supra* n. 34, p. 539. *Italics* in the original.
38. Zürn, *supra* n. 16.
39. Gronau and Schmidtke, *supra* n. 34, p. 536.
40. Zürn, *supra* n. 16, p. 70.
41. Zürn, *supra* n. 16, p. 70.
42. Zürn, *supra* n. 16, pp. 72–77.

norm-setter in this regard.[43] It seems appropriate to describe this legitimation effort as the "democracy narrative," since the European Commission is making use of democratic arguments to build its story. In the Financial Times it was for example written how Vestager relates the investigations into the tax practices of Apple to the technology companies that are "undermining democracy."[44] This democracy narrative of the European Commission also includes fairness-related arguments to complete the plot. In the press release concerning the Fiat and Starbucks investigations, Verstager asserts for example how "(a)ll companies, big or small, multinational or not, should pay their fair share of tax."[45]

There is a convincing argument to be made that this democracy narrative amounts to a somewhat calculating form of marketing which is merely focused on the mere consolidation and expansion of authority. Of course there is no need to be naive about the intentions of the European Commission. International organizations (including the European Commission) are increasingly attentive to public opinion and are actually very skilled at "selling" its policies to the public through centralized communication initiatives.[46] It would however be somewhat premature to pigeonhole this democracy narrative straightaway as a merely Machiavellian effort to "manipulate" the legitimacy beliefs of the Member States and the EU citizenry.

The sense of bewilderment about the tax ruling initiatives of the European Commission should in the first place be related to a lack of normative agreement about the functions and goals of EU fiscal state aid control. Theorists of the output-driven "school" of legitimacy take for granted that there is a "normative consensus" about the "shared social purpose" that an institution is supposed to perform. Scharpf agrees with Majone in this regard and writes how this kind of legitimacy "presupposes a normative consensus on the validity of certain norms, or the desirability of certain outcomes."[47] It does seem impossible though to find consensus about the "normative consensus" of EU (fiscal) state aid control. There are indeed legal scholars who take for granted that the Member States were in agreement about the fact that Article 107 TFEU was explicitly not concerned with the elimination of harmful tax competition between the Member States.[48] Such a static interpretation does however appear to be at odds with

43. R. Christensen, The Rise of the EU in International Tax Policy, in *Global networks and European actors: Navigating and managing complexity* (G. Christou and J. Hasselbalch eds., Routledge, 2019, forthcoming).
44. https://www.ft.com/content/917bc018-c34a-11e7-b2bb-322b2cb39656#myft:saved-articles:page (last visited Apr. 15, 2019).
45. http://europa.eu/rapid/press-release_IP-15-5880_en.htm (last visited Apr. 15, 2019).
46. M. Ecker-Ehrhardt, *Self-legitimation in the face of politicization: Why international organizations centralized public communication*, 13(4) The Review of International Organizations, 519–546 (2018).
47. Scharpf, *supra* n. 22, p. 21.
48. *See* F. Vanistendael, *Fiscal support measures and harmful tax competition*, 9(3) EC Tax Review 156 (2000); E. Traversa and A. Flamini, *Fighting harmful tax competition through EU state aid law: Will the hardening of soft law suffice?*, 14(3) Eur. St. Aid L.Q. 323–331 (2015); and E. Forrester, *Is the state aid regime a suitable instrument to be used in the fight against harmful tax competition?*, 27(1) EC Tax Review 30–31 (2018).

the dynamic development of EU (fiscal) state aid control throughout the years.[49] It is, in other words, difficult to reconcile this presumed normative consensus with the continuous political battle between the Member States and the European Commission about the terms of the incomplete contract concerning EU (fiscal) state aid control.[50]

It is therefore more likely to agree with the view of Zürn who convincingly argues that the mere (ex ante) granting of a certain *authority* to an international institution does in no way imply that the (ex post) social acceptance of the exercise of this authority can be taken for granted until the end of time.[51] Consequently, it is tempting to agree with Kleiner who writes how "(t)he acceptance of State aid control will continue to depend on the ability of the Commission to legitimize its action, by demonstrating its value-added in an increasingly complex and diverse Europe."[52]

[C] Legitimation Narratives and Three Different Models of EU Fiscal State Aid Control

At this point it is possible to establish the connection between EU fiscal state aid *law* and EU fiscal state aid *policy*.[53] The thesis is that legitimation narratives of the EC play an important role on the interface of the politics and law of EU fiscal state aid control. The European Commission will revert to such narratives to convince the Member States and the EU citizenry that its new *policy initiatives* deserve their recognition. Also the already discussed democracy narrative should be seen against the background of this authority to develop state aid policy. At the same time, the European Commission—and the national courts—rely heavily on legitimation narratives to continue to legitimize its authority to *control* fiscal state aids. It counts on appropriate legitimation narratives to perform the substantive state aid analysis in an objective (more or less mechanical) way. In this regard it is completely dependent on the coherence and the consistence of the notion of fiscal state aid that has been developed in the case law of the Court of Justice of the European Union (CJEU).

The next sections distinguish the *tax expenditure* narrative, the *discrimination* narrative and the *democracy* narrative to establish the connections between EU fiscal state aid law and EU fiscal state aid policy. These narratives represent three paradigmatic competing normative visions of EU fiscal state aid control. The tax expenditure narrative is a truly technocratic narrative that can be related to a model of EU fiscal

49. Compare J. López, *The concept of state aid under EU law. From internal market to competition and beyond* (Oxford: Oxford University Press 2015).
50. On this incomplete contract and the "dilemma of discretion," *see* T. Doleys, *Managing the Dilemma of Discretion: The European Commission and the Development of EU State Aid Policy*, 13(1) Journal of Industry, Competition and Trade 23-38 (2013).
51. Zürn, *supra* n. 16, p. 65.
52. Kleiner, *supra* n. 12, p. 23.
53. Please note that this chapter does not analyze in greater detail the somewhat ambiguous institutional framework of EU fiscal state aid control. The European Commission has after all both the authority to merely *control* fiscal state aids and the authority to develop state aid *policy* in a rather autonomous way. Compare M. Blauberger, State aid control from a political science perspective, in *Research Handbook on European State Aid Law* 28, 33 (E. Szyszczak ed., Cheltenham: Edward Elgar Publishing Limited 2011).

state aid control which attempts to safeguard the autonomy of the Member States to the greatest possible extent. It is a typical example of technocratic governance in the sense that it is based on the premise that independent experts are able to "measure" the effects of fiscal state aids with scientific objectivity. The discrimination narrative is a truly legal narrative that can be related to a model which explicitly attaches value to the further completion of the internal market. It is a narrative that counts on legal, rather formalistic, concepts to assess fiscal state aids. Lastly, the democracy narrative is a truly political narrative that can be related to a model of EU fiscal state aid control that explicitly attempts to realize deeper integration between the economies of the Member States. This narrative is actually work in progress in the sense that it is being used by the European Commission to legitimize its current progressive interpretation of the notion of fiscal state aid. Section 5 will deal with this narrative in greater depth.

Sections 3 and 4 will however first of all outline the tax expenditure narrative and the discrimination narrative in greater detail and assess them in order to acquire a better understanding of continuous uncertainty about the notion of fiscal state aid and the related legitimacy concerns about EU fiscal state aid control. This assessment is based on the analysis of the empirical sources of legitimacy in the preceding sub-sections. The relevant yardstick is therefore that when there are different views on the *performance* of EU fiscal state aid control, only an objective—i.e., more or less mechanical—*process* of establishing fiscal state aids would be able to guarantee a sufficiently consistent and coherent notion of fiscal state aid. The analysis in the next sections will illustrate that such an objective process is actually not available which proves to be the core of the described problems of EU fiscal state aid control.

§2.03 THE TAX EXPENDITURE NARRATIVE AND ITS DISCONTENTS

[A] The Tax Expenditure Narrative

The tax expenditure narrative constitutes the legitimation narrative in the first (paradigmatic) model of EU fiscal state aid control.[54] It is a narrative that attempts to relate the authority of the European Commission to a model which attempts to safeguard the autonomy of the Member States to the greatest possible extent. The tax expenditure narrative is a typical example of technocratic governance in the sense that it is based on the premise that independent experts are able to "measure" the effects of fiscal state aids with scientific objectivity. It is a view that counts heavily on the role of scientific knowledge to strengthen the empirical legitimacy of governance institutions.[55] This legitimation narrative therefore shows a strong resemblance with the view that there should be an explicit economic ascertainment that a disputed state measure has the

54. Compare Kleiner, *supra* n. 12, pp. 3–4.
55. Compare S. Ashenden, Legality, legitimacy, and the circumstances of sociology, in *Legality and Legitimacy: Normative and Sociological Approaches* (C. Thornhill and S. Ashenden eds., Baden-Baden: Nomos, 2010).

effect of distorting trade and competition in the particular case at hand.[56] Consequently, it is a narrative that explicitly relates EU fiscal state aid control to competition law.[57]

This technocratic basis can be traced straight back to the academic origins of the tax expenditure concept. It is a notion that has taken root in a period of sheer optimism about the possibilities to develop a "science of public policy."[58] Stanley Surrey developed the notion with a view to obtain more insight in the pattern of expenditures of a government.[59] Burton and Sadiq compellingly write in this regard how "Surrey hoped that his rational approach to tax expenditure management would dispel subjective judgements from the realm of tax policy."[60] The technocratic idea was therefore that tax experts would be able to keep in check democratically enacted tax laws on the basis of an academic consensus about the principles of tax policy.[61]

Tax expenditures may be defined as those provisions of the taxing system "whose function and effect are to implement government spending programs."[62] These tax expenditures can (theoretically at least) be distinguished from "those provisions necessary to implement the normative tax structure" which would equal the benchmark tax system.[63] It is the promise of the academic ascertainment of a benchmark tax system that explains why it is actually rather sensical that this tax expenditure concept developed into a promising legitimation narrative for EU fiscal state aid control. Such a benchmark tax system is useful to determine the, as Schön calls it,[64] "hypothetical taxes" that would have been due if the state had *not* decided to refrain from imposing the tax.[65]

Supporters of the tax expenditure narrative claim that the concept should make it possible to assess fiscal state aids on the basis of an objective criterion. Schön stresses how, ideally, the benchmark tax system should be based on the economic foundations of the tax.[66] In this regard he takes the view that "(i)t is generally accepted amongst the Member States of the European Union that each tax shall raise revenue according to the

56. *See* Kleiner, *supra* n. 12, p. 3 and Hofmann, *supra* n. 10, p. 6. Also compare, e.g., J. da Cruz Vilaça, *Material and geographic selectivity in state aid – recent developments*, 4(8) European State Aid Law Quarterly 443-451 (2009).
57. Schön, *supra* n. 1, pp. 18–19.
58. M. Burton and K. Sadiq, Tax expenditure management. A critical assessment, Cambridge University Press, Cambridge, 2013, p. 9.
59. Compare S. Surrey, Pathways to tax reform: The concept of tax expenditures, Harvard University Press, Cambridge, Massachusetts, 1973. A critical and exhaustive overview of the development of the concept can be found in Burton and Sadiq, *supra* n. 58.
60. Burton and Sadiq, *supra* n. 58, p. 9.
61. Burton and Sadiq, *supra* n. 58, p. 9.
62. P. McDaniel and S. Surrey (eds.), International aspects of tax expenditures: a comparative study, Kluwer Law and Taxation Publishers, Deventer, 1985, p. 9.
63. McDaniel and Surrey, *supra* n. 62, p. 9.
64. W. Schön, World Trade Organization law and tax law, Bulletin for International Taxation, 2004, volume 58, p. 292.
65. Also compare Schön, *supra* n. 1, p. 4.
66. W. Schön, State aid in the area of taxation, in *EU state aids, fourth edition* (L. Hancher, T. Ottervanger, and P. Slot eds., London: Sweet & Maxwell, 2012) s. 10-022. Schön adds in s. 10-024 that this approach cannot be used in the context of regulatory taxes which have other objectives than the mere collection of tax revenues. Another issue is the determination of the "normal" tax rate. *See* s. 10-029.

taxpayers' 'ability to pay'."[67] Consequently, this ability to pay test would make it possible to identify the "structural component" of the tax.[68] This structural component, which, in his words, "is necessary to implement this fundamental structure of a tax" can be distinguished from the "tax expenditure component" that "consists of the provisions by which government spending objectives are carried out through the tax system."[69] In this view, "technical provisions," including the rules to prevent double taxation and tax avoidance, should be regarded as part of the structural component of the tax, since they constitute "the fine print of the general decision by a Member State to levy an income tax, a wealth tax and so forth."[70]

The European Commission had this legitimation narrative in mind when it started to investigate in a structural way how fiscal state aids should be distinguished from general tax measures.[71] In the "First survey on state aids" it was written for example that "tax reliefs granted to certain development areas (reduction in corporation taxes, or favourable depreciation terms) are regarded as tax expenditures, whereas the rate structure is regarded as an integral part of the benchmark tax system."[72] The European Commission found inspiration for this approach in the work of the Organisation for Economic Co-operation and Development (OECD) on tax expenditures.[73] Interestingly though, the European Commission was also carefully trying to manage expectations about the prospects of the tax expenditures concept to assess cases of fiscal state aid in a completely objective way. It took the view that there is a "grey area" to be found on "on the borderline between aid within the meaning of Article 92(1) and general measures."[74] The European Commission acknowledged that further research would be necessary in order to "elucidate this 'grey area'."[75] This grey area kind of disappeared in the 1998 Notice (on the application of the state aid rules to direct business taxation) when the European Commission made rather sharp distinctions in this regard.[76] It acknowledged in a rather firm way that "tax measures of a purely technical nature" do not constitute state aid as long as these apply without distinction to all firms.[77] With this rather Solomonian Judgment it kept "provisions to prevent double taxation or tax avoidance" basically outside the scope of EU fiscal state aid control. Arguably, this categorical exception contributed to the presumption—also in

67. Schön, *supra* n. 66, s. 10-022.
68. *See also* Szudoczky, *supra* n. 1, pp. 184–188.
69. W. Schön, *Taxation and state aid law in the European Union*, 36 Common Market Law Review 926 (1999).
70. Schön, *supra* n. 69, p. 926.
71. Commission of the European Communities, *First survey on state aids in the European Commission*, s. 72 and s. 10.5 of the Technical Annex (Luxembourg: Office for Official Publications of the European Communities, 1989).
72. *See* First Survey on state aids, *supra* n. 71, s. 10.5 of the Technical Annex.
73. *See* First Survey on state aids, *supra* n. 71, s. 10.5 of the Technical Annex. Also compare Schön, *supra* n. 69, p. 923.
74. *See* First Survey on state aids, *supra* n. 71, s. 10.5 of the Technical Annex.
75. *See* First Survey on state aids, *supra* n. 71, s. 10.5 of the Technical Annex. Also compare K. Bacon, *State aids and general measures*, 17(1) Yearbook of European Law 270–271 (1997).
76. Commission notice on the application of the State aid rules to measures relating to direct business taxation, OJ C 384, Dec. 10, 1998, pp. 3–9.
77. Para. 13 of the 1998 Commission Notice.

academic literature—that Member States were almost completely autonomous to decide about their measures of international tax policy.[78]

[B] The Limits of the Tax Expenditure Narrative

Undoubtedly, the tax expenditure narrative has substantially affected the case law of the CJEU about the interpretation of the conditions of Article 107 TFEU.[79] Traces of the concept can definitely be found in the interpretation of the advantage criterion and—to some extent—in the selectivity concept.[80] It is even tempting to take the view that the tax expenditure narrative plays a role in the criticized conflation of these two conditions of Article 107 TFEU. There should however be no doubt that these traces of the concept do not quite pass the standard of scientific objectivity that forms the basis of this technocratic legitimation narrative. In others words, the decision-making process to establish the existence of fiscal state aid in this paradigmatic model is not an objective, mechanical exercise.

The main problem is that, as also Schön acknowledges,[81] the tax expenditure concept has been a controversial notion for economists ever since its very conception.[82] One group of scholars, such as Surrey and McDaniel, takes the view that it is indeed possible to discern generally shared principles of tax policy.[83] In their view, "there exist broadly shared views as to the elements that constitute a normative income, value added or wealth tax."[84] This position, like the above position of Schön, is actually a normative stance on the basis of an idealized economic definition of income.[85] Another group of scholars opposes this normative claim and takes the (positivist) view that the normative (benchmark) tax system can only be deduced from the particular taxing system that is in place.[86]

Against this background it is probably not very surprising that in the practice of EU fiscal state aid control the factual taxing system of a Member State has become the basis for the benchmark test. This practice does however seriously damage the objective character of this legitimation narrative, since the required academic backing is simply lacking. Unsurprisingly, it is exactly such a lack of an objective norm that is

78. *See* however R. Luja, Tax treaties and state aid: Some thoughts, 44 European Taxation 234-238 (2004) and C. Panayi, Limitations on benefits and state aid, 44 European Taxation 83-98 (2004).
79. At a general level, this concerns the similarities between the tax expenditure concept and the so-called "derogation method." It is obviously out of the scope of this chapter to study in detail the precise influence of this concept on this case law. A good starting point for such a study would be: M. Aldestam, *EC state aid rules applied to taxes: An analysis of the selectivity criterion* (Uppsala: Iustus Förlag, 2005).
80. Compare, e.g., R. Luja, *Assessment and recovery of tax incentives in the EC and the WTO: A view on state aids, trade subsidies and direct taxation.* Doctoral thesis 29-30 and 53 (Maastricht: University of Maastricht 2003).
81. Schön, *supra* n. 69, p. 927.
82. Compare Burton and Sadiq, *supra* n. 58, chapter 2.
83. Compare Burton and Sadiq, *supra* n. 58, p. 150.
84. McDaniel and Surrey, *supra* n. 62, p. 5.
85. K. Goudswaard en H. Vording, De analyse van belastinguitgaven, in *Gielebundel* 232 (C. van Raad and G. Frank ed., Deventer: Kluwer, 1990).
86. Goudswaard and Vording, *supra* n. 85, p. 232.

emphasized by critics such as Lang. He stresses that the determination of the distinction between the rule and the exception to that rule has evolved into a classical "chicken or egg" problem, since it is not clear what objective criteria should be used for these purposes.[87] In his view, neither the legislative technique nor the intentions of the legislator should be conclusive.[88] His criticisms are therefore actually in line with Bacon's early conclusions that this kind of application of the derogation test constitutes merely a "descriptive" rather than "prescriptive" analysis.[89] In other words, in the absence of proper objective criteria the determination of the benchmark tax system and the derogation from that benchmark becomes a self-referential activity. This toning down substantially undermines the technocratic character of the tax expenditure narrative. It illustrates that this narrative is not based on a mechanical decision-making process to analyze the existence of fiscal state aids.

This lack of an objective scientific basis to determine the relevant benchmark is even more pressing when it comes to the identification of fiscal state aids to taxpayers that perform cross-border transactions. In such situations it becomes relevant to determine whether and to what extent (soft) norms of international tax law should be taken into consideration. It is therefore not surprising that the relevance and the interpretation of the OECD Transfer Pricing Guidelines plays such a crucial role in the pending tax rulings cases. No doubt the application of such norms creates the danger that EU fiscal state aid control transforms into an instrument to establish the gradual harmonization of taxing systems in the Member States.[90] Against this background it is therefore understandable that the use of an autonomous benchmark tax system (i.e., a benchmark that is independent from the ideas and policies of the various Member States) has generally been dismissed in academic literature.[91]

From the point of view of the technocratic background of the tax expenditure narrative, it is however problematic that there are no objective scientific arguments to dismiss the use of such an autonomous, de facto European, benchmark. Unsurprisingly, the use of such a benchmark is generally dismissed on the basis of more normative reasons that relate to the desirable allocation of competences between the Member States and the institutions of the European Union (i.e., the European Commission and the CJEU). Schön refers to "sound 'fiscal federalism'"[92] and the "unquestioned sovereignty of the states to generally decide which economic transactions shall be subject to tax."[93]

87. M. Lang, State aid and taxation: Selectivity and comparability analysis, in *State aid law and business taxation* 34 (I. Richelle, W. Schön, and E. Traversa eds., Berlin and Heidelberg: Springer, 2016).
88. Lang, *supra* n. 87, p. 34.
89. Bacon, *supra* n. 75, p. 298.
90. V.H. Guerrero, *Defining the balance between free competition and tax sovereignty in EC and WTO law: The "due respect" to the general tax system*, 5(1) German Law Journal 95 (2004).
91. Compare, e.g., Schön, *supra* n. 66, s. 10-018 and F. Engelen and A. Gunn, State aid: Towards a theoretical assessment framework, in *State aid and tax law* 140–141 (C. Micheau and A. Rust eds., Alphen aan den Rijn: Wolters Kluwer, 2013).
92. Schön, *supra* n. 69, p. 915.
93. Schön, *supra* n. 66, s. 10-018.

At this point, it becomes clear how the tax expenditure narrative is explicitly linked to a certain normative conception of EU fiscal state aid control. It is a narrative that strives to relate the authority of the European Commission to a model of EU fiscal state aid control which safeguards the autonomy of the Member States to the greatest possible extent. Kleiner explains in this regard how this particular model starts from the assumption that the granting of a state aid is not necessarily undesirable, since such a state intervention may also have positive ramifications.[94] The main economic rationale for the supervision of state aids in this paradigm is mostly the need to eliminate negative *cross-border* externalities of *state* interventions.[95] This rationale is therefore very much in line with the tax expenditure narrative that is guiding this normative vision of EU *fiscal* state aid control. The starting point of this stance is that "it is up to the Member States to determine what to tax, whom to tax, and what tax rate to set."[96] Schön writes how in this regard that the rules on EU state aid control cannot bypass the imperative of national legislators to decide whether or not to tax a certain economic event.[97]

Such normative underpinnings would not damage the credibility of a technocratic legitimation narrative in case there is normative *consensus* in society about these underpinnings. In that case, the European Commission and the national judges could act on the basis of the tax expenditure concept and brush away the imperfections of the decision-making process that is guiding this narrative. The expansive case law of the CJEU about the notion of fiscal state aid has however made clear that there is no such normative consensus. The CJEU has been striving for a more expansive model of EU fiscal state aid control. It is this model that is at the basis on the discrimination narrative that is the subject of section 4.

§2.04 THE DISCRIMINATION NARRATIVE AND ITS DISCONTENTS

[A] What Is the Discrimination Narrative?

The discrimination narrative constitutes the legitimation narrative in the second (paradigmatic) model of EU fiscal state aid control.[98] It is a narrative that relates the authority of the European Commission to a vision of EU fiscal state aid control which explicitly attaches value to the further completion of the internal market.[99] Consequently, this provision is supposed to constitute a *complement* to the various fundamental freedoms in the sense that it guarantees free and undistorted trade on the

94. Kleiner, *supra* n. 12, p. 3.
95. After all, as explained by Verouden and Werner, such "cross-border externalities will drive a wedge between national interests and the collective (EU) interest". *See* Verouden and Werner, *supra* n. 10, p. 11.
96. Aldestam, *supra* n. 79, pp. 181–182.
97. Schön, *supra* n. 1, p. 5.
98. Compare Kleiner, *supra* n. 12, pp. 2–3.
99. Kleiner, *supra* n. 12, p. 2. Buendia Sierra and Smulders write in this respect that "State aid 'DNA' shares more chromosomes with internal market rules than with antitrust rules." J.L. Buendia Sierra and B. Smulders, The limited role of the "refined economic approach" in

internal market.[100] After all, in this view, the proper functioning of the internal market would be hampered when a Member State could neutralize the removal of discriminatory trade barriers with the introduction of state aids.[101] This would hamper competition on the European internal market as a whole which is considered to be undesirable.[102]

The main characteristic of this narrative is that the assessment of a fiscal state aid is above all a legal exercise.[103] Unlike the tax expenditure narrative, this legitimation narrative does however not count on "external," social scientific (such as economic) concepts to ascertain the compatibility of a tax measure with Article 107 TFEU. It is a view that counts heavily on the role of "law" to strengthen the legitimacy of governance institutions.[104] In this view, as Biondi puts it, "the logic of the internal market principles" should be at the basis of the interpretation of Article 107 TFEU.[105] Consequently, as explained by Kleiner, this position "leads to a vision of State aid as a legal process of formal typology, categorizing some State actions as aid and designating formal areas of derogation to the general prohibition of State aid."[106] He adds how "a strict legal tradition has developed in which State aid is deemed illegal, unless certain (largely form-based) criteria are met."[107] This characterization is undoubtedly a reference to the development of the discrimination test in the case law of the CJEU.

It is exactly this preference for the discrimination narrative that unites a second school of thought about EU fiscal state aid control. This concerns the group of scholars that challenges the application of the benchmark tax system to determine the selectivity of a tax measure.[108] Lang explains in this regard how Article 107 TFEU does not constitute "a general requirement of equal treatment, but a prohibition of providing for unequal treatment that may cause distortion of competition."[109] Other scholars, such as Wattel[110] and Szudoczky,[111] point out that the case law of the CJEU about Article 107

---

achieving the objectives of state aid control: Time for some realism, in *EC State Aid Law*, 9 (Liber Amicorum Francisco Santaolalla Gadea, Alphen aan den Rijn: Kluwer Law International, 2008).

100. De Cecco, *supra* n. 10, p. 38.
101. Kleiner, *supra* n. 12, p. 2.
102. In this view, cross-border externalities are not only causing harm to other Member States, but also to the internal market in a broader sense. *See* Verouden and Werner, *supra* n. 10, pp. 12–13.
103. Hofmann, *supra* n. 10, p. 9.
104. Compare S. Ashenden, *supra* n. 55.
105. A. Biondi, *The rationale of state aid control: A return to orthodoxy*, 12 Cambridge Yearbook of European Legal Studies 42 (2010).
106. Kleiner, *supra* n. 12, p. 2.
107. Kleiner, *supra* n. 12, p. 3.
108. Compare, e.g., M. Lang, *State aid and taxation: Recent trends in the case law of the ECJ*, 11(2) European State Aid Law Quarterly 411–421 (2012) and Lang, *supra* n. 87.
109. Lang, *supra* n. 87, p. 36.
110. P. Wattel, *Forum: Interaction of state aid, free movement, policy competition and abuse control in direct tax matters*, 5(1) World Tax Journal 128–144 (2013) and P. Wattel, Comparing criteria: State aid, free movement, harmful tax competition and market distorting disparities, in *State aid law and business taxation* 59–71 (I. Richelle, W. Schön, and E. Traversa eds., Berlin and Heidelberg: Springer, 2016).
111. R. Szudoczky, *Convergence of the analysis of national tax measures under the EU state aid rules and the fundamental freedoms*, 15(3) European State Aid Law Quarterly 357–380 (2016).

TFEU is, *as a matter of fact*, more and more in line with its case law about the fundamental freedoms. This means most of all that the identification of cases of fiscal state aid is actually very similar to the Rule of Reason test that is being applied to interpret the fundamental freedoms.[112]

The use of the discrimination narrative results in a substantially broader scope of application of EU fiscal state aid control than the tax expenditure narrative. Whereas the latter narrative starts from the view that fiscal state aids may prima facie be "good," the discrimination narrative considers that state aids are "per se" distortive to the functioning of the internal market.[113] De Cecco refers in this regard to the indispensability of a "wide net" as to "safeguard the Commission's control over potentially distortive public intervention."[114] Such a strict monitoring is indispensable in order to avoid that the introduction of one particular tax measure in a single Member State has the effect that a process of harmful tax competition between the Member States is set in motion.[115] In this view, it is therefore the authority of the European Commission to monitor the adverse effects of such a tax measure on the other Member States *and* on the internal market as a whole.[116] This would also include Pistone's view that Article 107 TFEU should target the so-called "smart tax competition."[117] Consequently, the discrimination narrative, which relates the authority of the European Commission to the shared social purpose of the internal market, has the effect that the Member States have substantially less leeway to implement *competitive measures of* international tax policy on the internal market than the tax expenditure narrative would create.

[B] The Limits of the Discrimination Narrative

Whereas the tax expenditure narrative (unsuccessfully) attempts to create a truly technocratic "story" for EU fiscal state control, the discrimination narrative is explicitly based on the authority of a "self-sufficient" system of EU law and the capacity of the judiciary to interpret this system. In other words, to paraphrase Scharpf, the acceptability of the discrimination narrative builds on "legitimation beliefs that place trust in the internal control mechanisms within the legal system, and in the validation of judicial law-making through specialized discourses within the legal profession that are, it is hoped, anchored in broadly held notions of public interest and justice."[118] Characteristic for this legitimation narrative is therefore that it does not revert to objective scientific concepts that are external to the law to justify the actions of the European Commission. It starts from the presumption that there are self-contained

112. It should be added that Wattel also identifies some elementary differences between the state aid rules and the free movement rules. *See* Wattel, *supra* n. 111, p. 129.
113. Kleiner, *supra* n. 12, p. 3.
114. De Cecco, *supra* n. 10, p. 96.
115. De Cecco, *supra* n. 10, pp. 42–43.
116. De Cecco, *supra* n. 10, p. 43.
117. P. Pistone, *Smart tax competition and the geographical boundaries of taxing jurisdictions: Countering selective advantages amidst disparities*, 40(2) Intertax 85–91 (2012).
118. Scharpf, *supra* n. 17, p. 190.

(i.e., autonomous) *legal* concepts in place that make it possible to interpret the application of Article 107 TFEU in every particular case.

There is an intense discussion in legal scholarship about the question whether and to what extent this discrimination narrative constitutes an objective activity. Is it for example possible to choose the criteria to establish the comparability of two situations in an objective way?[119] And how should the trade-off be made between, on the one hand, the safeguarding of undistorted competition on the internal market and, on the other hand, the safeguarding of the national policy objectives that have found their way "into" the democratically legitimized direct tax systems of the Member States?[120] Is the legal system able to carry these burdens in an objective way or are these the kind of normative questions that should be dealt with in the political process? Unsurprisingly, Schön is therefore very critical of this approach when he writes that "(w)e should not try to transform state aid control in the field of taxation into a wide-reaching anti-discrimination prohibition streamlining national legislation."[121]

This chapter however does not analyze these arguments of the "participants" of EU law in detail, but it takes an "observer" perspective to illustrate that this discrimination narrative cannot be seen as a completely objective "story." The best way to illustrate this concern is to address the well-known distinction between negative and positive integration. Despite of the many different interpretations of the selectivity criterion, tax lawyers actually take for granted that Article 107 TFEU constitutes negative integration only.[122] This constraint is actually supposed to limit the exercise of authority of the European Commission in the sense that Article 107 TFEU is supposed to be restricted to setting limits (i.e., through prohibitions) to the autonomy of the Member States only. Consequently, Article 107 TFEU is not supposed to bring about "policy integration" (i.e., positive integration).[123]

Unfortunately though, this neat theoretical distinction cannot be squared with the broad discrimination narrative that is supposed to complete the internal market. This reality is that a broad discrimination-based interpretation of Article 107 TFEU gives rise to *both* negative *and* positive integration. This Janus-faced character of EU fiscal state aid control can be illustrated with the help of the position of Ismer and Piotrowski who conclude—on the basis of the infamous Gibraltar case[124] of the CJEU that the broad discrimination-based selectivity test requires the Member States to ensure the "external consistency" of their taxing systems.[125] Their position implies de

119. Szudoczky, *supra* n. 1, pp. 188–194 and Szudoczky, *supra* n. 111, pp. 366–370.
120. Szudoczky, *supra* n. 111, p. 370.
121. Schön, *supra* n. 1, p. 19.
122. P. Wattel, Chapter 3. General EU law concepts and tax law, in *European tax law: Volume I – General topics and direct taxation* 24 (P. Wattel, O. Marres and H. Vermeulen eds., Deventer: Wolters Kluwer, 2018).
123. P. Wattel, Introduction, in *European tax law. Volume I – General topics and direct taxation.* Student edition 4 (P.J. Wattel, O. Marres, and H. Vermeulen eds., Deventer: Wolters Kluwer, 2018). Wattel also qualifies Art. 107 TFEU as a form of negative integration.
124. It is obviously outside the scope of this chapter to analyze whether this can indeed be derived from this case.
125. *See* R. Ismer and S. Piotrowski, *The selectivity of tax measures: A tale of two consistencies*, 43(10) Intertax 559–570 (2015), R. Ismer and S. Piotrowski, *Selectivity in corporate tax matters after World Duty Free: A tale of two consistencies revisited*, 46(2) Intertax 156–166 (2018).

facto that the Member States need to adhere to certain standards of international taxation, such as the criteria laid down in the Code of Conduct.[126] Ismer and Piotrowski explicitly maintain that their position amounts to a form of negative integration.[127] One might however equally describe such minimum standards as a form of positive integration. These standards are actually a perfect example to illustrate how, in the words of De Cecco, the application of EU fiscal state aid control, "promotes the emergence of new regulatory realities, or it subjects previously unregulated areas of national concern to a common regulatory process."[128] It therefore concerns both negative *and* positive integration at the same time.[129]

This Janus-faced character of EU fiscal state aid control results in the first place from the character of EU law in general. The discrimination narrative counts on the fact that EU law does—as a matter of fact—not have quite an autonomous and neutral character.[130] Ever since the publication of the famous work of Cappelletti, Seccombe and Weiler it is generally accepted that legal integration has come to serve as an important instrument to establish further economic integration in the EU. Augenstein paraphrases Weiler in this regard and writes how, "law is both the *object* and the *agent* or *instrument* of integration: while law is a product of the polity, the polity is also to some extent the creature of the law."[131] This instrumental use of EU law therefore basically implies that "(l)aw functions as a mask for politics."[132]

Such an instrumentalist tendency is particularly imperative when the CJEU interprets the fundamental freedoms and the EU state aid provisions as broad (material) principles of non-discrimination, since such an interpretation blurs the distinction between negative and positive integration.[133] Ortino makes convincingly clear that the interpretation by the CJEU of such a broad non-discrimination test has characteristics of both negative and positive integration.[134] It has a negative *function* in the sense that it "invalidates *ipso facto* discriminatory rules," but it also has a positive function given the fact that "it provides for a normative criterion which Member States must follow in enacting new regulation."[135] Obviously, in case the CJEU would accept that there is an EU arm's length principle, it is possible to observe the same "harmonizing" effect in the sense that the Member States will need to adhere to that minimum standard.

126. Ismer and Piotrowski, *The selectivity of tax measures, supra* n. 125, p. 569.
127. Ismer and Piotrowski, *The selectivity of tax measures, supra* n. 125, pp. 569–570.
128. De Cecco, *supra* n. 10, p. 39.
129. *See* De Cecco, *supra* n. 10, pp. 5–6.
130. *See* Peters, *supra* n. 15, pp. 81–82 with further references.
131. D. Augenstein and M. Dawson, What law for what polity? "Integration through law" in the European Union revisited, in *"Integration through law" revisited. The making of the European polity* 1 (D. Augenstein, Farnham: Ashgate, 2012).
132. A.-M. Burley and W. Mattli, *Europe before the Court: A political theory of legal integration*, 47(1) International Organization 44 (1993).
133. An excellent overview of this issue and the distinction between negative and positive integration can be found in F. Ortino, *Basic legal instruments for the liberalization of trade: A comparative analysis of EC and WTO law*, 17–24 (Oxford and Portland Oregon: Hart Publishing, 2004).
134. Ortino performs an analysis of Art. 28 EC (i.e., Art. 34 TFEU), but the line of reasoning should not be fundamentally different for the interpretation of Art. 107 TFEU as a broad non-discrimination test.
135. Ortino, *supra* n. 134, p. 19.

All in all, the conclusion is that—in this paradigmatic understanding—the discrimination narrative is not a sufficiently objective exercise. The decision-making process to establish the existence of fiscal state aid in this paradigmatic model is not a sufficiently mechanical process. In close conjunction with the instrumental character of EU law, the broad discrimination-based interpretation of Article 107 TFEU does not guarantee a neutral process to establish the existence of fiscal state aids. Just like the tax expenditure narrative, the discrimination narrative is also based on the assumption of a normative consensus about the goals and functions of this model of EU fiscal state aid control. This means, in other words, that the eventual performance of the narrative is supposed to correct this weakness of the decision-making process to define fiscal state aids. There is not such a consensus though about these normative foundations. Proponents of the discrimination narrative might argue that the eventual shared social purpose (i.e., the establishment of the internal market) constitutes an objective point of reference which makes a more or less mechanical exercise possible. Such an argument should however be dismissed. Despite the definition in the TFEU, the precise meaning of the concept of an "internal market" is at best ambiguous. Will there for example be a day when the internal market is actually complete or is it actually better to evaluate the current functioning of the internal market?[136] And, most importantly, what kind of internal market do we want to establish?[137] The shared social purpose of this model of EU fiscal state aid control therefore suffers from what Habermas would call "the impotence of the ought."[138] Under these conditions it is therefore very difficult to assume that the discrimination narrative will be able to evolve into a coherent and consistent decision-making process to assess fiscal state aids.

§2.05 THE RISE OF THE DEMOCRACY NARRATIVE AND ITS IMPLICATIONS

The lack of normative consensus about the shared social purpose of EU fiscal state aid control in combination with the described shortcomings of the tax expenditure narrative and the discrimination narrative creates both threats and opportunities for the European Commission. It is a challenging environment in the sense that it will continuously have to convince the Member States and the EU citizens that it is exercising its authority to control fiscal state aids in an adequate manner. Without such support the Member States would, for example, eventually lose their willingness to comply with the recovery decisions. It is therefore of crucial importance for the European Commission to keep into consideration that any purposeful attempt to

136. N. Shuibhne, Introduction, in *Regulating the internal market* 1 (N. Shuibne ed., Cheltenham and Northampton: Edward Elgar Publishing, 2006).
137. J. Snell, The internal market and the philosophies of market integration, in *European Union Law* 300–324 (C. Barnard and S. Peers eds., Oxford: Oxford University Press, 2014).
138. J. Habermas, *Between Facts and Norms: Contributions to a Discourse Theory of Law and Democracy*, 56 (Cambridge: Polity Press, 1997) (translation of Faktizität und Geltung. Beiträge zur Diskurstheorie des Rechts und des demokratischen Rechtsstaats, Suhrkamp Verlag, Frankfurt, 1992; translated by William Rehg).

legitimize its authority is restricted by the fact that such an attempt needs to be grounded in the shared social purpose that it is supposed to establish.[139]

At the same time, the current environment also creates opportunities for the European Commission. As there are currently no strictly objective reasons that limit its authority, there is actually no reason *not to* take a "creeping normative role." The CJEU's extensive interpretation of Article 107 TFEU has made it possible for the European Commission to bypass the resistance of the Member States to comply with EU (fiscal) state aid control.[140] Even more, the instrument has evolved into an excellent instrument to escape from the "joint-decision trap" that has been blocking progress in the field of EU tax governance for a long time.[141] This phenomenon implies, simply put, that the institutional framework of the EU blocks progress in some policy areas, given the fact that all Member States take part in a bargaining style decision-making process that requires unanimity in order to establish results. Genschel illustrates how the European Commission is actually able to "nudge" the Member States away from these kinds of deadlocks.[142] Wattel hints at such nudges when he argues that the European Commission is using the tax ruling initiatives to "stimulate" the development of various other initiatives including a system of automatic notification of tax rulings, the common corporate tax base ("CCTB") and the further expansion of the room to manoeuvre for the Code of Conduct Group for Business Taxation.[143]

The result of these considerations is that the first two models of EU fiscal state aid control are in fierce competition with, what Kleiner calls, the "political integration model" of EU (fiscal) state aid control.[144] This is a vision of EU fiscal state aid control which explicitly aims at the establishment of deeper integration between the economies of the Member States.[145] Consequently, EU fiscal state aid is, to borrow Kleiner's words, mostly regarded to be "a means to controlling governments and coordinating their economic policies."[146] As such, it is, in the words of Hofmann, "leading to a more coordinated and harmonized common economic policy."[147] The main characteristic of this model is therefore that EU fiscal state aid control should be able to stipulate "binding" guidelines about the way the Member States should design their economic

139. Zürn, *supra* n. 16, p. 69.
140. C. Romariz, *Revisiting material selectivity in EU state aid law – or "the ghost of yet-to-come,"* 13(1) Eur. St. Aid L.Q. 46 (2014).
141. *See* the seminal F. Scharpf, *The joint-decision trap: Lessons from German federalism and European integration*, 66 Public Administration 239–278 (1988). He developed his position in F. Scharpf, *The joint-decision trap revisited*, 44(4) Journal of Common Market Studies 845–864 (2006) and F. Scharpf, The JDT model: Context and extensions, in *The EU's decision traps: Comparing policies* 217–236 (G. Falkner ed., Oxford: Oxford University Press, 2011).
142. *See* P. Genschel, One trap, many exits, but no free lunch: How the joint-decision trap shapes EU tax policy, in *The EU's decision traps: Comparing policies* 54–72 (G. Falkner ed., Oxford: Oxford University Press, 2011).
143. P. Wattel, The cat and the pigeons: Some general comments on (TP) tax rulings and state aid after the Starbucks and Fiat decisions, in *State aid law and business taxation* 34 (I. Richelle, W. Schön, and E. Traversa eds., Berlin and Heidelberg: Springer, 2016).
144. Kleiner, *supra* n. 12, pp. 4–5.
145. Kleiner, *supra* n. 12, p. 4.
146. Kleiner, *supra* n. 12, p. 4.
147. Hofmann, *supra* n. 10, p. 9.

policies.[148] It is therefore a model of positive integration that is able to trump the democratic "input" of (some of) the Member States.[149] Consequently, EU fiscal state aid control is able to establish tax policy convergence in the EU against the explicit will of the Member States.[150] In this view, positive integration is interpreted in a more extensive—(neo-) functionalist—way implying that also other actors than the Member States are able to force the convergence of the tax laws of the Member States.

Characteristic for this vision of EU fiscal state aid control is that the authority of the European Commission to design EU policy plays a crucial role. This implies that this institution is increasingly acting as a "supra-national enterpreneur" that "acts strategically in order to overcome Member State resistance and to turn potential powers granted by the Treaty into actual powers."[151] The central role of the European Commission in this model of EU fiscal state aid control can be illustrated with the fact that this institution is increasingly concerned with convincing not only the Member States, but also the EU citizens that it has the rightful authority to perform EU fiscal state aid control in an extensive manner. It is exactly in this very context that the already mentioned democracy narrative plays a crucial role. This democracy narrative is a true "narrative" in the sense that it anticipates cleverly on the room for manoeuvre that has been created by the extensive interpretation of the notion of fiscal state aid by the CJEU. The European Commission is responding to the changing social norms about the taxation of multinational companies and is trying to convince the EU citizens that is has the legitimate authority to tackle these kind of problems. As such it is illustrating that the Member States are no longer completely in charge of the establishment of the goals and functions of EU fiscal state aid control. It would however be incorrect to describe these legitimation efforts as mere strategy and manipulation only. The democracy narrative is simply the logical consequence of the efforts of the CJEU to expand the notion of fiscal state aid in a gradual way at the expense of the consent of the Member States.[152] In other words, in the absence of a clear normative consensus amongst the Member States about the essence of EU fiscal state aid control it is actually not surprising that the European institutions increasingly acquire more authority to set out the direction for the future.

Given the scope of this chapter it is not possible to reflect in more detail on the implications and the normative desirability of the rise of this democracy narrative and the related paradigmatic model of EU fiscal state aid control. It actually gives rise to many interesting questions that should be raised in future research. The main point of discussion at the moment is the *direction* of tax policy convergence that it is able to establish. This is the very question that Schön posed about tax harmonization, as pursued by the Member States, at the beginning of the millennium. That question is

148. Kleiner, *supra* n. 12, p. 5.
149. Compare, De Cecco, *supra* n. 10, pp. 131–133.
150. C. Peters, *Tax policy convergence and EU fiscal state aid control: In search of rationality*, 28(1) EC Tax Review 6–17 (2019).
151. M. Blauberger, State aid control from a political science perspective, in *Research Handbook on European State Aid Law* 28, 31 (E. Szyszczak ed., Cheltenham: Edward Elgar Publishing Limited 2011).
152. Romariz, *supra* n. 141, p. 46.

whether EU fiscal state aid control should be "solely directed at the abolition of impediments to the internal market," or whether it should be "employed to strengthen the fiscal powers of the national governments and to guarantee equity and and neutrality within the domestic tax systems."[153] The message of the democracy narrative clearly illustrates in which direction the European Commission would like to develop it. Future research will also have to address more explicitly the nature of EU fiscal state aid control as an "exit mechanism" to bypass the joint-decision trap that is at the heart of the current system of EU tax governance. As such it will be necessary to analyze the normative desirability of various alternative exit mechanisms, including qualified-majority voting, the application of Articles 116–117 TFEU and a broad interpretation of Article 107 TFEU.

§2.06 CONCLUSION AND WAY FORWARD

The starting point of this chapter was that EU fiscal state aid control is currently suffering from two related problems. These are the difficulties with the definition of the notion of fiscal state aid and the concerns about the legitimacy of EU fiscal state aid control. The subsequent analysis in this chapter has made clear that these related problems originate in the first place from a political battle about the essence of EU fiscal state aid control. There is no normative agreement on the supposedly "performance" of the institutions of EU fiscal state aid control. This is a problematic state of affairs, since the legitimacy of these institutions eventually depends on the shared social purpose that it is supposed to be establishing. The chapter identified three competing visions about the goals and functions of EU fiscal state aid control and characterized these on the basis of the decision-making "process" that is guiding the determination of fiscal state aids. The underlying assumption of this point of departure was that when there are different views on the performance of EU fiscal state aid control, only an objective—i.e., more or less mechanical—process of establishing fiscal state aids would be able to guarantee a sufficiently consistent and coherent notion of fiscal state aid.

Both the tax expenditure narrative and the discrimination narrative are founded on the promise of such an objective exercise. The tax expenditure narrative is built on the assurance that independent experts are able to "measure" the existence of fiscal state aid with scientific objectivity, whereas the discrimination narrative depends completely on the guarantee that legal, rather formalistic, concepts are able to identify fiscal state aids in an objective way. The analysis of these narratives in this chapter has made clear that both narratives fail to deliver their promises of an objective, more or less mechanical, process of establishing fiscal state aids. In the end, both narratives count on a minimum amount of normative consensus about the performance of the underlying model of EU fiscal state aid control. The tax expenditure narrative depends

153. W. Schön, Tax competition in Europe – General Report, in *Tax competition in Europe* 1, 9 (W. Schön ed., Amsterdam: IBFD Publications BV 2003).

on a sense of agreement that the autonomy of the Member States should be safeguarded to the greatest possible extent whereas the discrimination narrative implicitly assumes that EU fiscal state aid control is supposed to complete the internal market.

Consequently, it is actually not surprising that there is currently no coherent and consistent notion of fiscal state aid. The interpretation of the notion in the case law of the CJEU probably reflects traces of both narratives—including their underlying normative assumptions—and therefore it is actually not surprising that a sound theoretical framework to assess cases of fiscal state aid is currently lacking. This unfortunate state of affairs implies that the debate about the legal notion of fiscal state aid has become bogged down in a rather circular discussion about the desirable remaining national sovereignty of the Member States.[154] Moreover, it is fair to conclude that the dark horse in this story of faltering narratives is the European Commission. In the absence of both normative consensus about the goals and functions of EU fiscal state aid control and a proper mechanical decision-making process to assess fiscal state aids, it is actually not surprising that the European Commission has been able to acquire a "creeping normative role." It is taking advantage of powerful narratives, such as the democracy narrative, to transform EU fiscal state aid control into an instrument that is gradually able to establish deeper integration between the economies of the Member States. The discontent of tax lawyers about the legitimacy of these actions is therefore likely to continue. At the same time, it is fair to conclude that exactly the use of legitimation narratives (such as the democracy narrative) has proven to be an effective way of "mediaton" between the legal realm and the political and societal context of EU fiscal state aid control. In this sense, the "creeping normative role" of the European Commission is actually aligning with the changing social norms about the taxation of multinational companies.

For the time being, we therefore have to accept—and probably even appreciate—that there are competing visions about the goals and functions of this institution. The establishment of the objectives of EU fiscal state aid control principally constitutes a political activity rather than a merely economic or legal one.[155] This explains why EU state aid law has been constantly evolving ever since it was introduced in EU law.[156] It also illustrates that it is not very "useful" to stick to some "original intent" of EU fiscal state aid control as a guiding principle for the interpretation of present-day challenges. Present-day discussions about the scope of EU fiscal state aid control are merely another illustration of the fact that the expectations about competition law in the EU are considerably changing. In this way, the state aid discussion about tax rulings is actually related to the vivid debate about the scope and interpretation of EU merger control and the discussion about the need for EU industrial policy.[157]

154. *See* Kyriazis, *supra* n. 8, p. 436.
155. Buendia Sierra and Smulders, *supra* n. 99, p. 4.
156. Compare López, *supra* n. 50 and A. Biondi and E. Righini, An evolutionary theory of state aid control, in *The Oxford Handbook of European Union Law* 670–690 (A. Arnull and D. Chalmers eds., Oxford: Oxford University Press, 2015).
157. Compare the interview with Vestager in the Financial Times. https://www.ft.com/content/1d3abbd0-3b6e-11e9-b72b-2c7f526ca5d0 (last visited Apr. 15, 2019).

The final consideration of this chapter is therefore that it is fair to conclude that EU fiscal state aid control is currently standing at cross-roads. One direction would be to try to eliminate the political forces altogether by safeguarding the technocratic nature of the institution. This would imply that the Member States take back control and reach a normative consensus about the goals and functions of that institution. Moreover, it would imply that rational and efficient answers are available to solve the inherently political problems of EU tax governance. No doubt this alternative would definitely contribute to the so-much needed legal certainty, but the challenge will be to find expert knowledge about (international) taxation that makes a truly objective analysis possible. The weaknesses of the tax expenditure approach are after all a clear illustration of the fact that it is very difficult to count on academic criteria to "measure" fiscal state aids in an objective way. In this regard it is not quite helpful that there is a considerable variety of academic perspectives to study the topic of state aid.[158]

The other direction would be to accept wholeheartedly the intrinsic political nature of EU fiscal state aid control and to consider it as an intrinsic element of the evolving system of multilevel tax governance in the EU. Without a doubt, the discrimination narrative that the CJEU is currently developing is paving the road for this direction. The democracy narrative (and the related model of deeper economic integration between the Member States) has after all been able to develop for a good reason. When the European Commission is playing such a dominant role in this vision of EU fiscal state aid control, we will however have to think carefully about the sources of its legitimacy. Is it really desirable that its legitimation narratives serve as the "mediator' between the legal realm and the political and societal context or does this kind of mediation require truly democratic mechanisms?[159] And what does such a more political role imply for the much needed independence of the European Commission? And how can a more political role of the European Commission be squared with the need for national judges to perform substantive state aid analyses in an autonomous way? The most important conclusion of the project that was at the basis of this book is after all that the role of these national judges in the evolving system of multilevel tax governance in the EU is still insufficiently clear at the moment. Future research about the empirical and normative legitimacy of EU fiscal state aid control is therefore highly needed to shine a light on these important topics.

158. S. Martin and P. Valbonesi, State aid to business, in *International handbook on industrial policy* 134 (P. Bianchi and S. Labory eds., Cheltenham/Northampton: Edward Elgar, 2006).
159. In any case there would need to be more transparency and accountability about the way the European Commission is making new fiscal state aid policies. Currently, it is after all not clear at all which interest groups are actually influencing the European Commission to make such choices.

CHAPTER 3

Fiscal Selectivity: A Notion in Need of Clarity

*Paul-John Loewenthal**

§3.01 INTRODUCTION

Notwithstanding its crucial importance for assessing national tax measures under the State aid rules, the Court of Justice ('the Court') has only recently begun to crystallise the notion of selectivity in relation to such measures. That is because, prior to 2013, most of the notable State aid judgments in the field of direct taxation were in response to requests for a preliminary ruling from the national courts of the Member States. That trend started to change once the Commission began adopting more State aid decisions in the field of direct taxation,[1] beginning with the decision on the Spanish rules on the amortisation of goodwill,[2] the decision on the loss carry forward rules in Germany,[3] and the decision on the Spanish tax lease scheme.[4] Since 2014, the Commission has

* Member of the Legal Service of the European Commission. All views expressed in this article are purely those of the author and may not in any circumstances be regarded as stating an official position of the European Commission.

1. From 1991 to 2012, 65 tax-related State aid cases were formally examined by the Commission. See European Parliament resolution of 25 November 2015 on tax rulings and other measures similar in nature or effect (2015/2066(INI)), para. 66. Of those sixty-five cases, twenty-nine ended in negative decisions, fifteen with recovery. Of the twenty-nine negative decisions, twenty-three were adopted under the mandate of Commissioner Mario Monti.
2. Commission Decision 2011/282/EU of 12 January 2011 on the tax amortisation of financial goodwill for foreign shareholding acquisitions C 45/07 (ex NN 51/07, ex CP 9/07) implemented by Spain (OJ 2011 L 135, p. 1).
3. Commission Decision 2014/200/EU of 27 July 2013 on the aid scheme SA.21233 C/11 (ex NN/11, ex CP 137/06) implemented by Spain – Tax scheme applicable to certain finance lease agreements also known as the Spanish Tax Lease System (OJ 2014 L 114, p. 1).
4. Commission Decision 2011/527/EU of 26 January 2011 on State aid C 7/10 (ex CP 250/09 and NN 5/10) implemented by Germany – Scheme for the carry-forward of tax losses in the case of restructuring of companies in difficulty (Sanierungsklausel) (OJ 2011 L 235, p. 26).

adopted a flurry of State aid decisions in relation to national tax measures, in particular on individual tax rulings granted to multinational corporations and on progressive turnover taxes adopted by Hungary and Poland. Appeals against those decisions are currently pending before the General Court.[5] In the meantime, several references for a preliminary ruling have been made to the Court regarding the compliance of national tax measures with the State aid rules, which raise fundamental issues on selectivity.

The Court has since pronounced itself on a number of those decisions and references, but its judgments and opinions still raise questions in relation to several fundamental aspects of the notion of selectivity. This chapter seeks to crystallise that notion to the extent permitted by the case-law, to identify those issues on which clarity is still needed, and to propose workable solutions.

§3.02 SELECTIVITY AND THE FISCAL SOVEREIGNTY OF THE MEMBER STATES

The prohibition on the grant of State aid is laid down in Article 107(1) of the Treaty on the Function of the European Union ('TFEU'). The purpose of that prohibition is to ensure that the Member States do not distort competition on the internal market by favouring certain companies over others through financial incentives. It is obvious that where a Member State provides certain companies with subsidies competition will be distorted on the market in that those companies will receive a financial benefit that their competitors are denied. It is equally obvious that the same distortion can be caused by a Member State granting certain companies an exemption or reduction from a tax that their competitors are required to pay.

As the Court has repeatedly held, Article 107(1) TFEU does not distinguish between measures of State intervention by reference to their causes or aims, but defines them in relation to their effects.[6] Article 107(1) TFEU clearly states that aid can be granted 'in any form whatsoever', that is, in the form of a subsidy or in the form of a reduction or exemption from charges that an undertaking would normally have to bear under the ordinary rules of taxation.[7] The State aid rules therefore also clearly apply to national tax measures.[8]

5. *See* Cases T-750/15, *Netherlands v. Commission* and T-636/16, *Starbucks v. Commission*; Cases T-755/15, *Luxembourg v. Commission* and T-759/15, *Fiat v. Commission*; Case T-131/16, *Belgium v. Commission* (Belgian Excess Profit); Cases T-778/16, *Ireland v. Commission* and T-892/16, *Apple v. Commission*; Case T-783/16, *Government of Gibraltar v. Commission*; Case T-816/17, *Luxembourg v. Commission* and Case T-318/18, *Amazon v. Commission*; and Case T-516/18 *Luxembourg v. Commission* and T-525/18 *Engie v. Commission*. *See also* Joined Cases T-836/16 and T-624/16, *Poland v. Commission* (Polish tax on retail turnover) and Case T-20/17, *Hungary v. Commission* (Hungarian tax on advertisement turnover).
6. Case C-159/01, *Netherlands v. Commission*, EU:C:2004:246, para. 51 and the case-law cited.
7. At one point it was estimated that as much as 40% of State aid measures were fiscal in nature, *see* European Commission, State aid scorecard 2004. Ten years later, that figure was estimated at 25%, *see* State Aid Scorecard 2014.
8. *See* Joined Cases C-182/03 and C-217/03, *Belgium and Forum 187 ASBL v. Commission*, EU:C:2006:416, para. 81; Case C-417/10, *3M Italia*, EU:C:2012:184, para. 25, and Order in Case C-529/10, *Safilo*, EU:C:2012:188, para. 18.

State aid control has been a part of the European Union's (EU) competition law framework since 1957 and the Court has long acknowledged that a favourable tax treatment can have the exact same effect as a direct subsidy in causing distortions to the market.[9] More specifically, in a 1974 judgment concerning a measure that exempted the Italian textile sector from certain fiscal contributions, the Court unequivocally rejected Italy's argument that, since direct taxation fell within the exclusive competence of the Member States, that measure could not give rise to State aid.[10]

However, in the absence of harmonisation at EU level in the field of direct taxation, the Member States enjoy sovereignty over their national tax systems.[11] The Member States are thus free to decide whether to tax a particular event and at what rate. This means that a Member State is free to tax certain activities, even if other Member States do not. Similarly, a Member State may tax a particular event at 30%, while another Member State chooses to tax it at 15%. Those differences cannot give rise to the grant of State aid, even if they undoubtedly cause distortions to competition within the internal market. The fiscal sovereignty of the Member States means that there is nothing the EU institutions can do to tackle these forms of harmful tax competition between the Member States, short of legislative harmonisation on the basis of Article 115 TFEU,[12] which requires unanimity in the Council.

The question therefore arises: where to draw the line between the fiscal sovereignty of the Member States and the application of the State aid rules? The case-law provides a very simple and straightforward answer: fiscal sovereignty ends where discrimination begins.[13] Where a Member State adopts a tax measure that discriminates in favour of certain companies over comparable companies within the same Member State, State aid is present. That is because the State aid assessment of a tax measure granted by Member State X to company Y only enquires into whether that measure results in a reduction of company Y's tax liability in Member State X as compared to similar companies. The fact that company Y has established itself in and operates from Member State X because it has a low corporate income tax rate is irrelevant in the context of a State aid assessment. Similarly, the fact that the part of company Y's profit not subject to Member State X's tax jurisdiction is not subject to tax in other tax jurisdictions has no bearing on a finding of State aid. A State aid assessment only considers whether Member State X has taxed company Y in the same manner as similarly situated companies subject to the same tax in that tax jurisdiction. It is this

9. Case 30/59, *De gezamenlijke Steenkolenmijnen in Limburg v. High Authority*, EU:C:1961:2. Case 6/69 *France v. Commission*, EU:C:1969:68, para. 17.
10. Case 173/73, *Italy v. Commission*, EU:C:1974:71, paras 12 and 13.
11. *See* Case 204/90, *Bachmann*, EU:C:1992:35, para. 23 and Case C-374/04, *Test Claimants in Class IV of the ACT Group Litigation*, EU:C:1992:35, para. 50.
12. The Commission has often employed Art. 115 TFEU to propose legislation aimed at tackling harmful tax competition between Member States. For example, harmonised rules on tax transparency and the automatic exchange of information on tax rulings entered into force in January 2017. In May 2017 the Anti-Tax Avoidance Directive (ATAD) was adopted, which aims at preventing tax avoidance via non-EU countries. The Commission has also proposed establishing a common consolidated corporate tax base (CCCTB) within the EU, transparency rules for intermediaries who design and promote tax planning schemes, and a digital turnover tax.
13. Case C-374/17, *A Brauerei*, EU:C:2018:1024, para. 35 and Joined Cases C-20/15 P and C-21/15 P, *Commission v. World Duty Free Group*, EU:C:2016:981, para. 54.

notion of discrimination that is embodied in the condition of selectivity, one of the constituent elements for a finding of State aid under Article 107(1) TFEU.

§3.03 DISTINGUISHING BETWEEN SELECTIVITY AND ADVANTAGE

Selectivity is one of six conditions for the finding of State aid under Article 107(1) TFEU, alongside the existence of an undertaking, imputability and State resources, the grant of an advantage, a distortion of competition, and an effect on intra-EU trade. Although it is often said that the selectivity condition is the cornerstone of the State aid analysis into tax measures, the Court did not specifically refer to selectivity in its enumeration of the conditions laid down by Article 107(1) TFEU until its 2016 *Lübeck* judgment.[14] Leaving aside the fact that that case had nothing to do with fiscal State aid, the reference to the selectivity condition was made in combination with the condition of advantage, in that reference was made to a 'selective advantage' as a constituent element for a finding of aid.

The fact that the Court combined the conditions of selectivity and advantage demonstrates the closeness of those two conditions, especially in the field of fiscal State aid. Nevertheless, the Court has stressed that selectivity must be clearly distinguished from the concomitant detection of an economic advantage.[15] A distinction is made between the conditions of advantage and selectivity to ensure that not all State measures that confer an advantage constitute State aid, but only those which grant such an advantage in a selective manner to certain undertakings or certain categories of undertakings or to certain economic sectors.[16]

Whether a Member State has conferred an advantage on a particular undertaking for the purposes of Article 107(1) TFEU is determined in the abstract. The financial situation of the undertaking following the measure is compared with its financial situation if the measure had not been taken. Thus, the comparison to be made in determining the existence of an advantage is by reference to the effect of the measure itself.[17] A measure gives rise to an advantage for an undertaking where, as a result of the measure, the beneficiary gains a financial advantage that it would not have gained but for the adoption of the measure in question. In other words, an advantage will be granted where, as a result of the measure, the beneficiary's net financial position is improved.[18] In the case of tax measures, an advantage may be granted through

14. Case C-524/14 P, *Commission v. Hansestadt Lübeck*, EU:C:2016:971, para. 40.
15. Case C-15/14 P, *Commission v. MOL*, EU:C:2015:362, para. 59.
16. Joined Cases C-20/15 P and C-21/15 P, *Commission v. World Duty Free Group*, EU:C:2016:981, para. 56 and Case C-6/12, *P Oy*, EU:C:2013:525, para. 18.
17. Case 173/73, *Italy v. Commission*, EU:C:1974:71, para. 13.
18. Case C-417/10, *3M Italia*, EU:C:2012:184, para. 38; Case C-172/03, *Heiser*, EU:C:2005:130, para. 36; Case C-126/01, *GEMO SA*, EU:C:2003:622, paras 28 to 31; Case 156/98, *Germany v. Commission*, EU:C:2000:467, para. 25; and Case C-387/92, *Banco Exterior de España*, EU:C:1994:100, para. 13.

different types of reduction in an undertaking's tax burden and, in particular, through a reduction in the tax rate, taxable base or the amount of tax due.[19]

Whether a measure is selective depends on whether the advantage to which it gives rise is conferred on 'certain undertakings or the production of certain goods'. Recent judgments of the Court equate the selectivity condition to that of establishing discrimination, namely whether a measure discriminates in favour of its beneficiary/-ies as compared to undertakings in a comparable factual and legal situation.[20] Seen in this manner, establishing selectivity consists in determining whether one or certain undertaking(s) enjoy an advantage with regard to comparable undertakings and, if they do, whether that differentiated treatment can be justified by the nature or logic of the system of which the measure forms a part.

Although the Court has insisted on making a distinction between the conditions of advantage and selectivity, it has not maintained a rigorous separation between those conditions when examining fiscal measures under the State aid rules. For example, the Court has repeated on several occasions that the identification of the reference framework, i.e., the benchmark for establishing selectivity, 'is of particular importance in the case of tax measures since the very existence of an advantage may be established only when compared with "normal" taxation'.[21] Similarly, in the *Forum 187* judgment, the Court held that '[i]n order to decide whether a method of assessment of taxable income [...] confers an advantage on [its beneficiary], it is necessary [...] to compare that [method] with the ordinary tax system, based on the difference between profits and outgoings of an undertaking carrying on its activities in conditions of free competition'.[22] In other words, the Court did not simply examine in the abstract whether the financial situation of the beneficiaries following the measure was improved, as is required for a finding of advantage; it compared the tax treatment of the beneficiaries as a result of the measure with the tax treatment of other undertakings under the ordinary tax system, which is a selectivity assessment.

This combination of the conditions of advantage and selectivity in relation to fiscal measures makes sense, since it is a direct consequence of the fiscal sovereignty of the Member States in the field of direct taxation. As explained below, part of the

---

19. Case C-66/02, *Italy v. Commission*, EU:C:2005:768, para. 78; Case C-222/04, *Cassa di Risparmio di Firenze and Others*, EU:C:2006:8, para. 132; Case C-522/13, *Ministerio de Defensa and Navantia*, EU:C:2014:2262, paras 21 to 31.
20. Joined Cases C-20/15 P and C-21/15 P, *Commission v. World Duty Free Group*, EU:C:2016:981, para. 54. *See also* Case C-524/14 P, *Commission v. Hansestadt Lübeck*, EU:C:2016:971, para. 53: 'The examination of whether such a measure is selective is thus, in essence, coextensive with the examination of whether it applies to that set of economic operators in a non-discriminatory manner [...]. The concept of selectivity [...] is thus linked to that of discrimination.' The *World Duty Free* judgment contains no less than nine mentions of the notion of discrimination (paras 54, 71, 74, 75, 83, 86, 92, 93 and 94), while the *Lübeck* judgment refers to that notion on four occasions (paras 53, 57 and 64). Finally *see* Opinion of Advocate General Bobek in Case C-270/15 P, *Belgium v. Commission*, EU:C:2016:289, paras 21 and 29: 'selectivity implies differentiation or inequality' and 'the key notion is in fact that of discrimination'.
21. Case C-88/03, *Portugal v. Commission*, EU:C:2006:511, para. 56; Case C-524/14 P, *Commission v. Hansestadt Lübeck*, EU:C:2016:971, para. 55; and Case C-203/16 P, *Dirk Andres v Commission* ('*Sanierungsklausel*'), EU:C:2018:505, para. 88.
22. *See* Joined Cases C-182/03 and C-217/03 *Belgium and Forum 187 v. Commission* EU:C:2005:266, para. 95.

selectivity analysis consists in establishing that a measure derogates from the normal system of taxation in the Member State concerned. Consequently, establishing that a tax measure constitutes a derogation from the normal rules of taxation in that its beneficiary/-ies pay less tax than would otherwise be due establishes not only the selectivity of the measure (in that there is discrimination between comparable undertakings) but also the existence of an advantage (in the form of a tax reduction).

§3.04 HOW TO ESTABLISH SELECTIVITY IN THE CASE OF INDIVIDUAL MEASURES, SCHEMES AND DISCRETIONARY ADMINISTRATIVE PRACTICES

The distinction between the conditions of advantage and selectivity means that measures of purely general application that confer an advantage, but which do not favour certain undertakings or the production of certain goods, do not constitute State aid, since they are not selective.[23] Therefore, a key aspect to assess selectivity is to determine whether a measure is of general application or, on the contrary, it applies only to certain (groups of) undertakings or certain sectors of the economy in a given Member State that are comparable to other undertakings.

The Court's recent case-law therefore draws a distinction between individual measures and general schemes when it comes to establishing selectivity. In the case of an individual measure, 'the identification of the economic advantage is, in principle, sufficient to support the presumption that it is selective'.[24] Where that presumption is relied upon, it is not necessary for the Commission to determine whether other economic operators are in a comparable factual and legal situation to the beneficiary of the measure to establish selectivity.[25] Rather, it is for the Member State that adopted the measure to demonstrate that all comparable companies can benefit from a similar advantage. In contrast, when examining a general scheme, it is necessary to identify whether the measure confers an advantage to the exclusive benefit of certain undertakings or certain sectors of the economy or whether it is generally available to all undertakings in a comparable situation.

Regulation (EU) 2015/1589, which is considered to codify the case-law on State aid procedure prior to its adoption,[26] provides a definition of aid schemes and individual aid. Article 1(d) of the regulation defines an aid scheme as 'any act on the basis of which, without further implementing measures being required, individual aid awards may be made to undertakings defined within the act in a general and abstract manner and any act on the basis of which aid which is not linked to a specific project may be awarded to one or several undertakings for an indefinite period of time and/or for an indefinite amount'. The first part of that provision defines 'general schemes', the

23. Case C-6/12, *P Oy*, EU:C:2013:525, para. 18 and the case-law cited.
24. Case C-211/15 P, *Orange v. Commission*, EU:C:2016:798, paras 53 and 54, Case C-270/15 P, *Belgium v. Commission*, EU:C:2016:489, paras 48 et 49 and Case C-15/14 P, *Commission v. MOL*, EU:C:2015:362, para. 60.
25. Case T-314/15, *Greece v. Commission*, EU:T:2017:903, para. 79.
26. Case C-139/07 P, *Commission v. Technische Glaswerke Ilmenau* EU:C:2010:376, para. 55.

second part 'individual schemes'. Article1(e) of the regulation defines individual aid in a negative manner as 'aid that is not awarded on the basis of an aid scheme and notifiable awards of aid on the basis of an aid scheme'. It follows from that negative definition that an aid measure can be either an aid scheme or an individual aid.

While several approaches have been proposed and applied to establish selectivity in relation to general schemes, all of which are discussed in the following section, the case-law provides no guidance on how to establish selectivity in the case of an individual scheme. Considering the inherently individualised nature of such a measure, it would make sense for the same presumption of selectivity to apply to such schemes. Nevertheless, the restrictive interpretation recently given by the Court to the definition of an individual aid scheme under Article 1(d) of Regulation (EU) 2015/1589 in the 2018 *IFP* judgment suggests that the category of measures that could potentially fall within that definition is extremely limited.[27] Clarity on the notion of selectivity in relation to individual schemes therefore does not seem forthcoming.

Another test entirely applies to establish selectivity where a particular tax measure results from a discretionary administrative practice. Administrative discretion in itself is unproblematic from a State aid perspective. However, the Court has held that where a tax administration enjoys broad discretion to determine the beneficiaries or the conditions under which a particular tax advantage is provided on the basis of criteria unrelated to the tax system under which it is provided, that advantage may be presumed to be selective.[28] To establish selectivity in such cases, it is necessary to effectively demonstrate that the administrative practice on the basis of which a particular tax measure is granted is wholly discretionary, in that it is not limited by objective criteria related to the tax system under which it is granted.[29]

In sum, three, possibly four, different tests apply to establish selectivity in relation to tax measures depending on whether they are individual or general measures and whether they result from a wholly discretionary administrative practice.

§3.05 DIFFERENT APPROACHES TO ESTABLISH SELECTIVITY OF GENERAL SCHEMES

In its 2011 *Paint Graphos* judgment, the Court first devised a three-step approach to establish the selectivity of general fiscal schemes.[30] The first step consists in identifying the 'normal' tax regime applicable in the Member State against which the scheme is to be assessed: 'the reference framework'. The second step consists in determining whether that scheme involves a derogation from that framework insofar as it differentiates between economic operators who, in light of the objective of the reference framework, are in a comparable factual and legal situation. If the scheme is found to

27. Case C-438/16 P, *Commission v. France and IFP Énergies nouvelles*, EU:C:2018:737, paras 61 to 74.
28. Case C-6/12, *P Oy*, EU:C:2013:525, paras 24 to 27.
29. Case C-15/14 P, *Commission v. MOL*, EU:C:2015:362, para. 64.
30. In Case C-524/14 P, *Commission v. Hansestadt Lübeck*, EU:C:2016:971, the Court endorsed the application of the three-step analysis for all types of State aid schemes, not just fiscal schemes.

constitute a derogation from the reference framework, the third step consists in determining whether that derogation is justified by the nature and logic of the reference framework. The three-step approach has been endorsed in a number of subsequent judgments and extended to establish selectivity of non-fiscal measures. In State aid decisions adopted by the Commission, the burden of proof in relation to the first two steps lies with the Commission, while the burden of proof in establishing a justification (i.e., the third step) lies with the Member State.[31]

This three-step approach can be contrasted with the two-step approach applied in several fiscal State aid cases before and after the *Paint Graphos* judgment.[32] Under the two-step analysis, the first step consists in determining whether the scheme discriminates in favour of certain undertakings in that they are granted an advantage that comparable undertakings are denied. If discrimination is established, it will need to be determined, under a second step, whether that discrimination can be justified by the nature and logic of the reference framework. Just like under the three-step approach, the burden of establishing discrimination (i.e., the first step) lies with the Commission, while the burden of justifying that discrimination (i.e., the second step) lies with the Member State.

As Advocate General Bobek stated in his 2016 opinion in the *BSE* case, 'the only discernible difference between the two approaches is rather academic. It consists of splitting the first step into two separate steps in the three-step approach. Under both approaches, it is necessary to define the appropriate reference framework. However, within the two-step approach, that definition is less apparent, being hidden in the first step'.[33] According to Advocate General Wahl in his 2017 opinion in the *Sanierungsklausel* case, a clear distinction must be drawn between the first and second steps of the three-step approach, which implies that selectivity can only be established through that approach.[34] Advocate-General Bobek also prefers the three-step approach.

In contrast, the Court's recent judgments in the *Escuelas Pias* and *ANGED* cases[35] appear to apply a two-step approach to assess selectivity. In neither judgment does the Court identify a reference framework against which the measure under consideration should be assessed to establish a derogation and both judgments principally focus their analysis on whether that measure discriminates between comparable undertakings. Even the *World Duty Free* judgment, with its singular focus on discrimination, appears

31. C-279/08 P, *Commission v. Netherlands (NOx)* EU:C:2011:551, para. 62.
32. *See* Case C-487/06 P, *British Aggregates v. Commission*, EU:C:2008:757, para. 82 et seq., Case C-172/03, *Heiser*, para. 40 et seq. and Case 143/99, *Adria-Wien Pipeline and Wietersdorfer & Peggauer Zementwerke*, EU:C:2001:598, paras 41 and 42.
33. Opinion of Advocate General Bobek in Case C-270/15 P *Belgium v. Commission* EU:C:2016:289 para. 28.
34. Opinion of Advocate-General Wahl in Case C-203/16 P, *Andres (in administration Heitkamp BauHolding) v. Commission*, EU:C:2017:1017, para. 109: 'it should not be forgotten that the determination of the reference system should precede the comparison of undertakings'.
35. Case C-74/16, *Congregación de Escuelas Pías Provincia Betania*, EU:C:2017:496, paras 68 to 72 and Joined Cases C-234/16 and C-235/16, *ANGED*, EU:C:2018:281, para. 35.

to apply a two-step approach, although it invokes the three-step approach before doing so.[36]

These three- and two-step approaches can be contrasted with what has recently been dubbed the 'general availability' approach. That approach first made its appearance in the judgments of the General Court in the Spanish goodwill and Spanish tax lease cases. In the Spanish goodwill judgments, the General Court concluded that a measure allowing Spanish corporate taxpayers to deduct from their taxable base the goodwill resulting from an acquisition in a foreign company was not selective because any taxpayer could undertake such an acquisition.[37] Similarly, the General Court concluded that although the tax benefits of the Spanish tax lease scheme were only open to special purpose vehicles known as 'Economic Interest Groupings', that scheme was not selective since any undertaking belonging to any sector of the economy could invest in such vehicles.[38] Although the Court appeared to have rejected the general availability approach on appeals against both judgments – holding that the fact that the beneficiary undertakings belong to various economic sectors and the fact that the advantage offered by the measure is available regardless of the nature of the business of the recipient undertakings is insufficient to call into the question the selectivity of a measure[39] – that approach was subsequently revived as the 'traditional method' to establish selectivity by Advocate General Saugmandsgaard Øe in his 2018 opinion in *A Brauerei*.[40] According to that approach, 'an advantage is not selective if the conduct targeted by that advantage may be adopted by any undertaking'.[41] That approach 'does not require that all undertakings actually benefit from the [...] advantage in question (actual enjoyment test) but merely that all undertakings may benefit from it (availability test)'.[42]

It is clear that an approach according to which the potential availability of benefitting from a tax measure excludes selectivity would shield virtually every tax scheme from the application of the State aid rules.[43] For example, a Member State could adopt a scheme to lure multinationals by offering a full exemption from corporate income tax to branches or subsidiaries of foreign companies established in the Member

36. Admittedly, in para. 57 of the judgment, the Court distinguished between the identification of the reference framework and the finding of a derogation from that system, but the remainder of the judgment focuses heavily on whether the measure discriminates between undertakings in a comparable factual and legal situation in light of the objectives of the larger framework of which it forms a part, which is a combination of both steps.
37. Case T-219/10, *Autogrill España v. Commission*, EU:T:2014:939 and Case T-399/11, *Banco Santander and Santusa v. Commission*, EU:T:2014:938.
38. Joined Cases T-515/13 and T-719/13, *Spain and Others v. Commission*, EU:T:2015:1004, paras 116 to 118.
39. Joined Cases C-20/15 P and C-21/15 P, *Commission v. World Duty Free Group*, EU:C:2016:981, paras 80 and 81 and Case C-128/16 P, *Commission v. Spain*, EU:C:2018:591, para. 70.
40. Opinion of Advocate General Saugmandsgaard Oe in Case C-374/17 *A Brauerei* EU:C:2018:741.
41. *Ibidem*, para. 71.
42. *Ibidem*, para. 94.
43. The Advocate General's admission in para. 81 of his Opinion is telling in this respect: 'use of the traditional method of analysis, based on the general availability test, allows the rules on State aid, and primarily the action taken by the Commission, to be refocused on the measures which are the most damaging to competition within the internal market, namely individual aid and sectoral aid'.

State. Since a standalone company could potentially set up a subsidiary or branch in another tax jurisdiction, the benefit offered by that tax exemption would be 'generally available' to all taxpayers and thus not selective under the general availability approach. In its 2018 *A Brauerei* judgment, the Court categorically rejected the general availability approach in favour of the aforementioned three-step approach.[44] The following three sections examine how each of those three steps is assessed to establish selectivity.[45]

§3.06 THE IDENTIFICATION OF REFERENCE FRAMEWORK (THE FIRST STEP)

The first step of the three-step approach is the identification of the reference framework. The first time the Court used the term 'reference framework' in one of its judgments in relation to selectivity was in the 2006 *Azores* judgment.[46] That term had been transposed from the decision forming the subject-matter of that judgment in which the Commission assessed whether a fiscal scheme adopted by the Azores region that resulted in reduced rates of income and corporation tax as compared to the Portuguese tax rules gave rise to State aid.[47] In that context, the term 'reference system' was used to explain why the national tax system and not the fiscal scheme adopted by the Azores regional authorities was the appropriate benchmark to assess selectivity. In other words, the case primarily concerned regional, not material, selectivity. Nevertheless, the dictum of the Court in the *Azores* judgment according to which '[t]he determination of the reference framework has a particular importance in the case of tax

44. Case C-374/17, *A Brauerei*, EU:C:2018:1024, paras 25 to 27.
45. The Court is not the only institution grappling with how to establish that economic operators have been granted impermissible fiscal subsidies. WTO law includes in its definition of subsidies 'government revenue that is otherwise due [which] is foregone or not collected (e.g., fiscal incentives such as tax credits)'. *See* Art. 1.1(a)(1)(ii) of the Agreement on Subsidies and Countervailing Measures Agreement. According to the WTO Appellate Body, there must be some defined, normative benchmark against which a comparison can be made between the revenue actually raised and the revenue that would have been raised 'otherwise' to establish that a tax measure results in revenue being foregone. The basis of comparison must be the 'prevailing domestic standard' established by the tax rules applied by the Member in question, because '[w]hat is "otherwise due" [...] depends on the rules of taxation that each Member, by its own choice, establishes for itself'. Like the Court, the WTO Appellate Body has devised a three-step test to conduct that assessment, which differs from the three-step test to establish selectivity. First, the tax treatment that applies to the income of the alleged recipients, considering the objective reasons behind that treatment, must be identified. Second, a benchmark for comparison, i.e., the tax treatment of comparable income of comparably situated taxpayers, must be identified. This involves an examination of the structure of the Member's domestic tax regime and its organising principles. Third, the challenged tax treatment, and its reasons, must be compared with the identified benchmark tax treatment. *See* Appellate Body Report, US – FSC, paras 87 to 92; *See also* Appellate Body Report, US – Large Civil Aircraft (2nd complaint), paras 806–810.
46. Case C-88/03, *Portugal v. Commission*, EU:C:2006:511.
47. Commission Decision 2003/442/EC of 11 December 2002 on the part of the scheme adapting the national tax system to the specific characteristics of the Autonomous Region of the Azores which concerns reductions in the rates of income and corporation tax (OJ 2003 L 150, p. 52).

measures'[48] quickly found its way into almost all subsequent judgments on material selectivity.

The reference framework is, in essence, the benchmark for establishing whether a measure discriminates in favour of its beneficiaries as compared to similar undertakings. The identification of the reference system is the starting point for both the two- and three-step approaches to establish the selectivity of general schemes. That identification exercise has been described as 'the heart of the selectivity test' by Advocate General Bobek[49] and 'of crucial importance for the assessment of selectivity' by Advocate General Wahl,[50] only to be deemed indecisive by Advocate General Kokott.[51]

Considering the fiscal sovereignty of the Member States in devising their tax systems, the identification of the reference framework should be the focal point of any State aid assessment into national tax measures. That is because, as explained in §3.02 above, it is only where a Member State discriminates in favour of certain undertakings as compared to others under its normal tax rules that fiscal State aid can be present.

Where a particular tax measure provides for a clear exception to a general rule, the identification of the reference framework should be rather straightforward. Imagine a situation in which a Member State taxes all companies at a rate of 30% on their corporate profits, but provides an exemption for companies in the textile sector of 15% to stimulate growth in that sector. One would then be tempted to conclude that the 'normal tax regime', and thus the benchmark for comparison, is corporate taxation at 30%, while the derogation from that benchmark is taxation at 15% for textile manufacturers. However, even that straightforward scenario has given rise to less than straightforward results in the Court's case-law on fiscal selectivity. And what to make of the situation in which a Member State taxes manufacturers at 30% and service providers at 15%? What is the general rule in such a situation and what is the derogation? The answer to that question is decisive when considering that many tax systems tax different types of profit at different rates.

Given the central importance of identifying the reference framework for establishing selectivity, one would expect the case-law to provide clear guidance on how that identification is to occur. That is not the case. As Advocate General Wahl remarked in his opinion in the *Sanierungsklausel* case 'the Court's case-law remains silent on how the relevant reference system ought to be determined. The Court has simply explained that the reference system is the common or "normal" tax regime applicable in the Member State concerned'.[52] While the Court's case-law is not entirely silent on

48. Case C-88/03, *Portugal v. Commission*, EU:C:2006:511, para. 56.
49. Opinion of Advocate General Bobek in Case C-270/15 P *Belgium v. Commission* EU:C:2016:289 para. 29.
50. Opinion of Advocate-General Wahl in Case C-203/16 P *Andres (in administration Heitkamp BauHolding) v. Commission* EU:C:2017:1017, para. 99.
51. Opinion of Advocate General Kokott in Joined Cases C-234/16 and C-235/16 *ANGED*, EU:C:2017:853, para. 86: '[...] the determination of a "normal" tax system cannot be decisive. As the Court reiterated in World Duty Free, the examination of the difference in treatment in question in the light of the objective pursued by the law alone is decisive'.
52. *See* Opinion of Advocate General Wahl in Case C-203/16 P *Andres (faillite Heitkamp BauHolding) v. Commission* EU:C:2017:1017, para. 100.

how the reference system should be identified, the guidance it does provide leaves more questions than answers.

The one clear stance the Court has taken is that the identification of the reference system should not depend on the regulatory technique used by the Member State. This runs both ways. A Member State cannot evade the application of the State aid rules simply by designing a tax system that does not formally provide for an exemption from a general rule, but in fact discriminates between comparable undertakings. That was the case in *Gibraltar*, where the measure under assessment was a new corporate income tax regime adopted by Gibraltar according to which companies were taxed on the number of persons employed in Gibraltar (a payroll tax) and of the occupation of business property in Gibraltar (a property tax). The Court held that 'the fact that offshore companies are not taxed [under the regime] is not a random consequence of the regime at issue, but the inevitable consequence of the fact that the bases of assessment are specifically designed so that offshore companies, which by their nature have no employees and do not occupy business premises, have no tax base under the bases of assessment adopted in the proposed tax reform'.[53] Conversely, the Commission cannot conclude that a measure is selective simply because the measure constitutes a formal exemption to a general rule. In *Sanierungsklausel*, the Court set aside a judgment of the General Court and annulled a Commission decision finding that an exemption to the rule governing forfeiture of losses was selective because it was 'worded in the form of an exemption'.[54]

Beyond this clear rejection of formalism, the Court's guidance on how to identify the reference framework has lacked clarity and consistency.

In the 2011 *Paint Graphos* judgment, the Court identified the Italian rules on the taxation of corporate profits as the reference system for assessing a tax exemption for producers' and workers' cooperative societies, since 'the basis of assessment of [cooperatives] is determined in the same way as that of other types of undertaking' under those rules.[55] After concluding that that exemption constituted a derogation from that system, to which profit-making companies were not entitled,[56] the Court subsequently assessed whether cooperatives were in a comparable situation to profit-making companies. That line of reasoning is inconsistent with the very same three-step approach set out in that judgment. If the reference framework is the benchmark for comparison and the Court had already concluded that the tax exemption constituted a derogation under that framework, since it was unavailable to profit-making companies, there is no room for a subsequent comparability assessment after that conclusion has been reached.

In the 2011 *NOx* judgment, the Court appears to have combined the identification of the reference framework with the comparability assessment. It concluded that the Commission was right to find that a measure that only benefitted large industrial

53. Joined Cases C-106/09 P and C-107/09 P, *Commission v. Government of Gibraltar and United Kingdom*, EU:C:2011:732, para. 106.
54. Case C-203/16 P *Andres (faillite Heitkamp BauHolding) v. Commission* EU:C:2018:505, para. 146.
55. Joined Cases C-78/08 to C-80/08, *Paint Graphos*, EU:C:2011:550, para. 50.
56. *Ibidem*, paras 51 to 53.

undertakings producing NOx emissions was selective since 'every undertaking the operations of which produce NOx emissions must comply with obligations regarding the limitation or reduction of those emissions, whether or not it falls within the measure in question'.[57]

In the 2011 *Gibraltar* judgment, the Court identified the Gibraltarian corporate tax system as the reference framework because it formally applied to all undertakings established in Gibraltar.[58] However, no general rule under that system in fact taxed all Gibraltarian companies on their profit. Rather, since the bases for assessment under that system were the number of persons employed in Gibraltar and of the occupation of business property in Gibraltar, offshore companies were entirely exempt from taxation under that system. The Court's selectivity analysis therefore did not consist in establishing a derogation from a general rule, but in establishing de facto discrimination between comparable undertakings. The Court held that 'the regime at issue, by combining those bases, even though they are founded on criteria that are in themselves of a general nature, in practice discriminates between companies which are in a comparable situation with regard to the objective of the proposed tax reform, namely to introduce a general system of taxation for all companies established in Gibraltar'.[59] It is for this reason that the *Gibraltar* judgment is often cited as an example where the Court abandoned its reference framework-based approach, but that is not entirely accurate. The Court in fact refers to the Gibraltarian tax system as the reference framework in several parts of that judgment under which a discrimination would have occurred.[60]

While the 2016 *World Duty Free* and 2018 *Sanierungsklausel* judgments reaffirm the importance of identifying the reference framework for establishing selectivity, they do not identify the applicable frameworks for assessing the measures under assessment. In contrast, the 2017 *Escuelas Pias* and the 2018 *ANGED* judgments no longer emphasis the importance of identifying the reference framework. In *Escuelas Pias*, the Court merely concluded that a measure that exempted religious institutions from a tax that is normally payable by all taxpayers who carry out construction or renovation works was prima facie selective, without identifying that tax as the reference system. In *ANGED*, the Court went one step further, abandoning the identification of the reference framework altogether, instead focussing on whether the beneficiaries of the measure under assessment were in a comparable factual and legal situation to undertakings excluded from the scope of the measure.[61]

The problem with this shift in focus from the identification of the reference framework to the comparability assessment is that comparability only makes sense against a particular benchmark. While the focus in the recent case-law on discrimination instead of derogations is to be welcomed, since it rids the selectivity analysis of formalism, the search for a benchmark for comparison should not be confused with the

57. Case C-279/08, *Commission v. Netherlands*, EU:C:2011:551, paras 63 and 64.
58. Joined Cases C-106/09 P and C-107/09 P, *Commission v. Government of Gibraltar and United Kingdom*, EU:C:2011:732, paras 95 and 101.
59. *Ibid*, para. 101.
60. *Ibid*, paras. 94 to 96.
61. Joined Cases C-234/16 and C-235/16, *ANGED*, EU:C:2018:281, paras 42 to 50.

comparability assessment that is necessary for establishing discrimination.[62] As the Court stated in the *Sanierungsklausel* judgment, 'the determination of the set of undertakings which are in a comparable factual and legal situation depends on the prior definition of the legal regime in the light of whose objective it is necessary, where applicable, to examine whether the factual and legal situation of the undertakings favoured by the measure in question is comparable with that of those which are not'.[63]

The Court's 2018 *A Brauerei* judgment reaffirms the importance of identifying the reference framework and separating it from the comparability assessment. However, the Court does not give much guidance on how that identification is to take place. That judgment concerns an exemption to a German tax on the transfer of real estate property which applies where the transfer is the result of a merger between a company that holds 95% of the capital or business assets in another company for five years before and after the merger and that other company. At issue was whether the reference system comprised the real estate transfer tax, of which the exemption formed a derogation, or whether the tax and its exemption formed the reference system, the exemption being seen as a measure to temper the scope of application of the tax. In that judgment, the Court asserts, without more, that it 'is apparent from the description of the national law in the order for reference [that] the reference framework [...] is composed of German law rules on real property transfer tax which, taken together, determine the subject matter or the chargeable event covered by that tax'.[64] The only description of the national law in the judgment is that given earlier on the origin of the exemption, not the reference framework.[65] The Court explains that 'the exemption from the real property transfer tax [...] was inserted into that law [...] as a measure formally derogating from [the tax]'. The Court then explains that that exemption 'sought, in essence, to facilitate the restructuring of undertakings and, in particular, the structural changes involving the transfer of property between companies, in order make them more competitive in the face of the financial crisis affecting the Federal Republic of Germany since 2008'. Finally, the Court explains that 'it was only during the legislative process that a decision was taken to restrict the benefit of that tax advantage to certain groups of companies'. Those explanations appear to be part of the rebuttal to Germany's argument that the exemption was a general measure and therefore not selective,[66] and not a description of the national law on which the Court relied to identify the reference framework.

In short, the case-law gives insufficient guidance on how to identify the reference system against which a measure should be assessed to establish selectivity. An overall assessment of the case-law suggests that the starting point for the identification of the

62. *See* Opinion of Advocate General Bobek in Case C-270/15 P *Belgium v. Commission* EU:C:2016:289 para. 33: '[d]efining a suitable reference framework requires a decision on the set of undertakings that are in a comparable legal and factual situation'.
63. Case C-203/16 P, *Andres (faillite Heitkamp BauHolding) v. Commission* EU:C:2018:505, para. 89. *See also* Case C-524/14 P, *Commission v. Hansestadt Lübeck*, EU:C:2016:971, para. 60.
64. Case C-374/17, *A Brauerei*, EU:C:2018:1024, para. 37.
65. *Ibid*, paras 28 to 30.
66. *Ibid*, para. 34.

reference framework should be the purpose of the measure under assessment.[67] In *Paint Graphos*, the purpose of the measure was to exempt cooperatives from Italian corporate income tax, which was also identified as the larger framework under which that measure was adopted. In *NOx*, the purpose of the measure under assessment was to grant large industrial undertakings engaged in intra-EU trade free NOx credits. The larger reference framework under which that measure was adopted was the NOx emission reduction scheme established by the Netherlands, under which undertakings had to comply with obligatory emissions standards by reducing either their NOx emissions or by buying emission allowances from other undertakings, or by a combination of both. Similarly, in *Gibraltar*, the purpose of the measure, i.e., the discriminatory features of the tax reform establishing the taxable base of corporate taxpayers, was to exempt offshore companies from corporate taxation in Gibraltar. The larger framework under which that measure was adopted is thus the Gibraltarian corporate income tax system which 'formally applies to all corporate taxpayers'. Finally, in *A Brauerei*, the purpose of the measure under assessment was to exempt transfers resulting from the merger between a parent company and its (virtually) wholly-owned subsidiary from the general German law rules on the taxation of real property transfers, which the Court identified as the reference framework. A certain link thus exists between the measure under assessment and the reference framework under which it was adopted and, hence, under which it should be assessed for selectivity.

§3.07 THE COMPARABILITY ASSESSMENT FOR ESTABLISHING A DISCRIMINATION (THE SECOND STEP)

The second step of the three-step approach is determining whether the measure under assessment gives rise to a discrimination between comparable undertakings. The first judgment to set out how to assess comparability is the 2001 *Adria Wien* judgment. That judgment concerned an Austrian measure granting a rebate of energy taxes on natural gas and electricity only to undertakings whose activity was shown to consist primarily in the manufacture of goods. By way of a preliminary reference, the Austrian constitutional court asked the Court whether such a measure gives rise to State aid. The Court stated that, as regards selectivity, '[t]he only question to be determined is whether, under a particular statutory scheme, a State measure is such as to favour certain undertakings or the production of certain goods [...] in comparison with other undertakings which are in a legal and factual situation that is comparable in the light of the objective pursued by the measure in question'.[68]

67. By contrast, in his Opinion in Case C-374/17 *A Brauerei* EU:C:2018:741, para. 130, Advocate General Saugmandsgaard Oe states that 'the reference framework must be identified exclusively on the basis of the effects of the measures at issue'. However. he then proceeds to examine the various objectives put forth for the reference system to which the measure under assessment belongs in order to define the reference framework.

68. Case C-143/99, *Adria-Wien Pipeline and Wietersdorfer & Peggauer Zementwerke*, EU:C:2001:598, para. 41. The Court refers to Case C-75/97, *Belgium v. Commission*, paras 28 to 30 in support of that statement. That judgment concerned a Belgian law laying down the general

After repeating that statement in a subsequent judgment,[69] the focus of the comparability assessment appears to have undergone a significant shift. In a series of judgments from 2004 to 2006, the Court begins referring to 'the objective pursued by the system in question', rather than 'the objective pursued by the measure in question' for the purposes of assessing whether the beneficiaries of the measure under assessment are in a comparable situation to undertakings excluded from the scope of that measure.[70] However, in its 2011 *NOx* judgment, the Court surprisingly repeats the test laid down in the *Adria Wien* judgment and its focus on 'the objective pursued by the measure in question'.[71] Subsequent judgments of the Court from 2011 to the present,[72] including a number rendered by the Grand Chamber,[73] squarely affirm that whether undertakings are in a comparable factual and legal situation to establish selectivity depends on the objective pursued by the reference system under which the measure under assessment has been adopted.

Whether the focus of the comparability assessment is on the objective of the measure under assessment or the reference system under which it was adopted clearly has a significant impact on establishing whether a measure is selective. Imagine a measure that exempts manufacturers from paying an energy tax that service providers are required to pay. The exemption (the measure under assessment) and the energy tax from which it constitutes a derogation (the reference system) clearly pursue different objectives. The former seeks to exempt manufacturers from paying a tax on energy. From that perspective, manufacturers and service providers are in a different situation. The latter seeks to tax the consumption of energy sources. From that perspective, manufacturers and service providers are in a comparable situation, since they both consume energy sources to operate their business.

---

principles of social security for wage earners under which employers employing manual workers were granted a reduction in social security contributions for each of those workers. The Court performs no comparability assessment in those or other paragraphs of the judgment. It merely observes that increased reductions are granted only to undertakings belonging to certain sectors of the processing industry defined in the legislation and concludes that since undertakings belonging to the sectors of the processing industry not referred to in that legislation and undertakings in the tertiary sector and the building sector do not benefit from the increased reductions, the reduction is selective.

69. Case C-409/00, *Spain v. Commission*, EU:C:2003:92, para. 47. In that paragraph, the Court also refers to Case C-200/97, *Ecotrade*, EU:C:1998:579 in support of that explanation, although that judgment does not contain a similar test, since it concerns a measure adopted on the basis of a wholly discretionary administrative practice and not an aid scheme.
70. Case C-308/01, *GIL Insurance and Others*, EU:C:2004:252, para. 68; Case C-172/03, *Heiser*, EU:C:2005:130, para. 40; Joined Cases C-182/03 and C-217/03 *Belgium and Forum 187 v. Commission* EU:C:2005:266, para. 119; and Case C-88/03, *Portugal v. Commission*, EU:C:2006:511, para. 54.
71. Case C-279/08 P, *Commission v. Netherlands* EU:C:2011:551, para. 62.
72. Case C-323/16 P, *Eurallumina v. Commission* EU:C:2017:952, para. 60; Case C-74/16 *Congregación de Escuelas Pías Provincia Betania*, EU:C:2017:496, para. 69; Joined Cases C-234/16 and C-235/16 *ANGED* EU:C:2018:281, para. 37; Case 203/16 P, *Andres (in administration Heitkamp BauHolding) v. Commission* para. 83 and Case C-128/16 P *Commission v. Spain* EU:C:2018:591, paras 69 and 71.
73. Joined Cases C-106/09 P and C-107/09 P, *Commission v. Government of Gibraltar and United Kingdom*, EU:C:2011:732, para. 75; Joined Cases C-20/15 P and C-21/15 P, *World Duty Free Group*, EU:C:2016:981, para. 54 and Case C-374/17 *A Brauerei* EU:C:2018:1024, paras 33, 36 and 38.

Focussing solely on the objective of the measure, instead of the objective of the system of which it forms a part, would lead to no measure ever being considered selective, since the objective of every tax exemption is to favour a particular category of undertaking. It is therefore unsurprising that a closer reading of the *Adria Wien* and *NOx* judgments reveals that the Court went beyond a mere examination of the objective of the measures under assessment in concluding that those measures differentiate between undertakings in a comparable situation. In the *Adria Wien* judgment, the Court compared the tax treatment of undertakings whose activity was shown to consist primarily in the manufacture of goods as a result of the measure under assessment to the tax treatment of undertakings supplying services under the normal tax regime, even though the latter were not covered by the scope of the measure.[74] In the *NOx* judgment, the measure under assessment limited the possibility of trading emissions of nitrogen oxides (NOx) only to large industrial undertakings producing those kinds of emissions. The scope of the national measure was therefore circumscribed to those undertakings. Yet, in view of the general objective of the reference system, namely the protection of the environment, the Court held that all undertakings that were subject to the 'same kind of obligations', namely to reduce NOx emissions, were in a comparable legal and factual situation, irrespective of their size.[75]

The focus of the comparability assessment is thus on the objective of the reference system under which the measure under assessment has been adopted.[76] That demonstrates the importance of properly identifying the reference system in establishing selectivity in the case of schemes, since the objective of that system determines whether the beneficiaries of the measure under assessment are in a comparable situation to other taxpayers. That begs the question: which objective(s) should be taken into account for the comparability assessment?

Every piece of legislation pursues multiple objectives - some fiscal, some economic and some societal - and the outcome of the comparability assessment will vary considerably depending on the objective(s) used for establishing the benchmark for comparison. Imagine a measure granting a reduction in energy taxes for service providers. The larger framework under which the measure is adopted is the energy tax

74. Case C-143/99, *Adria-Wien Pipeline and Wietersdorfer & Peggauer Zementwerke*, EU:C:2001:598, para. 50 and 52.
75. Case C-279/08 P *Commission v. Netherlands* EU:C:2011:551, para. 66.
76. In his Opinion in Case C-270/15 P, *Belgium v. Commission*, EU:C:2016:289, paras 31 to 37, Advocate General Bobek identified three possible factors for assessing comparability: (1) the scope of the measure under examination, (2) the purpose of that measure and the objective of the broader reference framework of which it forms a part, and (3) the degree of competition between the beneficiaries of the measure and other undertakings. The Court appears to have given short shrift to the third factor in Case C-518/13, *Eventech*, EU:C:2015:9, para. 59, although Case C-5/14, *Kernkraftwerke Lippe-Ems*, EU:C:2015:354, paras 78 to 80 might suggest otherwise, and it has unequivocally chosen the second factor over the first as being decisive for the comparability analysis: comparability in light of the objective of the reference system. The problem with the third factor, i.e., competitive comparability, is that it undermines the main concern the State aid laws seek to address, namely subsidy wars between Member States. If a tax incentive granted to a sector a whole would be deemed non-discriminatory simply because that sector does not compete with other sectors, it would open the door for Member States to outbid each other through the grant of subsidies to attract undertakings from a particular sector.

that is normally applied for the consumption of energy products. The fiscal objective of that reference framework is to tax the consumption of energy products. In the light of that objective, service providers and manufacturing companies are in a comparable factual and legal situation, since they both consume energy products in their day-to-day operations. The economic objective of the tax is less clear. From the perspective of the legislator, it could be said to collect revenue for government expenditure. Focusing on that objective would result in the absurd result that the beneficiaries of the measure are in a comparable situation to all undertakings subject to any tax, since all taxes seek to collect revenue for government expenditure. The societal objective of the tax could be said to reduce energy consumption for environmental reasons. To the extent service providers consume less energy, they could be considered to be in a different situation to manufacturers in light of that objective. Then again, any undertaking subject to any environmental tax could be considered comparable to the beneficiaries of the measure in light of that objective.

While the Court has clearly held that only inherent objective(s) may be taken into account for assessing whether a discriminatory tax measure is justified by the nature and logic of the system (the third step of the three step approach), it has given scant guidance on the types of objective(s) that should be taken into consideration for assessing comparability (the second step). Different judgments point in different directions, some invoking solely fiscal objectives, others social objectives, and others differences that seem detached from the objectives of the reference system altogether.

An example of the latter is the *Paint Graphos* judgment. While the Court invoked 'the objective pursued by the corporation tax regime, namely the taxation of company profits' as the benchmark for comparison,[77] not a single provision of the Italian corporate tax regime is mentioned or assessed in the comparability assessment that follows. Instead, the Court refers to various objectives of EU legislation and a Commission Communication on the promotion of cooperative societies in Europe to highlight differences between cooperatives and other economic operators.[78] It concludes, on that basis, that cooperatives are not comparable to profit-making companies 'provided, however, that they act in the economic interest of their members and their relations with members are not purely commercial but personal and individual, the members being actively involved in the running of the business and entitled to equitable distribution of the results of economic performance'.[79] It then leaves it to the referring court to determine whether that was the case in relation to the producers' and workers' cooperative societies benefitting from the tax exemption in question.

Other cases lay the focus squarely on the fiscal objective of the reference system. In *Gibraltar*, the Court pointed to the 'the objective of the proposed tax reform' which was 'to introduce a general system of taxation for all companies established in Gibraltar'.[80] In the light of that objective, the Court found that offshore and onshore

77. Joined Cases C-78/08 to C-80/08, *Paint Graphos*, EU:C:2011:550, para. 54.
78. *Ibid*, paras 55 to 60.
79. *Ibid*, para. 61.
80. Joined Cases C-106/09 P and C-107/09 P, *Commission v. Government of Gibraltar and United Kingdom*, EU:C:2011:732, para. 101.

companies were in a comparable factual and legal situation and that the bases of assessment adopted in the proposed tax reform discriminated in favour of the former over the latter.[81] Similarly, in *A Braurei* the Court identified the objective of the German tax on the transfer of real property as the objective 'to tax the transfer of the right of ownership in a property from natural or legal person to another natural or legal person within the meaning of civil law'.[82] From the perspective of that objective, companies carrying out a restructuring procedure within a group, which benefit from an exemption from that tax, and standalone companies carrying out the same procedure, which cannot benefit from the exemption, are in a comparable factual and legal situation.[83] The Court therefore concluded that the tax exemption gave rise to prima facie discrimination between those two types of companies.

The *A Brauerei* judgment also seems to suggest that other intrinsic objectives of the reference system are only relevant for the purposes of assessing whether the measure under assessment is objectively justified and not for the comparability assessment.[84] An overly broad approach to the intrinsic objectives that may be taken into account for assessing comparability runs the risk of circularity. That is because, according to the case-law, the search for an objective justification also depends on objectives intrinsic to the reference system. In the *A Brauerei* judgment, the Court points in this regard to 'the objective related to the proper functioning of the general tax regime at issue [...] to avoid double and, hence, excessive taxation' as a means of justifying the discrimination resulting from the tax exemption. If that intrinsic objective could already have been taken into consideration during the comparability assessment, the Court would never have found a discrimination in the first place, since companies carrying out a restructuring procedure within a group and standalone companies carrying out the same procedure are in a different factual and legal situation in the light of that objective. That is because standalone companies are never at risk of double taxation when carrying out such a procedure. In contrast, if the same intrinsic objectives could be taken into account under the second and third steps of the three-step approach, no measure that is found to give rise to a discrimination would ever be objectively justified. Widening the scope of intrinsic objectives that can be taken into consideration for assessing comparability also places less of a burden on the Member States to justify the exercise of their fiscal sovereignty, since establishing a discrimination would be harder.

This is precisely the approach taken by the Court in the *ANGED* case.[85] In that judgment, the Court ruled that a tax based on the sales area of an undertaking that only applied to undertakings with a sales area surpassing a particular threshold was not discriminatory in light of the objective of the tax, which was 'to contribute towards environmental protection and town and country planning'. According to the Court, 'the environmental impact of retail establishments is largely dependent on their size' and 'a

81. *Ibid*, paras 106 and 107.
82. Case C-374/17, *A Brauerei*, EU:C:2018:1024, para. 39.
83. *Ibid*, para. 41.
84. *Ibid*, para. 49.
85. Joined Cases C-234/16 and C-235/16 *ANGED* EU:C:2018:281.

condition relating to sales area thresholds [...] in order to distinguish between undertakings with a greater or lesser impact, is consistent with the objectives pursued'. Thus, rather than look at the fiscal objective of the tax, i.e. to tax sales area, the Court looked at the tax's environmental objective to assess whether companies subject to the tax were comparable to those exempt from the tax. As regards the question whether the threshold was set in an appropriate manner to ensure that the tax did not discriminate between comparable companies, the Court left the determination of that threshold to the discretion of the national legislature and, without any further assessment, declared that the thresholds at issue could 'not be regarded as manifestly inappropriate for the purposes of the objectives pursued'.[86] Neither the Court nor the Advocate General required any evidence to conclude that the exemption from a tax on surface area, which was allegedly motivated by environmental and urban planning considerations, had been properly tailored to tax only those establishments that gave rise to environmental and urban planning concerns.

The approach seems at odds with an earlier judgment of the Court that also concerned an environmental levy. In the 2008 *British Aggregates* judgment, the Court annulled a Commission decision that had declared a British system of levies on the commercial exploitation of aggregates not to constitute aid. More specifically, the Court ruled that the Commission was wrong to conclude that that system was not selective, notwithstanding the fact that it foresaw an exemption from the levy for the extraction of by-products.[87] The Court accepted that the levy pursued an environmental objective, namely reducing the unnecessary extraction of virgin aggregate. However, the Court held that 'the need to take account of requirements relating to environmental protection, however legitimate, cannot justify the exclusion of selective measures, even specific ones such as environmental levies, from the scope of Article [107(1) TFEU] [...], as account may in any event usefully be taken of the environmental objectives when the compatibility of the State aid measure with the common market is being assessed pursuant to Article [107(3)]'.

§3.08 OBJECTIVELY JUSTIFYING DISCRIMINATION (THE THIRD STEP)

Once it has been established that a tax measure discriminates between comparable undertakings under a particular reference system, the final step that remains for establishing selectivity is assessing whether that discrimination can be objectively justified. The notion of objective justification is present in numerous internal market provisions. Unlike many of those provisions,[88] no mention is made of possible justifications in the text of Article 107(1) TFEU.[89] Rather, it is the Court that has established that a prima facie discriminatory measure can be objectively justified and thus be non-selective.

86. Ibid, para. 48.
87. Case C-487/06 P, *British Aggregates v. Commission*, EU:C:2008:757, paras 79 to 93.
88. *See* Arts 36, 45(3), 52, 65 TFEU.
89. In this manner, Art. 107 TFEU is similar to Art. 102 TFEU, which also contains no mention of possible justifications, but which the Court has read into that provision.

The first mention of a justification precluding the selectivity of a tax measure is in the Court's 1974 judgment on an Italian measure exempting the textile sector from certain fiscal contributions. In that judgment, the Court concluded that a partial exemption from social charges from which undertakings in that sector benefitted was selective 'without there being any justification for this exemption on the basis of the nature or general scheme of this system'.[90] That the justification must find its origin in the nature or general scheme of the reference system of which the measure forms a part has been repeated in all judgments rendered since.[91] According to the Court, a measure finds its origin in the nature and general scheme of the reference system where it directly results from the basic or guiding principles of that system.[92] This means that measures that are necessary to achieve the objectives underpinning the reference system can justify discrimination, whereas measures that seek to achieve an objective that is unrelated to that system cannot.[93]

It is clear that allowing objectives extrinsic to the reference system to objectively justify discriminatory tax measures would result in unpredictable outcomes, since selectivity would depend on the political choices of the legislator. However, the question that then arises is which objectives are intrinsic to a particular reference framework? From an overview of the case-law in which the Court has accepted environmental objectives as being inherent to the reference system, it appears that there must be some correlation between the tax system and the objective it seeks to achieve for that objective to be considered intrinsic to the system. Provided it can be shown that the reference system has been designed in an appropriate and proportionate manner to pursue a legitimate objective, that objective must be considered to form an intrinsic part of the reference system. Consequently, while the protection of the environment may be considered an intrinsic objective of a tax based on surface area, since the size of an undertaking corresponds to a certain extent to its impact on the environment,[94] or the protection of human health may be considered an intrinsic objective of a sugar or fat tax,[95] the same would not be true of a tax on profit allegedly pursuing those objectives.

It is in the 2011 *Paint Graphos* judgment that the Court has gone furthest in explaining how an objective justification can be successfully invoked. In that judgment, the Court affirms that 'tax exemptions which are the result of an objective that is unrelated to the tax system of which they form part cannot circumvent the [State aid

90. Case 173/73, *Italy v. Commission*, EU:C:1974:71, para. 15.
91. *See, e.g.*, Case C-88/03, *Portugal v. Commission*, EU:C:2006:511, para. 52 and Joined Cases C-20/15 P and C-21/15 P, *Commission v. World Duty Free Group and Others*, EU:C:2016:981, para. 58 and the case-law cited.
92. Joined Cases C-78/08 to C-80/08, *Paint Graphos* EU:C:2011:550, para. 68.
93. *Ibid*, para. 70.
94. In contrast, in para. 92 of the *British Aggregates* judgment, the Court appeared to rule out environmental protection as an inherent objective of a levy on the extraction of virgin aggregates and considered such an objective to only play a role in the compatibility assessment under Article 107(3) TFEU.
95. *See, e.g.*, Commission Decision of 24 April 2018 in Case SA.45862 (2018/N) Irish tax on Sugar Sweetened Drinks (OJ 2018 C 180, p. 1).

rules]'.[96] It adds that a tax exemption 'must be consistent not only with the inherent characteristics of the tax system in question but also as regards the manner in which that system is implemented' and that it is therefore necessary 'for the Member State concerned to introduce and apply appropriate control and monitoring procedures in order to ensure that specific tax measures introduced for the benefit of cooperative societies are consistent with the logic and general scheme of the tax system and to prevent economic entities from choosing that particular legal form for the sole purpose of taking advantage of the tax benefits provided for that kind of undertaking'. Finally, the Court holds that 'for tax exemptions such as those at issue in the main proceedings to be justified [...], it is also necessary to ensure that those exemptions are consistent with the principle of proportionality and do not go beyond what is necessary, in that the legitimate objective being pursued could not be attained by less far reaching measures'.[97]

These restrictive requirements, especially when compared to the fundamental freedoms case-law, means that discriminations resulting from national tax measures are extremely difficult to justify. It is therefore perhaps unsurprising that the Court did not repeat them in its *A Brauerei* judgment when accepting the need to avoid double taxation as a valid justification for discrimination,[98] the same justification it accepted in the *Paint Graphos* judgment under the aforementioned stringent conditions.[99]

Otherwise, the General Court has also acknowledged the principle of fiscal neutrality as an objective justifying discrimination.[100] Other justifications that could possibly meet the aforementioned requirements in relation to tax measures include the need to fight tax fraud or tax evasion,[101] the progressive nature of income tax in light of the ability to pay principle, and the objective of optimising the recovery of fiscal debts.[102] By contrast, the Court has explicitly rejected that regional development, social cohesion policy and employment policy objectives can justify discriminatory treatment.[103] Such extrinsic objectives may only play a role in the Commission's State aid assessment, if at all, in relation to compatibility.

96. *Ibid*, paras 69 and 70.
97. *Ibid*, para. 75.
98. Case C-374/17, *A Brauerei*, EU:C:2018:1024, para. 50.
99. Joined Cases C-78/08 to C-80/08, *Paint Graphos* EU:C:2011:550, para. 71.
100. *See, e.g.*, Case T-399/11 RENV, *Banco Santander and Santusa v. Commission*, EU:T:2018:787, para. 171.
101. Commission decision of 29 July 2016 in Case SA.42007 on Alternative income tax regime for the wholesale diamond sector in Belgium; [2016] OJ C 369/1.
102. *See* Commission Decision 2011/276/EU of 26 May 2010 on State aid C-76/03, Umicore SA [2011] OJ L 122/76. The decision concludes that no advantage was granted as a result of a tax settlement, but the appropriate conclusion appears to be one of a lack of selectivity, either because a similar settlement would have been available to comparable taxpayers or because any discrimination is justified by the need to optimally recover fiscal debts.
103. Case C-88/03, *Portugal v. Commission*, EU:C:2006:511, para. 82 and Case C-6/12, *P Oy*, EU:C:2013:525, para. 30.

§3.09 CONCLUSION

Whether a national tax measure gives rise to State aid essentially turns on the notion of selectivity. As things currently stand, the case-law gives limited guidance to assess whether such measures are selective and thus constitute State aid. As much as four different tests apply to assess the selectivity of fiscal measures depending on the nature of the measure and, in relation to schemes, as many as three different tests have been proposed to establish selectivity. Moreover, different approaches have been taken to identifying the reference framework, the comparability assessment and the search for possible justifications, again depending on the nature of the measure under assessment.

Beyond the Court's rejection of formalism, no guidance exists on how to identify the reference framework. As regards the comparability assessment, a tension exists between judgments that accept intrinsic objectives beyond the fiscal objective of the reference system to conduct that assessment and judgments that rely solely on its fiscal objective. A further tension exists between the intrinsic objectives that can be taken into account for comparability and those that can be invoked to justify discrimination. Finally, it is unclear whether the principles of necessity, appropriateness and proportionality play a role in devising justifications for discrimination.

Some have argued that the inconsistencies in the case-law can be explained by the fact that different rules apply when establishing selectivity in relation to exemptions from general tax measures (like in *Paint Graphos* and *A Brauerei*), special levies (like in *Adra Wien, NOx* and *ANGED*) and inherently discriminatory taxes (like in *Gibraltar*). That would bring the total number of tests to establish selectivity in relation to fiscal measures to ten!

Considering the importance of legal certainty in relation to taxation, such inconsistencies should be avoided at all cost. In the absence of harmonisation in taxation at the EU level, it is clear that a balance must be struck between the fiscal sovereignty of the Member States and the effective application of the State aid rules. However, the search for a general test that can apply to all types of fiscal measures while assuring that balance remains elusive. As testified by the recent *A Brauerei* judgment, the foreseeable approach to selectivity is one that the Court will likely develop case-by-case. Clarity in relation to the notion of fiscal selectivity therefore still seems out of reach.

CHAPTER 4

Mismatches in View of the Recent Fiscal State Aid Investigations: Genuine Situation or Intentional (Illegal) Arrangements?

Paulina Szotek & Alexandra Miladinovic

§4.01 INTRODUCTION

For more than two decades now, the Commission has been applying the prohibition against State aid under Article 107(1) of the Treaty on the Functioning of the European Union (TFEU) in the area of direct tax law. In the last couple of years, and in particular after the BEPS initiative, the focus has been increasingly placed on identifying fiscal State aid and challenging Member States' (MSs) tax measures.[1] Particularly, after hundreds of tax rulings issued by the Luxembourg tax authorities were leaked and made available to the public in the course of the LuxLeaks affair in 2014, the Commission started investigating the tax ruling practices of MSs.[2] The Commission's inquiry, apart from the scrutiny of various aid schemes (e.g., the *Belgian Excess Profit*

1. *See, e.g.*, Press Release IP/17/5343 (18 December 2017); Press Release, IP/18/4228 (20 June 2018); *see also* Dimitrios Kyriazis, *From Soft Law to Soft Law Through Hard Law: The Commission's Approach to the State Aid Assessment of Tax Rulings*, 3 EStAL, 428 et seq. (2016).
2. Tax rulings are instruments that may be binding or non-binding and they are issued by tax authorities to provide legal certainty to taxpayers before a taxable event materializes. Some rulings are specifically dedicated to solve issues mainly related to the application of transfer pricing legislations. The function of rulings is to determine the application of national tax law to a particular case in advance and to lay down the methods through which transfer pricing for intra-group transactions within a multinational enterprise is established to be considered at arm's length. See Commission Notice on the notion of State aid as referred to in Art 107(1) of the Treaty on the Functioning of the European Union, C/2016/2946, OJ C 262, 19.7.2016, p. 1–50 [hereinafter: Notion of Aid Notice], para. 169; Richard Lyal, *Transfer Pricing Rules and State Aid*, 38 Fordham Int'l L.J. 1017 (2015); Adrien Giraud and Sylvain Petit, *Tax Rulings and State Aid Qualification: Should Reality Matter?*, 16(2) EStAL 233 (2017).

Rulings Scheme or the *UK CFC rules*),[3] led to the initiation of formal investigation procedures with regard to rulings granted by some MSs.[4] While the Commission scrutinized transfer pricing rulings and, respectively, rulings governing the profit allocation in the larger part of the cases (e.g., *Fiat*, *Starbucks*, *Amazon*, *Apple*, *Huhtamäki*),[5] in two tax ruling cases so far it was concerned with mismatches (*Engie* and *McDonald's*).[6] Whereas the debates around transfer pricing rulings and especially the Commission's argumentation line based on the arm's length principle are worthwhile discussing as much,[7] this contribution will rather focus on the latter set of cases and will refer to the former where necessary.

In general, mismatches may occur once rules apply concurrently in a not coordinated manner. Mismatches between uncoordinated rules can lead both to an advantage or disadvantage.[8] For the purpose of State aid, they become relevant if the concurrent application of rules results in lower or non-taxation on a selective basis.[9] In the *Engie* case, the Commission addressed a mismatch which appeared in a pure intra-state situation and led to double non-taxation of income in Luxembourg.[10] The *McDonald's* case, by contrast, concerned a mismatch in an inter-state scenario which led to non-taxation in neither of the two states involved.[11] Although the exploitation of rules not being perfectly coordinated can cause a benefit for undertakings, the application of State aid law to mismatches is not entirely clarified.[12]

3. Commission Decision of 11 January 2016 on the Excess Profit Exemption State aid Scheme SA. 37667 (2015/C) (ex 2015/NN) implemented by Belgium, C(2015) 9837 final; for the negative decision in the UK CFC Group Financing Exemption case see Commission Decision of 2 April 2019 on the State aid SA.44896 implemented by the United Kingdom concerning CFC Group Financing Exemption, C(2019)2526 final.
4. E.g., Press Release, IP-14-663_EN (11 June 2014).
5. Commission Decision of 4 October 2017 on State Aid SA.38944 (2014/C)(ex 2014/NN) implemented by Luxembourg to Amazon, C(2017) 6740 final; Commission Decision of 30 August 2016 on State aid SA.38373 (2014/C) (ex 2014/NN) (ex 2014/CP) implemented by Ireland to Apple, C(2016)5605 final; Commission Decision of 21 October 2015 on State aid SA.38374 (2014/C ex 2014/NN) implemented by the Netherlands to Starbucks, C(2015) 7143 final; Commission Decision of 21 October 2015 on State aid SA.38375 (2014/C ex 2014/NN) which Luxembourg granted to Fiat, C(2015) 7152 final.
6. Commission Decision of 20 June 2018 on State aid SA.44888 (2016/C) (ex 2016/NN) implemented by Luxembourg in favour of ENGIE, C(2018) 3839 final; Commission Decision of 19 September 2018 on Tax Rulings SA.38945 (2015/C) (ex 2015/NN) (ex 2014/CP) granted by Luxembourg in Favour of McDonald's Europe, C(2018) 6076 final; for the opening decision in the Huhtamäki case see Press Release IP/19/1591 (7 March 2019) and Commission Opening Decision of 10 May 2019, State aid SA.50400 (2019/C)(ex 2019/NN-2) Possible State aid in favour of Huhtamäki, OJ 2019/C 161/02.
7. For further literature on the Arm's Length Principle *see, e.g.*, Bonnici, The European Commission's Arm's Length Standard: Relationship and Compatibility with the Arm's Length Principle under Transfer Pricing, ITPJ 2019, published online on 29 November 2018.
8. *See* e.g., OECD BEPS Action Plan on Base Erosion and Profit Shifting (2013) 9; also *see*, in particular, the final report on BEPS Action 2, OECD, Neutralising the Effects of Hybrid Mismatch Arrangements, Action 2 - 2015 Final Report (2015).
9. Rita Szudoczky, Double Taxation Relief, Transfer Pricing Adjustments and State aid Law: Comments in Isabelle Richelle/ Wolfgang Schön/ Edoardo Traversa (eds) State aid Law and Business Taxation (2016) 165.
10. Press Release, IP-18-4228 (20 June 2018).
11. Press Release, IP-18-5831 (19 September 2018); for the opening decision in the Huhtamäki case see Press Release IP/19/1591 (7 March 2019).
12. *See* Szudoczky/van de Streek, Revisiting the Dutch Interest Box under the EU State aid rules and the Code of Conduct: When a 'Disparity' is Selective and Harmful, Intertax 2010, 272.

Against this backdrop, we aim to shed some more light on this matter. First, we give an overview on the principle of autonomy and types of mismatches and present the different views on their compatibility with State aid rules. Second, we analyse particular aspects of the Commission decisions in the cases of *Engie, Huhtamäki*[13] and *McDonald's*. After a brief description of the cases, we extract the main arguments and make some comments on them. The focus of this part is specifically put on the Commission's final decision in the *Engie* case and the opening decision in the *Huhtamäki* case. It outlines the facts of these cases and the Commission's analyses, with a particular attention to the problem of the alleged misapplication of national legal provisions by Luxembourg. It discusses different aspects of these cases and looks for potential similarities and differences in the Commission's approaches. This analysis is completed with the general views on the *McDonald's* case. In this context, we aim at elaborating on the justification step within the selectivity analysis in more detail and discussing potential implications of the decision of the General Court in the *Magnetrol International* case.[14] This case concerns the *Belgian Excess Profit Ruling Scheme* and is the first in the row of the Commission's tax ruling cases decided by the European Union (EU) Courts. Although more case law is expected to follow soon, we want to pursue a brief analysis of this very first case since it could be of interest for the treatment of mismatches, and potentially allow a prognosis on the outcome of the other Commission decisions appealed. Last, we summarize our findings and end with a conclusion. Even though we might not be able to give final answers at this point in time, we aim at contributing to the academic debates and add some ideas to the discussions.

§4.02 TYPES OF MISMATCHES AND THEIR COMPATIBILITY WITH STATE AID LAW

Mismatches do not only occur within one jurisdiction (intra-state mismatch) but also due to the concurrence of two jurisdictions (inter-state mismatch). For State aid purposes, the first type of mismatch might be relevant when two or more rules within one state apply different legal consequences which, when applied at the same time, can lead to a selective tax advantage.[15] Thus, as will be later shown by example of the *Engie* case, the assessment of selectivity in terms of intra-state mismatches might be particularly challenging as there are two rules at stake which examined separately do not pose a risk of being contradictory to State aid rules - they are only selective if applied simultaneously.[16] In purely internal situations, the advantage can be attributed to one MS.

13. Case SA. 50400 (Alleged aid to Huhtamäki), IP/19/15/91. At the time when this article had been written, only the opening decision was available.
14. Judgement of the General Court of 14 February 2019, Joined Cases T-131/16 and T-263/16, *Magnetrol International*, ECLI:EU:T:2019:91.
15. Rita Szudoczky, Double Taxation Relief, Transfer Pricing Adjustments and State aid Law: Comments in Isabelle Richelle/ Wolfgang Schön/ Edoardo Traversa (eds) State aid Law and Business Taxation (2016) 165.
16. *See* Ibid., 177 et seq.

The relevance of the second type, i.e., inter-state mismatches, in respect of the State aid prohibition is disputed.[17] In general, the Court of Justice of the European Union (CJEU) recognizes the tax sovereignty of MSs.[18] According to the principle of autonomy, which is also a fundamental principle of EU law, MSs are free to apply their tax laws without the necessity to adjust to the laws applied somewhere else.[19] Each tax system is autonomously applicable. In the absent of coordination, the autonomous application of tax systems could produce a mismatch.[20] This mismatch can have a detrimental effect on the internal market. As put by A.G. Geelhoed, 'distortions of economic activity [are] resulting from the fact that different legal systems must exist side by side. In certain cases, these distortions provide disadvantages for economic actors; in other cases, advantages. While in the first case they are "restrictive," in the second case they stimulate cross-border establishment activity'.[21]

According to settled case-law, negative impacts for taxpayers deriving from the parallel application of two or more tax systems do not fall foul of, in particular, the fundamental freedoms.[22] Thus, consequences that occur due to the parallel existence of two tax regimes in two different countries are not covered by the scope of the freedoms.[23] It has been clarified that the 'Treaty offers no guarantee to a citizen of the Union that transferring his residence to a Member State other than that in which he previously resided will be neutral as regards taxation. Given the disparities in the tax legislation of the Member States, such a transfer may be to the citizen's advantage or not, according to circumstances.'[24] The exercise of sovereign power involves neither any obligation for adjustments to the tax treatment in another state, nor any provision of compensation for taxpayers for such deterioration.[25] As a result, it can be concluded

17. *See, e.g.*, De Brue, Editorial XL. Can Tax Treaties Confer State Aid?, EC Tax Review 2017, 232.
18. According to settled CJEU jurisprudence, 'it is settled case-law that, in the absence of unifying or harmonising measures adopted by the Community, the MS remain competent to determine the criteria for taxation of income and wealth', *see, e.g.*, Judgement of the CJEU of 28 February 2008, Case C-293/06, Deutsche Shell GmbH, para. 41; also *see* CJEU, Case C-290/04, FKP Scorpio Konzertproduktionen, para. 54; CJEU, Case C-374/04, Test Claimants in Class IV of the ACT Group Litigation, para. 52; CJEU, C-231/05, Oy AA, para. 52.
19. *See, e.g.*, Judgement of the CJEU of 12 February 2009, C-67/08, Block, para. 31, in which the Court held that 'in the current stage of the development of Community Law, the Member States enjoy a certain autonomy in this area provided they comply with Coummunity law, and are not obliged therefore to adapt their own tax systems to the different systems of tax of the other Member States in order, inter alia, to eliminate the double taxation arising from the exercise in parallel by those Member States of their fiscal sovereignty'.
20. *See Kokott*, Das Steuerrecht der Europäischen Union (2018) § 2 para. 156.
21. Case C-374/04, Test Claimants in Class IV of the ACT Group Litigation, AG Opinion, 23 February 2006, para. 38.
22. Judgment in *Kenny*, 1/78, EU:C:1978:163, at para. 18; Judgment in *Van Dam*, 185/78 to 204/78, EU:C:1979:177, at para. 10.
23. Judgment in *Walt Wilhelm*, 14/68, EU:C:1969:4, at para. 13.
24. Judgment in *Block*, C-67/08, EU:C:2009:92, at para. 35; also *see* Judgment in *Alevizos*, C-392/05, EU:C:2007:251, at para. 76; Judgment in *Renneberg*, C-527/06, EU:C:2008:566, at para. 40; Judgment in *Schulz-Delzers and Schulz*, C-240/10, EU:C:2011:591, at para. 42; Judgment in *National Grid Indus*, C-371/10, EU:C:2011:785, at para. 62.
25. *See* Judgement of the CJEU of 26 February 2015, C-144/13, C-154/13, C-160/13, *VDP Dental Laboratory and Others*, para. 63.

that unfavourable results stemming from mismatches are not protected by the freedoms – even though this outcome constitutes a barrier for economic integration and the internal market, and obviously contradicts most international attempts for a coordinated approach among states to avoid negative aspects hampering economic relations. The fundamental freedoms cannot serve as a basis to challenge different tax policy decisions of the MSs insofar as there is no harmonization.[26]

Whereas one can find settled jurisprudence concerning the fundamental freedoms,[27] which should not be discussed here in more details,[28] there is not much case-law for the field of State aid in terms of mismatches. Since it is argued by many that both the fundamental freedoms and the rules governing the State aid prohibition form two sides of one coin, the majority pronounces that the principle of autonomy should lead to the same results also for the State aid rules.[29] Accordingly, the State aid rules should not be applicable whenever there is a tax benefit that is conferred on an undertaking resulting from a mismatch between tax legislations.[30] Even in the fundamental freedoms analysis, the EU Court has apparently admitted that there could be exceptions to the rule.[31] Accordingly, the CJEU specified that disparities do not fall within the scope 'so long as they affect all persons subject to them in accordance with objective criteria and without regard to their nationality'.[32] Therefore, disparities could well be covered by the scope of the freedoms if they produce a discrimination or restriction.[33] The same is true for State aid. Mismatches in an inter-state scenario are not automatically outside the scope of Article 107 TFEU.

Similar to the fundamental freedoms, one out of four criteria of Article 107 TFEU requires the respective advantage to be attributable to a MS. The prevailing view considers relevant the imputability of the aid to only one MS and, thus, this criterion should not be satisfied in case of disparities.[34] Since the benefit results from the interaction of two tax systems, it is not possible to assign it to only one of the states involved, and therefore the measure should fall outside the scope of State aid law.[35]

26. Opinion of AG Geelhoed in *Test Claimants in Class IV of the ACT Group Litigation*, C-374/04, EU:C:2006:139, para. 47; Judgment in *Columbus Container Services*, C-298/05, EU:C:2007:754, para. 51; Judgment in *Block*, C-67/08, EU:C:2009:92, para. 31.
27. *See* on disparities and the fundamental freedoms, e.g., Judgement of the CJEU of 12 July 2005, C-403/03, *Schempp*, para. 45; CJEU of 29 April 2004, C-387/01, *Weigl*, para. 55; CJEU of 15 June 2004, C-365/02, *Lindfors*, para. 34; CJEU of 29 November 2011, C-371/10, *National Grid Indus*, para. 62.
28. For further academic literature on the impediments for free movement resulting from disparities see, Christoph Marchgraber, Double (Non-)Taxation and EU Law (2018) section 2.3.3.
29. *See, e.g.*, Juliane Kokott, Das Steuerrecht der Europäischen Union (2018) § 2 para. 160.
30. *Ibid.*
31. *See* Christoph Marchgraber, Double (Non-)Taxation and EU Law (2018) section 2.3.3.
32. Judgment in *Perfili*, C-177/94, EU:C:1996:24, at para. 17; Judgment in *Schempp*, C-403/03, EU:C:2005:446, at para. 34.
33. *See Kokott*, Das Steuerrecht der Europäischen Union (2018) § 2 para. 196.
34. *See, e.g.*, *Szudoczky/Van de Streek*, Revisiting the Dutch Interest Box under the EU State Aid Rules and the Code of Conduct: When a 'Disparity' is Selective and Harmful, Intertax 2010, 272.
35. Rita Szudoczky, Double Taxation Relief, Transfer Pricing Adjustments and State aid Law: Comments in Isabelle Richelle/ Wolfgang Schön/ Edoardo Traversa (eds) State aid Law and Business Taxation (2016) 177 et seq.

However, this solution might not be as convincing as it might appear at first glance. It should be clear from the outset that the imputability of a State measure to one single MS cannot be decisive when there is a situation in which two MSs collaborate in order to provide an advantage to an undertaking: If, for example, two MSs agree in the course of a bilateral tax ruling or advance pricing agreement (APA) not to impose any taxes on a particular undertaking operating in those two states, the measure is imputable to both MSs. This situation should clearly be covered by the State aid rules even though the proportion of aid granted by each state might not be established without difficulties. The proportion of the aid granted by one State or the other should not be relevant for the classification as State aid if the competition is distorted by State involvement. Due to the imputability of an aid to two states at the same time, the State aid rules can theoretically apply as well in a scenario which involves one MS and a third State – at least for the part of the MS, which is obliged to respect Article 107 TFEU. Once both States are involved in the process of granting State aid, the advantage cannot be attributed to only one of those States. However, this does not alter the fact that one of those States, i.e., the MS, has to observe State aid law and that – from an isolated country-perspective – State aid could be granted at least partly by it. Indeed, imputability to two states would leave some open issues regarding recovery due to the proportional amount of aid to be recovered – particularly in case of third-state involvement since only MSs are obliged to recover State aid. Nevertheless, a situation of State aid through involvement of two states should be covered by Article 107 TFEU regardless whether both or only one of the states is a MS.

In an official document, the Commission lists some more examples of deliberate mismatches that could fall within the ambit of the State aid prohibition.[36] It names, for example, situations in which tax authorities, by means of a ruling, confirm a tax treatment in violation of the normal interpretation of national law. Moreover, a deliberate mismatch could be in place if a special legislation is introduced which creates a mismatch that specifically applies to a selective group of undertakings, like 'a special definition of debt or equity [...] introduced just for international transactions, which would not apply as part of the normal tax system domestically'. In academic literature, the same was concluded for participation exemption regimes and tax treaty exemptions without subject-to-tax clauses as well as unilateral downward transfer pricing adjustments.[37] Hence, the dividing line between deliberate mismachtes, which are covered by the State aid rules and genuine mismatches, which are not, might not entirely be clear in each case.[38] Some of the Commission's latest decisions challenged different cases of mismatches which shall be discussed and analysed in the following chapters.

36. Directorate General for Internal Policies. Policy Department A: Economic and Scientific Policy, EU State Aid Law and National Tax Rulings, IP/A/TAXE/2015-02, PE 563.453, October 2015, 15.
37. *See* Rita Szudoczky, Double Taxation Relief, Transfer Pricing Adjustments and State aid Law: Comments in Isabelle Richelle/ Wolfgang Schön/ Edoardo Traversa (eds) State aid Law and Business Taxation (2016) 182 et seq.
38. *See* Werner Haslehner, Double Taxation Relief, Transfer Pricing Adjustments and State aid Law in Isabelle Richelle/ Wolfgang Schön/ Edoardo Traversa (eds) State aid Law and Business Taxation (2016) 136 et seq.

§4.03 MISMATCHES DUE TO DIFFERENT QUALIFICATIONS BY ONE AND BY MORE THAN ONE STATE

On 20 June 2018, the Commission made a final decision on the Luxembourg tax treatment of *Engie* (formerly GDF Suez).[39] The Commission concluded that Luxembourg deviated from the 'normal interpretation' of its national law in applying it to two sets of rulings granted to *Engie's* entities concerning the tax treatment of certain interest-free convertible instruments (so-called 'ZORAs'). In fact, the Commission submitted that Luxembourg tax authorities agreed to create a type of *lacuna* in applicable national law, whereby profits generated by *Engie's* two companies in Luxembourg were exempt from corporate taxation due to a specific financial arrangement. Although a considerable amount of time passed since the final decision had been issued, financial instruments that give raise to interest payment deductions without a corresponding inclusion remain one of the biggest concerns of the Commission under State aid rules.

While the *Engie* case applies to a purely internal situation of Luxembourg domestic tax treatment, the Commission has also opened State aid investigations into the tax treatment of financial intra-group arrangements between entities situated in two different states.[40] On 7 March 2019, the Commission opened a formal investigation into rulings obtained by a Luxembourg subsidiary (*Huhtalux*) of the Finnish *Huhtamäki* group.[41] In particular, the Commission's State aid assessment relates to the treatment of interest-free loans granted to *Huhtalux* by another financing group company situated in Ireland. The Commission raised doubts as to whether deductions of interest payment in case of an intra-group interest-free loan arrangement derogate

39. Commission Decision of 20 June 2018 on State aid SA.44888 (2016/C) (ex 2016/NN) implemented by Luxembourg in favour of ENGIE, C(2018)3839 final; *see* on the case *Gormsen*, European State aid and Tax Rulings (2019) 35 et seq.
40. In the Case SA.38375 (2014/C ex 2014/NN) concerning aid which Luxembourg granted to Fiat from 21 October 2015, the Commission decided that the transfer pricing method applied to intra-group financial transactions, and endorsed in the tax rulings by the Luxembourg tax authorities, did not reflect the market outcome. In result, taxable profits of Fiat entity in Luxembourg were understated. Moreover, in the Case SA.46470 (2017/NN) – Netherlands (Possible State aid in favour of Inter IKEA) from 18 December 2017, the Commission expressed its doubts whether the price paid by Inter IKEA Systems in the Netherlands for the acquisition of the intellectual property from another group company, the interest paid on the inter-company loan, and agreed price adjustment mechanism correspond to a reliable approximation of a market-based outcome. The Commission submits that as a consequence of the interest payments, a significant part of Inter IKEA Systems' profits was shifted to its parent entity in Liechtenstein. The Fiat case concerns the methodology for establishing a transfer price in the specific intra-group loan arrangement, and the IKEA case mainly concerns the arm's length nature of some of the terms of the loan agreement for the interest payment as well as the deduction of provisions for future interest related to the certain price adjustment mechanism that may not be compliant with Dutch law. It is therefore beyond the scope of this article to discuss those cases in relation to potential mismatches resulting from certain intra-group financial arrangements. Detailed aspects of the Fiat and IKEA decisions that are problematic from a fiscal perspective are subject to assessment by Paulina Szotek as a part of her PhD research on the topic of 'Group Taxation, State aid and Transfer Pricing' at the Maastricht University.
41. Case SA. 50400 (Alleged aid to Huhtamäki), IP/19/15/91.

from Luxembourg law. According to the tax treatment agreed with the Luxembourg tax authorities, *Huhtalux* could book such an interest payment as an expense and deduct it from its taxable profits. The Commission claims that *Huhtalux* does not effectively pay any such interest to another group entity in Ireland, and thus it has doubts whether Luxembourg tax authorities should have accepted deductibility of such expenses corresponding to fictitious interest payments (deemed deduction). Therefore, the main concern of the Commission is the fact that no independent third party in the market would have demanded and obtained such deductions when it did not effectively pay any interest to another unrelated undertaking. Accordingly, such an arrangement ultimately aims at reducing *Huhtalux's* taxable base in Luxembourg, where the company is taxed on lower profits due to the deduction. The *Huhtamäki* case concerns a unilateral State aid assessment of intra-group financial arrangements based on the factual situation of only one company involved in such transaction, and the underlying national tax treatment of a single element of this arrangement, namely the interest deduction by Luxembourg.

The discussable aspect of these different approaches in the two cases relates to the concept of intentional and genuine mismatches, and different approaches to establish the conditions of advantage and selectivity. As rightfully put forward by the Commission, Article 107(1) TFEU defines aid measures in relation to their *economic effects* in the market, not in relation to the legislative techniques used.[42] Consequently, in case of the intra-group loan arrangement, a prima facie selective advantage can potentially be established when the combined effect of the deductibility of interest and the exemption/non-inclusion of the corresponding income results in non-taxation of profits, both through a derogation from generally applicable national rules (i.e., the reference framework), and by discriminating between undertakings in the same factual and legal situation. This can be fully ascertained when the case concerns a purely internal transaction or series of transactions taking place within one MS. This is because in practice, the selectivity requirement rests on a domestic treatment of undertakings and on finding a derogation from the reference framework, as acknowledged by the CJEU.[43] National treatments granting artificial advantages to only certain undertakings have to be scrutinized by the Commission. Nevertheless, State aid law has no vocation to redress distortion of business competition left by diversity among national laws.[44] In that case, general measures are excluded from State aid scrutiny and MSs are allowed to compete by their means, which ensures regulatory neutrality.

42. Judgement of the CJEU, Joined cases, C-106/09P and C-107/09P, *Commission v. Government of Gibraltar, UK and Northern Ireland*, paras. 88–92.
43. Judgement of the CJEU, Case C-143/99, *Adria-Wien Pipeline and Wietersdorfer & Peggauer Zementwerke*, paras. 34 et seq. Judgment of the CJEU, Case C-15/14 P, *Commission v MOL*, para. 60. Judgment of the CJEU, Case C-20/15 P and C-21/15 P, *Commission v World Duty Free Group and Others*, para. 56.
44. Ever since the Spaak Report it is stated that 'Certain regimes of intervention that formally constitute aids or subsidies are not specifically aimed at certain undertakings or sectors, but affect general economy. In such case, the Commission has no jurisdiction to decide by itself on the incompatibility, but needs the approval of the Council acting unanimously during the first stage, by a qualified majority thereafter.' Spaak, Paul-Henri. (1956) *Intergovernmental Committee on European Integration. The Brussels Report on the General Common Market (abridged, English translation of document commonly called the Spaak Report) [June 1956].*

Although, general measures can distort competition within the internal market, such distortions must be resolved through harmonization by the EU Council acting under Articles 114 to 118 TFEU.[45]

Consequently, it can be questioned whether any potential advantage for the *Huhtalux* entity arose solely due to the derogatory and discriminative treatment of the debt element of the intra-group loan by Luxembourg, or whether the alleged non-taxation was a result of diparency among national laws of two MSs. In the latter event, the Commission would have to conclude that any potential non-taxation resulted from disparities between Irish and Luxembourg general tax systems (i.e., genuine mismatch). Consequently, the Commission could potentially reach a different decision when it would take into account the taxable treatment at the group level and find out that the preferential overall result stems from a deliberate mismatch looking at each country-perspective separately. Contrary to the *Huhtamäki* case, the Commission performed an analysis on the existence of a selective advantage in the *Engie* case with reference to the combined effect of the deductibility of the expenses linked to interest payments at the level of subsidiaries in Luxembourg, and the exemption of the corresponding income at the level of the holding companies in the same state. Due to the fact that financial intra-group transactions were made in a purely domestic setting (i.e., Luxembourg), the Commission applied its State aid assessment by looking at all of the elements that were part of this arrangement, as well as preceding and subsequent transactions between different entities of the *Engie* group. Therefore, the question arises whether the Commission in the *Huhtamäki* case, similarly to its approach in the *Engie* case, should have evaluated the combined effect of the deductibility of expenses linked to interest payments in Luxembourg, and the treatment of payments for the loan in Ireland at the *group level*. And if so, how to establish selectivity in the latter case? Before elaborating on arguments put forward in the *Huhtamäki* case, we will discuss different aspects of the *Engie* case and later contrast similarities and differences between the Commission's approach with the newly opened *Huhtamäki* case. This analysis involves the Commission's views in the final decision in the *McDonald's* case.[46]

§4.04 DIFFERENT APPROACHES TO ESTABLISH A SELECTIVE ADVANTAGE IN CASE OF MISMATCHES

[A] The *Engie* Case

In the *Engie* case, the Commission contested two sets of tax rulings obtained by the *Engie* group in Luxembourg.[47] The first set includes five individual rulings concerning

45. E.g., as happened through the adoption of the Anti-Tax Avoidance Directive (ATAD), Council Directive (EU) 2016/1164 of 12 July 2016 laying down rules against tax avoidance practices that directly affect the functioning of the internal market, OJ L 193.
46. Commission Decision of 19 September 2018 on Tax rulings SA.38945 (2015/C) (ex 2015/NN)(ex 2014/CP) granted by Luxembourg in favour of McDonald's Europe, C(2018) 6076 final.
47. Commission Decision of 20 June 2018 on State aid SA.44888 (2016/C) (ex 2016/NN) implemented by Luxembourg in favour of ENGIE, C(2018) 3839 final [hereinafter: ENGIE decision], paras 28 et seq.

the purchase, sale and trading of gas and gas derivative products, which the Commission combined into a single bulk of '2008 LNG tax rulings'. Another two rulings concern the financing and treasury arrangements of the *Engie* group, and are collectively described as the '2010 GSTM tax rulings'. The facts of and the treatments awarded by the rulings and the analysis of subsequent tax implications (i.e., when the same instrument is qualified as both debt and equity) for the *Engie* group are discussed respectively in view of the Commission's findings of a selective advantage. The facts of the Engie case are explained in Figures 4.1 and 4.2.

Facts of the Case

1. 2008 LNG ZORA

Figure 4.1 Overview of the Structure and Agreements – 2008 LNG ZORA (Based on the Facts Presented by the Commission in Paragrahs 33–34 of the Decision)

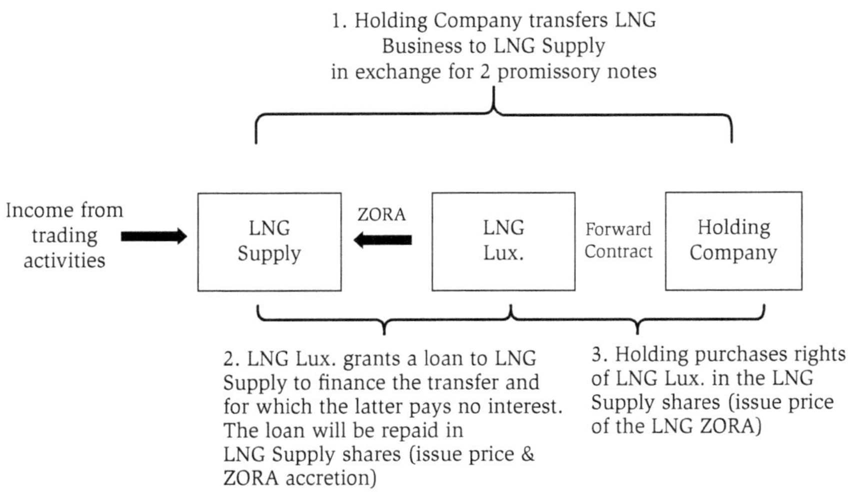

2. 2010 GSTM ZORA

Figure 4.2 Overview of the Structure and Agreements – 2010 GSTM ZORA (Based on the Facts Presented by the Commission in Paragrah 61 of the Decision)

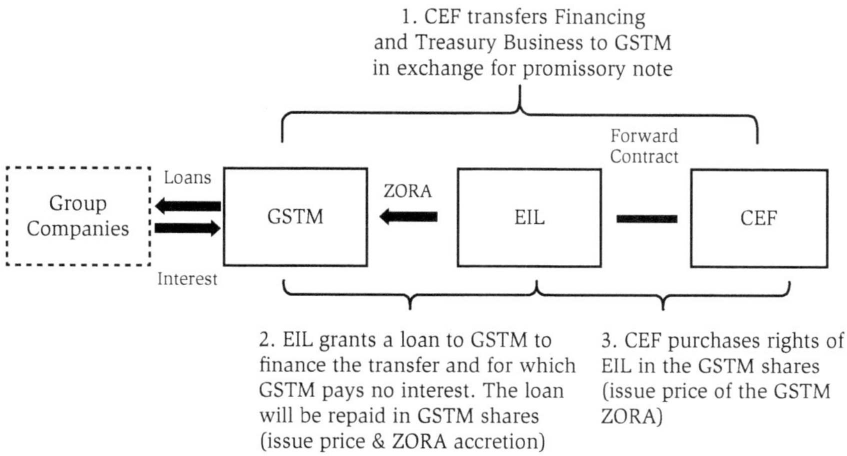

3. LNG Supply[48] *and GSTM*[49]

The treatment accorded in the '2008 LNG tax rulings' made it possible for the LNG Supply to be taxed on the fixed margin of yearly profits.[50] The same dealing was granted to the GSTM in the '2010 GSTM tax rulings'.[51] Effectively, for both these companies the difference between their respective fixed margins and profits actually recorded could be treated as a deductible expense linked to the ZORAs.[52,53] In that respect, the ZORA accretions (i.e., an increase on the value of the issue price of the ZORAs) could be recorded as debt on the balance sheets of GSTM and LNG Supply and considered as an expense that these companies could deduct every year with the result that they would always be taxed only on the agreed particular margins.

After the implementation of the '2008 LNG tax rulings' and the '2010 GSTM tax rulings', the LNG ZORA and the GSTM ZORA were reported as a liability in the balance sheet of LNG Supply and GSTM, and were included in the companies' tax returns at the amount equal to the nominal value of their respective ZORAs. In each subsequent year, an amount equal to the yearly ZORA accretions was recorded as liability of LNG Supply and GSTM against the corresponding expense in the profit and loss account, and was

48. GDF Suez LNG Supply S.A.
49. GDF Suez Treasury Management S.a.r.l.
50. ENGIE decision, para. 29.
51. ENGIE decision, para. 30.
52. Interest-free mandatory convertible loans.
53. ENGIE decision, para. 157.

deducted from the companies' tax base. In case of the LNG Supply ZORA, in 2014, a partial conversion took place in accordance with which both - part of the nominal value of ZORA as well as part of the accretions were reduced. At the same time, LNG Supply increased its capital to partially reimburse the ZORA, which had no tax consequences for LNG Supply. A year later, LNG Supply was in a loss-making position, which resulted in ZORA accretions to become negative. As a consequence, the remaining ZORA accretions as well as the outstanding nominal value of ZORA were reduced. LNG Supply remained taxed at the fixed margin, agreed in the tax rulings. For GSTM, the agreed fixed margin changed in 2011, and for which calculations were not performed by reference to the tax ruling requests, thus never accepted by the Luxembourg tax administration.

4. LNG Lux. and EIL[54]

According to the tax rulings of LNG Lux. as well as EIL, the companies could maintain the value of ZORA in their accounts at book value, or either increase or decrease value from the acquisition price to redemption price. It was also agreed with the tax administration that during the lifetime of their respective ZORAs, LNG Lux. and EIL could choose not to book any taxable income or tax deductible expense related to ZORAs. At conversion of ZORAs into shares, the companies could choose to apply Article 22 bis LIR[55] as an optional regime with the effect that this conversion would not give rise to capital gains for tax purposes, and thus no corporate income tax (CIT) would be due. It practice, this treatment meant that the ZORA accretions were not subject to tax at the level of LNG Lux. or EIL. Effectively, LNG Lux. decided to book the value of ZORA as assets, and maintained it at its nominal amount until a partial conversion in 2014. Upon a partial conversion of ZORA, both value of ZORA as well as LNG Forward Contract, which was booked as liabilities in the tax return for the same amount as a nominal amount of the value of the ZORA, decreased and had no impact on the LNG Lux. profit and loss account. However, LNG Lux. did not opt for an optional regime of Article 22 bis LIR. In the subsequent years the value of ZORA decreased due to negative ZORA accretions, and LNG Lux. also decided twice to decrease value of ZORA to that amount to which the value decreased, and to reduce the value of the Forward Contract to the same amount. EIL decided to maintain the value of ZORA at book value in line with the option granted in the '2010 GSTM tax rulings'.

5. Holding Company and CEF[56]

Holding Company and CEF agreed with Luxembourg tax authorities that they could record the payments under their respective Forward Contracts in accounts as 'Financial Fixed Assets', which ought to be valued at cost price, and both companies would not

54. Electrabel Invest Luxembourg SA.
55. Art. 22bis of the Luxembourg Income Tax Code ('LIR') (loi modifiée du 4 decembre 1967 concernant l'impôt sur le revenu).
56. Compagnie Européenne de Financement C.E.F. S.A.

book any taxable income or any deductible expense before the conversion of ZORAs and the transfer of shares. In both cases, it was established that the participation exemption regime under Article 166 LIR would apply from the moment of the purchase by the Holding Company and CEF under their respective Forward Contracts of the rights to shares. Any taxable income related to the ownership by the Holding Company of the LNG Supply shares and by CEF of GSTM shares in the frameworks of the ZORA conversions would be tax exempt at the level of the Holding and CEF. In 2012, Holding Company booked in its tax returns participation in LNG Supply for the amount equal to the nominal of the LNG ZORA under the category of participation exemption. The year after, at the conversion, the cancellation of the LNG Supply shares generated capital gain, which remained entirely untaxed also due to applicability of the participation exemption regime. In the subsequent years, Holding Company booked an adjustment on the Forward Contract reflecting the decrease in value of ZORA following negative ZORA accretions. This impairment adjustment was reflected as a change in the company's profit and loss account. In case of CEF, its participation in GSTM for an amount equal to the nominal value of the GSTM ZORA appeared in CEF's tax return under participation eligible under Article 166 LIR.

[B] Existence of a Selective Advantage in the *Engie* Case

In the *Engie* case, the Commission presents the whole spectrum of analysis of a selective advantage. It refers to the presence of a selective advantage at the *individual companies'* level[57] as well as at the whole *group's* level.[58] Although advantage and selectivity ought to be considered separately,[59] the case-law seems to indicate that the criteria of advantage and selectivity are often evaluated together, or at least are not very clearly distinguished. It has been suggested by some scholars that the assessment of fiscal aid generally suffers from the lack of a coherent and functionally consistent approach, merely due to this blurred line between the selectivity and advantage criteria.[60] This position can be illustrated in the *Forum 187* case,[61] where the Court analyzed the tax treatment of the beneficiaries that gave rise to an advantage on the basis of comparison with the tax treatment of other undertakings under the ordinary tax system in Belgium.

57. ENGIE decision, part 6.2.
58. ENGIE decision, part 6.3.
59. Judgment of the CJEU, Case C-15/14 P, *Commission v. MOL*, para. 59.
60. T. Jaeger, Tax Incentives under State Aid Law: A Competition Law Perspective in I. Richelle, W. Schön and E. Traversa eds., *State Aid Law and Business Taxation*, Springer, 2016, p. 51; R. Luja, State Aid Benchmarking and Tax Rulings: Can We Keep It Simple? in I. Richelle, W. Schön and E. Traversa eds., *State Aid Law and Business Taxation*, Springer, 2016, p. 118.
61. Joined Cases C-182/03 and C-217/03, *Belgium and Forum 187 v. Commission*, judgment of 22 June 2006, ECR I-5479. 'In order to decide whether a method of assessment of taxable income [...] confers an advantage on (its beneficiary), it is necessary [...] to compare that method with the ordinary tax system.'

Therefore, albeit not clearly distinguishing advantage from selectivity, the Commission's analysis does not depart from the approach applied in the case-law of the Court.

Moreover, the Commission elaborated on the process of defining a reference system and finding a derogation therefrom. Thus, the Commission defines as a reference framework the entire CIT system of Luxembourg refusing to narrow it down to only certain provisions of the Luxembourg tax code (i.e., concerning the determination of the tax base, the linking of the commercial and tax balance sheets, the prudence principle, and the deductibility of business expenses).[62] Yet, it also assesses the selectivity against a narrower reference system, consisting of the participation exemption regime and the taxation of profit distributions.[63]

When analyzing selective advantage at the *individual company's* level, the Commission defined as a reference system the whole Luxembourg CIT system, the objective of which is to tax profits of all resident companies, and according to which the taxable profit of corporate taxpayers is determined on the basis of its accounting profits. Part of this broadly defined reference framework is the principle of 'linking the tax balance sheet and the commercial balance sheet'. It means that, the accounting profit of a company is included in its tax base, unless a specific provision of law indicates otherwise. Such a special provision of law the Commission considered the principle of prudence, which allows only for a temporary difference between the moment LNG Supply and GSTM book the ZORA accretions as expenses and the moment in which LNG Lux and EIL book the corresponding income. However, in the treatment of *Engie's* loans, there was not only a temporal non-taxation. Profits exempted from taxation due to the participation exemption regime of Article 166 LIR economically corresponded to the amounts deducted as expenses (i.e., ZORA accretions) at the levels of LNG Supply and GSTM, which led to the outcome that virtually all the profits realized by these companies have effectively been left untaxed. Consequently, LNG Supply and GSTM were merely taxed on the fixed margins agreed in their tax rulings with Luxembourg tax authorities, and any profits exceeding the fixed margin remained untaxed. After the profit distribution, they were also not taxed in the hands of the Holding Company or CEF due to the application of participation exemption regime.

In that respect, the Commission decided that the contested tax rulings constituted a derogation giving rise to a favourable treatment compared to other undertakings in a comparable factual and legal situation in light of the objective of the system. In the light of that objective, all corporate taxpayers that are capable of generating profit are, as a matter of principle, in a comparable factual and legal situation when it comes to assessing their CIT liability in Luxembourg. Hence, the nature of the income realized by the company (i.e., profit distribution eligible under Article 166 LIR or other commercial profit realized by the company), and the rest of conditions set out under Article 166 LIR did not have any bearing on the objective of the system, which is the taxation of the profit of all companies subject to tax in Luxembourg.

62. ENGIE decision, part 6.2.1.
63. ENGIE decision, part 6.2.2.

Moreover, the Commission opposed the view put forward by Luxembourg and *Engie* stating that, in line with the principle of legality, the way in which taxes are determined is clearly established by law, which must be interpreted according to the letter of law and not with reference to its objective. In addition to this statement, both parties argued that the Commission did not define the reference system correctly, and that it should be limited to only certain provisions of the Luxembourg tax code (i.e., concerning the determination of the tax base, the linking of the commercial and tax balance sheets, the prudence principle and the deductibility of business expenses). In the Commission's view, narrowing the reference system from a general CIT system to specific articles that target certain taxation or certain undertakings would indicate that the choice of the reference framework depends on whether the MS in question has adopted specific tax rules, rather than looking at the objective of the system. It would, in turn, render State aid control ineffective, as the establishment of the derogation would depend on the regulatory technique of a MS. To the contrary, in the State aid assessment it is the effect of the measure that needs to be considered, and not the techniques used. Consequently, whenever the application of one or more provisions of the law to a specific case gives rise to an exception to the general rule set out in the reference system (in this case, the taxation of the profit of all companies subject to tax in Luxembourg), then that tax treatment must be considered as constituting a derogation. If such derogation gives rise to a discrimination vis-à-vis undertakings in a comparable legal and factual situation in the light of the objective of the system, the tax treatment in question must be considered *a priori selective*, and this irrespective of whether the terms of the provisions applied have been respected or not. This indicates that the Commission considers intentional mismatches created due to (mis-) application of different articles of law, and which result in a derogation from the objective of the general rule of the CIT system (and therefore in differential treatment of certain undertakings), as problematic from the State aid perspective due to the effect created by such mismatches.

In the *Engie* case, the Commission also assessed the selectivity against a *narrow reference system*, consisting of the participation exemption regime and the taxation of profit distributions. It established that under the ordinary Luxembourg CIT system, the participation exemption applies on post-tax profit (i.e., it cannot be applied to amounts deducted from the tax base of the distributing entity). Therefore, under the narrower reference framework composed exclusively of the rules concerning the participation exemption and the taxation of profit distributions, the participation exemption is applicable to income which does not correspond to amounts deducted from the tax base of the participating entity, and this regardless of whether such income is qualified as a profit distribution or a capital gain. Thus, also in this case the Commission derived the conclusions by considering the treatment applicable at both levels - the Holding Company and LNG Supply as well as CEF and GSTM. On this basis it could establish inconsistency with general national rules, according to which deduction of interest expenses and no inclusion of corresponding interest income cannot be made in the same transaction.

[C] The *Huhtamäki* Case

In the newly opened *Huhtamäki* case, the Commission assesses the selective advantage at the individual company's level. The subject of this investigation is the Luxembourg tax treatment of expenses linked to the zero-interest loan granted by *Huhtalux's* affiliated company located in Ireland. Similar to the *Engie* case, in case of *Huhtamäki*, Luxembourg allowed for the deduction of interest in a ruling where there was no corresponding taxation of such interest at the other side of this financial transaction. The Commission might have seen non-taxation due to this arrangement; however, it may well turn out that the assessment of the economic effect of this non-taxation can hardly be attributed to Luxembourg only.

Facts of the case

Figure 4.3 Overview of the Structure and Agreements – Huhtalux Tax Rulings (Based on the Facts Presented by the Commission in Paragraphs 13–41 of the Decision)

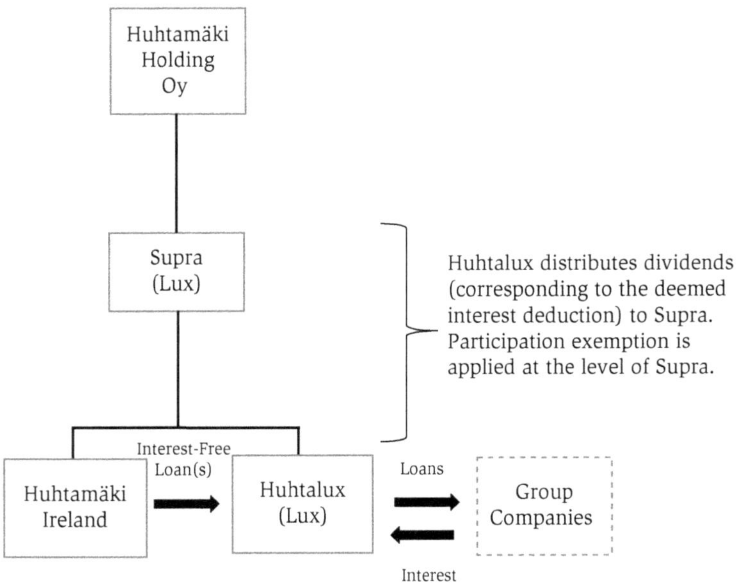

The rulings contested by the Commission refer to the determination of the tax liability of *Huhtalux* with respect to income arising from the intra-group financing transactions, under which *Huhtalux* carried out on-lending activities. It received financing from *Huhtamäki Ireland* in the form of 'Interest Free Loan(s)' and subsequently financed group companies based in the United States (the US) through 'Interest-Bearing Loans'. The rulings confirmed the computation of *Huhtalux's* taxable profits in accordance with the arm's length principle (i.e. arm's length remuneration for its financing activity). The interest related to the 'Interest-Free Loan(s)' was not recorded in the commercial accounts of *Huhtalux*, but it was recognized in its tax profit and loss account as a deductible cost. The deductible amount (i.e., 'deemed interest') corresponded to the difference between the profit effectively realized by the company from its on-lending financing activity and the arm's length compensation set in the form of the minimum profit margin (the 'Profit Margin'). The profits corresponding to the deemed interest deducted by *Huhtalux* were subsequently redistributed to *Supra*, which could, instead of distributing it further to *Huhtamäki Holding Oy*, capitalize *Huhtamäki Ireland* that could in turn further on-lend this cash to *Huhtalux* on an interest free basis. In effect, the taxable profits of *Huhtalux* were reduced by the 'deemed interest' deducted (i.e., the difference between the actual profits and the market remuneration[64]).

The Commission concluded that *Huhtalux* received a selective advantage in the form of deemed interest deduction recorded in its tax profit and loss account, which did not correspond to the actual expense recorded in the commercial accounts. In effect, part of the profits realized by *Huhtalux* and reflected in its commercial accounts remained untaxed, and after redistribution to *Supra* the same profits were exempt from taxation due to the participation exemption regime. The Commission argues that the accounting profits should be the starting point and the basis for taxing corporate profits under the reference framework, which is the general CIT system in Luxembourg.

[D] Existence of a Selective Advantage in the *Huhtamäki* Case

At the time when the first ruling was granted to *Huhtalux* (i.e. 2009), Luxembourg tax law did not provide for integrated transfer pricing legislation.[65] Any transfer pricing adjustments in accordance with the arm's length principle could be made based on different tax provisions and concepts under Luxembourg domestic tax law. The new transfer pricing legislation that completed the existing rules and concepts entered into force in the beginning of 2015 and formalized the application of the arm's length principle (Article 56 of the Luxembourg Income Tax Law (LITL)). The new Article 56 LITL was inspired by a similar provision of the Dutch Income Tax Code (Article 8b(1) CIT) and provided a legal basis for transfer pricing adjustment of profits of associated enterprises. This provision applied to cross-border transactions as well as transactions between related companies in Luxembourg and did not apply regarding the determination of commercial income.

In addition to Article 56 LITL, the hidden dividend distribution and hidden capital contribution rules were of relevance in determining whether associated companies

64. The market remuneration (i.e., the arm's length compensation) was calculated as a gross remuneration for functions performed expressed in basis points of the nominal outstanding amount of the interest-bearing loan, and a risk premium expressed in basis points and calculated on the outstanding amount of the interest-bearing loan.
65. *See, e.g.*, Hoor, Oliver. Luxembourg Reshapes Its Transfer Pricing Landscape, European Taxation 2015, 131.

adhered to the arm's length principle.[66] Both these concepts were modelled in accordance with the doctrine developed by the German Reich Tax Court (*Reichsfinanzhof* - RFH) and the German Federal Tax Court (*Bundesfinanzhof* - BFH).[67] The general practice of Luxembourg law prescribed a priority of these norms, which operated independently of one another, but could be applied simultaneously. Consequently, the hidden dividend distribution and hidden capital contribution concepts should take precedence over Article 56 LITL due to the fact that their scope of application and tax consequences differed. Article 56 LITL aimed at adjusting the taxable basis of the company according to the arm's length conditions, whereas the assumed capital contributions and assumed dividends distributions required tax adjustment at the level of both companies to the transaction.

Therefore, it had to be established whether a particular agreement between related companies reflected arm's length conditions that were generally acceptable for Luxembourg tax purposes, or there were advantages granted by related entities, which would be subject to reclassification as hidden dividend distributions or hidden capital contributions. Both these concepts had their origin in the principle that disconnected, for tax purposes, the company, which was itself subject to tax, and its shareholders (so-called *Trennungsprinzip*[68]). The main objective of these rules were to avoid a reduction of the company's taxable income that was motivated by the shareholding relationship. Therefore, when advantages were shifted between related companies, tax adjustment under Luxembourg law was generally based on the concepts of hidden dividend distributions and hidden capital contributions. In addition, Article 56 LITL was applicable when such advantages shifted between related companies could not be classified as assumed dividend distribution or assumed capital contributions.

The legal literature refers to different practices and rules applicable to situations where free-interest loans were granted between affiliated companies. In the past, some authors argued in favour of downward adjustment under the hidden capital contribution concept where a free-interest loan was provided to a Luxembourg company.[69] Others mentioned the German *"Nutzungseinlagen"* doctrine applied where shareholders granted services to a company for partial or no consideration (e.g., interest-free loan or rent-free lettings of real estate).[70] In such cases, advantages granted would not qualify as assets and could not be reflected in the company's balance sheet (i.e., under the Luxembourg GAAP rules), which in consequence meant that only assets could be contributed to the company. With reference to principles established by the Courts, this remained a situation irrespective of any increase in the company's profits resulting

66. *See, e.g.*, Hoor, Oliver. Hidden Dividend Distribution in Luxembourg: A Technical Guide, European Taxation 2011, 383 and Neefs. Philippe & Hoor, Oliver. Hidden Capital Contributions in Luxembourg - Clearing the Mist, European Taxation 2009, 241.
67. Ibid.
68. Separate entity approach.
69. *See, e.g.*, Hoor, Oliver. Luxembourg Reshapes Its Transfer Pricing Landscape, European Taxation 2015, 131.
70. Neefs, Philippe & Hoor, Oliver. Hidden Capital Contributions in Luxembourg - Clearing the Mist, European Taxation 2009, 241.

from the difference between the arm's length price and the price agreed between the parties.[71] Accordingly, these advantages could not be classified as hidden capital contributions for which it was essential that the contributions were reflected in the company's balance sheet resulting in either decrease or increase in assets and liabilities.[72] Despite that, where services were provided for no consideration (e.g. free-interest loans) between sister companies, such advantage could be classified as a deemed dividend distribution to the common shareholder, if all the predefined conditions and underlying tests (e.g., net equity test; motivation test; prudent business manager test; taxable income test) were fulfilled as analysed on a case-by-case basis. However, if neither of the above concepts applied, Article 56 LITL provided a clear legal basis for a downward profit adjustment in accordance with the arm's length principle when a Luxembourg company received such interest-free loan or free service from an associated company.[73]

In the opening decision, the Commission does not refer to the above technicalities and mechanisms of the Luxembourg system, hence disregarding these characteristics as belonging to the general or "normal" corporate income tax system. According to the Commission, the reference system should be based on such elements as the tax base, the taxable person, the taxable event, and the tax rates. The ruling given to *Huhtalux* determined its corporate tax liability in Luxembourg, and therefore the Commission considered it appropriate to take into account a broad legislative framework in order to avoid artificially taking some provisions out of its framework. Therefore, the reference system is the general CIT system, in which accounting profits are the basis for determining taxable profits, unless specific provisions of the law indicate otherwise. The company's tax liability is a starting point, determined based on the actual transactions leading to income actually realized and expenses actually incurred and booked in the commercial accounts.

The Commission found a derogatory nature of the ruling in allowing a deduction from the tax base of a deemed interest expense connected to the free-interest loan. The deemed interest was a deductible expense in the tax profit and loss account, which did not correspond to an actual expense incurred by *Huhtalux*, and recorded in the commercial profit and loss account. In effect, a substantial part of the profits realized by *Huhtalux* on its financing activities and recorded as profits in its commercial accounts remained untaxed and subsequently redistributed to *Supra* as dividends exempted from taxation in Luxembourg. The Commission claims that such treatment derogates from the reference system (i.e., CIT system in Luxembourg), according to which the accounting should be the starting point and the basis for taxing the corporate income. By stating that, the Commission puts forward that the tax treatment, as endorsed by Luxembourg, allowed the group to pay less tax than other stand-alone or group companies, the transactions of which are priced in accordance with market

71. *See, e.g.*, BFH, Decision of 9March 1962, I 203/61 S, BStBI III 1962, p. 338 and BFH, Decision of 14 March 1989, I R 8/85, BStBI II 1989, p.633.
72. The concept of hidden capital contributions relates only to contributions that remain undisclosed in agreements entered into by related entities.
73. *See, e.g.*, Hoor, Oliver. Luxembourg Reshapes Its Transfer Pricing Landscape, European Taxation 2015, 131.

terms. Hence, the Commission does not follow one of the approaches in the *Engie* case of narrowing down the reference framework; Instead, it applies a broad reference system in its analysis, being the general CIT system of Luxembourg. It takes the approach applied previously in the tax ruling and transfer pricing cases, disregarding any reference to comparability between intra-group transactions. In the transfer pricing cases, the Commission argues that the nationally implemented transfer pricing rules or provisions implementing the arm's length concept cannot be taken as the reference framework, which would create an artificial distinction between companies on the basis of their corporate structure.[74] Therefore, according to the Commission, the Organisation for Economic Co-operation and Development (OECD) Transfer Pricing Guidelines are there to ensure that group companies are treated in the same way as unrelated undertakings, and they do not create any 'special rules' for multinationals, what would in turn immediately imply selective treatment.

Additionally, the Commission does not accept the arm's length principle and other national rules based on that concept as being part of the reference framework. It states that possibility to apply downward or upward adjustment under former Article 56 LITL (i.e., the deemed deductions) gave tax authorities a wide margin of discretion to apply the arm's length principle. At the time when the ruling was granted, there were no objective criteria determining how such downward adjustment should be applied, and how to determine the amount of such adjustment. Thus, the Commission claims that even if this article prescribed downward adjustments, the application of it in the *Huhtamäki* case would be a priori selective, due to the discretionary nature of this provision. It is, however, difficult to imagine a transfer pricing system that would be fully based on objective criteria applied consequently in every single case, without analyzing intra-group transactions on a case-by-case basis for comparability purposes under the arm's length principle. Does the Commission imply the existence of a 'hypothetical' system[75] containing an objective set of criteria, which predefine the outcome of intra-group pricing (i.e., effect)? And could the Luxembourg tax authorities have been aware of the existence of such a system at the time they considered the treatment of *Huhtalux* under national rules? If the doctrine applied in a country generally allows for taxation and consequently deduction of fictitious interest, and tax authorities determine the taxable profits in accordance with national rules, which are internally consistent, there should be no question of derogation from the reference system. That system would be the only one that the tax authorities could have been aware of at the moment when a particular tax treatment was confirmed. If the fictitious interest rates were established on the basis of the arm's length principle (i.e., reflecting what the third parties would have agreed to), is Luxembourg to be blamed for any

74. E.g., Commission Decision of 4 October 2017 on State aid SA.38944 (2014/C) (ex 2014/NN) implemented by Luxembourg to Amazon, paras. 591 et seq.
75. *See, e.g.*, Judgment in Joint Cases T-836/16 and T-624/17 Poland v Commission. According to the Court, in order to analyse derogation from a reference system, one has to consider real characteristics of the 'normal' reference system identified in the first place, and not refer to a hypothetical elements and characteristics that the legislator has not considered when designing such a system.

eventual non-taxation of part of the profits of *Huhtamäki*? Or perhaps this result is due to differences between national tax systems of Luxembourg and Ireland?

Looking at the totality of the transaction, and including Luxembourg doctrine and rules as part of the reference framework,[76] may reveal that any potential non-taxation of profits due to this intra-group loan arrangement is a mere result of disparities between national tax systems of Ireland and Luxembourg. The question is how likely the Commission is to move away from its analysis on the basis of an 'EU arm's length standard' which it developed in its transfer pricing ruling cases.[77] This notion is not derived from international sources (i.e., Article 9 OECD Model Tax Convention (OECD MC)[78]) or national doctrines, as followed and implemented by States, but directly from Article 107 (1) TFEU.[79] This approach implies the existence or an emergence of a special rule under the State aid framework by means of which a selective benefit is determined in an individual intra-group transfer pricing arrangement. In that respect, the Commission claims that the arm's length test was confirmed as a yardstick already in 2006 in the decision on the Belgian Coordination Centres and does not represent a new method. However, the main question to be answered by the Courts in the

76. The Commission would have to determine if deemed capital controbution, or deemed dividend distribution, or Art. 56 LITL was to be applied in that case, and whether tax authoritied deviated from these rules for the benefit of Huhtalux.
77. For this notion also *see Szotek*, Is the Council about to confirm the existence of an EU at arm's length principle? July 2017, Kluwer International Tax Blog.
78. Art 9 OECD MC has been adopted to reflect some guiding principles in the taxation of multinational groups whose divisions do business one with another across national borders. Art 9 OECD MC has a long history dating back to 1963 and reads: '(When) conditions are made or imposed between ... two (associated) enterprises in their commercial or financial relations which differ from those which would be made between independent enterprises, then any profits which would, but for these conditions, have accrued to one of the enterprises, but by reason of those conditions, have not so accrued, may be included in the profits of that enterprise and taxed accordingly'. For greater clarity and to diminish difficulties with applying the underlying concepts, the OECD has been providing a number of comments, which continued to expand as complexity of cross-border transactions grew. Recent Art 9 of the OECD MC contains two paragraphs: the first one resembling the original wording of this article and providing the authoritative statement of the arm's length principle and the second paragraphs providing for a guiding principles of a corresponding adjustment of the profits charged in another State. However, the primary source of the OECD principles is the comprehensive Transfer Pricing Guidelines for Multinational Enterprises and Tax Administrations ('TPG'), published first in 1995 with the most recent updates published in 2017. For the historical perspective on Art 9 OECD MC *see* C. Adams and R. Coombes, *Global Transfer Pricing: Principles and Practice*, LexisNexis: UK, 2003; J. Wittendorff, *Transfer Pricing and the Arm's Length Principle in International Tax Law*, Kluwer, 2010; R.S. Collier and J.L. Andrus, *Transfer Pricing and the Arm's Length Principle after BEPS*, Oxford University Press, 2017.
79. On 19 July 2016, the Commission Notice on the Notion of State Aid was published to clarify the EC's understanding of Art 107(1) of the TFEU, as interpreted by the European Courts. In the section dealing with the interpretation of the selectivity criterion in relation to administrative tax rulings (*see* s. 5.4.4.1, para.172 of the Notice), the EC states: 'This arm's length principle necessarily forms part of the Commission's assessment of tax measures granted to group companies under Art. 107(1) of the Treaty, independently of whether a Member State has incorporated this principle into its national legal system and in what form.' It can be derived from it that the Commission applies its own understanding of an arm's length concept in State aid investigations into transfer pricing.

proceeding cases is whether the Court in fact implied an obligation to apply the arm's length principle in Article 107(1) TFEU in the *Forum 187* case.[80]

[E] The *Engie* Case Contrasted with the Approaches Taken in *McDonald's* and *Huhtamäki*

The approach taken in the *Engie* case can be contrasted with the Commission's finding in the *McDonald's* case, in which it had to assess whether there was a misapplication of the double taxation treaty between Luxembourg and the US under the general Luxembourg CIT system, which resulted in a selective advantage for *McDonald's*.[81] The Commission reached the conclusion that there was no derogation from the reference system by Luxembourg tax authorities. Hence, different from the finding in the *Engie* case, the Commission in the *McDonald's* case concluded that through the interpretation of the tax treaty the Luxembourg tax authorities did not misapply the national law, and thereby did not confer a selective advantage on particular undertakings. In the *McDonald's* case, the national rules were internally consistent and the underlying treatment of *McDonald's* did not deviate from them. Hence, the Commission accepted that Luxembourg did not derogate from the letter of law by applying the respective treaty provision. According to the Commission, the disparencies arose due to different classification of a permanent establishment under Luxembourg and the US national legal provisions. In a situation in which Luxembourg generally exempts profits of foreign branch from taxation also due to the applicability of a respective tax treaty, and the other state does not make use of its right to tax assigned under the double tax treaty, because of its national interpretation of the term 'business' for defining the existence of PE, does not make Luxembourg accountable for any mismatch resulting in double non-taxation. In the Commission's view, the exemption of the business income of the US Franchised Branch of *McDonald's* Europe from CIT in Luxembourg obviously was the result of a genuine mismatch. However, in *Engie* it found the application of the law incorrect even though the national tax authorities perhaps only applied the provisions as they were laid down in Luxembourg tax law (and thereby just applied what was in the law).

Moreover, the fact of opening the proceedings in the *Huhtamäki* case indicates that the Commission does not consider it to be a clear case of genuine mismatches. In the *Huhtamäki* case, the Commission is concerned with unilateral downward adjustment of profits by Luxembourg. This was a result of Luxembourg allegedly misapplying its national rules on deductibility of interest paid by *Huhalux* to its affiliated entity in Ireland.

The Commission have not found any connecting factor, which requires to take into account the tax treatment in the other state, and which may potentially lead to the conclusion that the non-taxation of profits is a mere result of genuine mismatches due to differences in general national provisions of Ireland and Luxembourg. If that was the

80. Judgement of the CJEU, Joined Cases C-182/03 and C-217/03, *Belgium and Forum 187/ Commission*, judgment of 22 June 2006, ECR I-5479.
81. On the McDonald's case *see Gormsen*, European State aid and Tax Rulings (2019) 32 et seq.

case, Luxembourg might allow deductibility of fictitious interest payments in an intra-group transaction, and Ireland may recognize and tax economically corresponding profits or not. Both states would apply their rules correctly. If in both countries these rules are internally consistent, and interest rates reflect the 'market conditions' and what third parties would have agreed to, any non-taxation may be the result of genuine mismatches that are beyond State aid control. Alternatively, the Commission could also establish a selective advantage on the basis of a one-country perspective with reference to the Luxembourg tax treatment of a part of this loan arrangements if it could prove, for example, that there is a rule in national law or a doctrine, which does not allow the deduction of interest in case of zero-interest loans in this particular case.[82]

[F] Relevance of Justification and Possible Implications of the *Magnetrol International* Case

At the third step of the selectivity analysis, it is up to the MSs to justify a prima facie selective advantage on the ground that the measure stems from the nature or guiding principles of the law. The prerequisite according to which a proper justification of prima facie selective advantages requires the measure not only to derive from the basic or guiding principles of the tax system at stake, but also to meet the condition of proportionality. This was first expressed by the CJEU in the *Paint Graphos* judgement.[83] In this decision, the Court held that for a measure 'to be justified by the nature or general scheme of the tax system of the Member State concerned, it is also necessary to ensure that those exemptions are consistent with the principle of proportionality and do not go beyond what is necessary, in that the legitimate objective being pursued could not be attained by less far-reaching measures'.[84]

In the *Engie* case, the Commission reveals that in its view an exemption from taxation aiming at avoiding economic double taxation may be justified by the nature and overall structure of the tax system.[85] Thus, the Commission agrees that application of the participation exemption under Article 166 LIR might be a valid ground for justification as to avoid economic double or triple taxation as it may result directly from the basic or guiding principles of the tax system. However, it considers the combined application of the exemption and the deduction not to be proportionate to justify the prima facie selective advantage. In fact, the economic effect of these tax treatments was that the individual companies of the *Engie* group (i.e., the Holding Company and CEF) as well as the entire *Engie* group per se actually benefited from double non-taxation. Therefore, the application of the tax exemption on distributed profits in this case goes

82. For example, on the basis of the German 'Nutzungseinlagen'- doctrine, as suggested by Prof. Luja; *see Luja*, Fictional interest payments and abuse of European Tax Law: new State aid challenges? Blog entry of 12 March 2019, accessible under https://www.maastrichtuniversity.nl/blog/2019/03/fictional-interest-payments-and-abuse-european-tax-law-new-state-aid-challenges.
83. Judgement of the CJEU, Joined Cases, C-78/08-C-80/08, *Paint Graphos*.
84. Judgement of the CJEU, Joined Cases C-78/08-C-80/08, *Paint Graphos*, para. 75.
85. ENGIE Decision, para. 228 and subseq., and 285 and seq.

beyond what is necessary and proportionate to achieve the objective to avoid economic double taxation.

In addition, this combined effect that results in non-taxation of profits in Luxembourg should also not escape the tax authorities' analysis under anti-abuse provisions.[86] Interestingly, in the Commission's view, these rules may be considered as being part of the reference framework consisting, on the one hand, of the general income tax system and its objective of the taxation of corporate profits as well as, on the other hand, anti-abuse tax rules aimed at avoiding that taxpayers circumvent its main objective. It can be questioned whether the Commission tends to rely on the general principle of anti-abuse as recently confirmed by the CJEU in the field of direct taxation,[87] which should naturally be part of each MSs national CIT system, irrespective of states having implemented national anti-abuse rules and in what form.

In that respect, the Commission decision on the UK Controlled Foreign Company (CFC) rules and the Group Financing Exemption, concluded in April 2019, should be analysed.[88] In the final decision, the Commission's choice of the reference framework was narrowed to the objective of the CFC rules.[89] These rules allow the UK to tax the income of overseas subsidiaries, controlled by a UK parent company where that income is considered as artificially derived from the UK. The investigation in the UK CFC case concerned the 'Finance Company Partial Exemption' referred to by the Commission as the Group Financing Exemption. It provides that a business with offshore financing arrangements may, under certain circumstances, be subject to a reduced CFC charge in respect of finance income (reduced by between 75% and 100%). The Commission found out that an exemption for arrangements where the group loans are financed with funds or assets, which derive from capital contributions from the UK, constituted a derogation from the reference system.[90] However, according to the Commission, the derogation can be justified since the exemption avoids a complex and disproportionately burdensome intra-group tracing exercise.[91] In its analysis, the Commission seems to refer to the proportionality test within the justification step of the selectivity assessment, by which the Group Financing Exemption provides for a clear situation that is justified to ensure the proper functioning and effectiveness of the CFC rules. Thus, the Commission found the CFC rules to be proportionate and therefore justified.[92]

---

86. ENGIE Decision, part 6.4.
87. Judgement of the CJEU, Joined cases C-115/16, C-118/16, C-119/16 and C-299/16, *N Luxembourg 1*, para. 101.
88. European Commission Press Release: State aid: Commission concludes part of UK tax scheme gave illegal tax advantages to certain multinational companies; remaining part does not constitute aid (SA.44896); Commission Decision of 2 April 2019 on the State aid SA.44896 implemented by the United Kingdom concerning CFC Group Financing Exemption, C(2019)2526 final.
89. Commission Decision of 2 April 2019 on the State aid SA.44896 implemented by the United Kingdom concerning CFC Group Financing Exemption, C(2019)2526 final, para. 107.
90. *Ibid.*, para. 151.
91. *Ibid.*, para. 161 et seq.
92. *Ibid.*, para. 162.

However, the Commission does not find such a justification valid in every case. Interestingly, in the *Huhtamäki* case, the Commission did not find the downward adjustment proportional. Instead, it proposed that the taxpayer itself could respect the objective of avoidance of double (non-)taxation and ensure equal treatment if it effectively paid the interest and recorded expenses without any deviation from the general principle according to which companies are taxed, as a starting point, on the basis of their commercial profits reflected in their accounts. Thus, the solution proposed by the Commission is that *Huhtalux* should effectively pay the interest to its sister company in Ireland reflecting a situation between independent parties on the market and then, deductible expenses connected to that transactions would effectively be reflected in the commercial accounts leading to lower taxable profits. This would, in view of the Commission, avoid any double (non-)taxation and any discrimination vis-à-vis independent companies. This reasoning in combination with a broad reference system established by the Commission indicates that it is aiming at tackling with State aid rules all sorts of fictitious (interest) payments regardless of the national rules and concepts applicable to such intra-group arrangements. Hence, are other national systems, which eliminate benefits originating from the group relation from the taxable income by a transfer pricing adjustment (e.g., deemed royalty payment), in danger under State aid rules? If the Commission considers that a less-far-reaching measure to attain the objective of avoiding double (non-)taxation would be the actual payment in the intra-group context, then any fictitious or informal contribution could fall automatically under derogation from the reference system as established by the Commission in the *Huhtamäki* case.

It is not the first time when the Commission aims at disregarding intra-group transactions and payments. In the *Starbucks* case,[93] the Commission concluded that when there was no internal or external Comparable Uncontrolled Price (CUP) identified for royalties' payment, such as the one between two Starbucks' entities, Dutch tax authorities should have disregarded this transaction in the intra-group context. Leaving aside discussions on particular technicalities and difficulties in trying to identify sufficient comparables on the basis of the CUP method for controlled transactions involving intangibles, the take away from the Commission's approach is that accepting any kind of intra-group transaction which does not exist, or is rare on the market, is a derogation from a national CIT system, which cannot be justified.

However, with reference to the UK CFC case and the Commission's findings on proportionality as an element of justification may indicate that double non-taxation or unilateral exemptions could potentially be justified in cases of cross-border transactions, which involve unproportionately burdensome intra-group tracing exercises. These observations are also, to the certain extent, confirmed by the General Court in the *Magnetrol International* case.[94] Let us first recall the facts of this case.

93. Commission Decision of 21 October 2015 on State aid SA.38374 (2014/C ex 2014/NN) implemented by the Netherlands to Starbucks, C(2015) 7143 final.
94. Judgement of the General Court, Joined Cases T-131/16 and T-263/16, *Magnetrol International*.

Facts of the case

The Belgian Excess Profit Tax Scheme[95]

Under the Belgian Excess Profit Tax Scheme, Belgian entities that are part of a Multinational Enterprise (MNE) (hereinafter 'Belgian group entities') could reduce their tax base through deduction of excess profits from their actual profits.[96] Such excess profit is calculated by estimation of the hypothetical average profit that a comparable standalone company would be expected to make under comparable circumstances and subtracting that amount from the profits actually recorded by the Belgian group entity. The purpose of the scheme was to make sure that the latter is only taxed at the amount that constitutes an arm's length profit. Thus, profits should have been excluded that exceeded this amount by profits resulting from, e.g., group synergies or other effects due to group participations. Therefore, the scheme allowed an annual pro-active downward adjustment of the CIT base of Belgian group entities through the exemption of their 'excess profits' (*see* Figure 4.4).

Figure 4.4 Belgian Excess Profit Tax Scheme

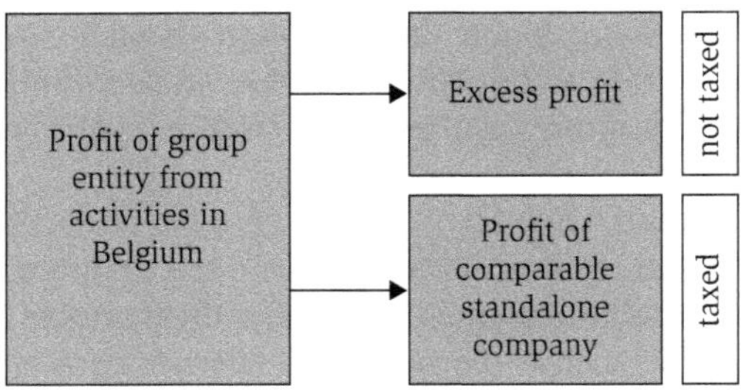

To benefit from the scheme, the Belgian group entity had to request a ruling from the Belgian tax authorities. In calculating the excess profits, the Belgian authorities followed a two-step approach: First, the Belgian group entity was identified as being the 'central entrepreneur' of the MNE and was allocated the residual profit stemming from the transactions. This profit was typically higher than the profit which a comparable standalone company would record in comparable circumstances. Second, the Belgian tax authorities applied the Transactional Net Margin Method (TNMM) to calculate a hypothetical average profit (i.e., arm's length profit) for the Belgian group entity based on a benchmark study. In the end, the excess profit was established by deducting the arm's length profit from the profit determined in the first step of the procedure. This excess profit was exempted under the scheme.

95. Commission Decision of 11 January 2016 on the Excess Profit Exemption State aid Scheme SA. 37667 (2015/C) (ex 2015/NN) implemented by Belgium, C(2015) 9837 final.
96. For a detailed description of the scheme, *see* Commission Decision of 11 January 2016 on the Excess Profit Exemption State aid scheme SA.37667 (2015/C) (ex 2015/NN) implemented by Belgium C(2015)9837 [hereinafter: Belgian Excess Profit Scheme Final Decision], paras. 13–22.

The Commission argued in its decision that the approach to establish the excess profit involved that the parties in a controlled transaction are tested with the TNMM, a one-sided transfer pricing method, at different stages in the transfer pricing assessment.[97] In the first step, the TNMM was applied to the non-Belgian group entities that were the least complex entities in the transactions with the lowest risks as opposed to the Belgian group entity that was having the function of the central entrepreneur. In this function, the Belgian group entity should have been allocated all of the residual profits. However, in the following step of the analysis, the TNMM was applied to the Belgian group entity. This, in turn, presupposed that it was the least complex entity only performing routine functions, to estimate its hypothetical average profit. As a consequence, the inconsistent application of the TNMM to the two parties to the controlled transactions led to the result that an untaxed amount was generated as the combined operating profit would not equal the sum of the profits that derive from the application of the TNMM on both parties. Moreover, according to the Commission, the unilateral adjustment made by the Belgian tax authorities to the Belgian group entity's profits that were actually recorded, precluded other jurisdictions from taxing the excess profit. The reason for other jurisdictions to not recognize the right to tax profits arising specifically from group synergies was that the taxing right only pertained to Belgium being the tax jurisdiction where they were actually recorded. Therefore, through the exemption of the excess profits in Belgium, a completely untaxed tax base was formed, and such an approach did not comply with the arm's length principle.[98]

The General Court annulled the Commission decision on procedural grounds and therefore gave only little insight on the material matters of the case.[99] However, the Court clarified certain aspects that could give some indications for the purposes of mismatches and potential possibilities to justify unilateral adjustments.

In the appeal, Belgium submitted that the Commission exceeded its competences since the determination of taxable income is an exclusive competence of the MSs.[100] The General Court recalled what was already settled case law on the fact that direct taxation including administrative practices of MS to designate tax bases and the spread of the tax burden across different factors of production and economic sectors is not excluded from the State aid rules.[101] In that context, Belgium argued that it had no

97. *See* Belgian Excess Profit Scheme Final Decision, paras. 153 et seq.
98. *See* Belgian Excess Profit Scheme Final Decision, para. 134.
99. Judgement of the General Court of 14 February 2019, Joined Cases T-131/16 and T-263/16, *Magnetrol International*, paras. 135 et seq.
100. Judgement of the General Court, Joined Cases T-131/16 and T-263/16, *Magnetrol International*, para. 63.
101. On this plea of law, the General Court responded as follows and repeated what is already settled case law: 'interventions by Member States in areas which have not been harmonised in the European Union, such as direct taxation, are not excluded from the scope of the State aid rules. Accordingly, the Commission may find that a tax measure constitutes State aid provided that the conditions for making such a finding are met' (Judgement of the General

jurisdiction to tax the excess profits, and that the national transfer pricing provision of Article 185(2)(b) of the Belgian Tax Code aimed at avoiding double taxation, a competence that exclusively belonged to Belgium. Due to the fact that Belgium limited its taxing rights and unilaterally excluded the excess profits that ought to be attributed to another jurisdiction, it was argued that the Commission should not question the non-taxation of these profits in Belgium.

The General Court considered these arguments in terms of the plea on the Commission's competences to examine the measures in question. It put forward that the need to avoid double taxation, understood as an objective pursued by the national tax authorities' practice, cannot justify an exclusive competence of a state in that respect. However, it may be interesting to see if the Court would be willing to accept a justification of avoiding double taxation with respect to a measure that would pursue such an objective, and under the condition that this measure would be a part of the general tax system established by the Commission (i.e., in the analysis of selectivity). A possibility that the Court may even consider such justification of a MS is indicated by the fact that in the *Magnetrol International* case, it actually put forward that it does not appear that the non-taxation of excess profit, as applied by the Belgian tax authorities, pursued the objective of avoiding double taxation. However, it has also been indicated that unilateral measures allowing downward adjustments may be difficult to justify, even if they have the objective of avoiding double taxation. In that sense, the Court already gave a sign that it might have sided with the Commission on the point that Article 185(2)(b) of the Belgian Income Tax Code provided for a downward profit adjustment only if that profit has been included in the profit of another company, and that it should have been verified by the competent authorities that it had actually been taxed in another country. This means that only measures that are apt to tackle actual double taxation and have features of corresponding downward adjustments are more likely to be justified under State aid rules.

Thus, it seems that the Court gave some indications on the application of the State aid rules in the field of domestic transfer pricing legislation. While it could be argued that transfer pricing legislation or downward adjustments should be outside the scope of the State aid rules because any potential non-taxation could be a result of disparities between the countries applying different administrative approaches to establish taxable profits, it appears that the Court might have a different stance. In mentioning that rules which are introduced by states to prevent double (non-)taxation have to meet certain conditions to be justified, it does not seem to be excluded that downward adjustments which do not hinge upon inclusion in the other State may be covered by

Court, Joined Cases T-131/16 and T-263/16, *Mangetrol International*, para. 63.) It further explained that '[i]t is true that, in the absence of EU rules governing the matter, it falls within the competence of the Member States to designate tax bases and to spread the tax burden across the different factors of production and economic sectors. However, that does not mean that every tax measure which affects inter alia the tax base taken into account by the tax authorities falls outside the scope of Art. 107 TFEU. If such a measure in practice discriminates between companies [...] it may be regarded as State aid for the purpose of Art. 107(1) TFEU.' (Judgement of the General Court, Joined Cases T-131/16 and T-263/16, *Mangetrol International*, para. 64 et seq.).

State aid law. Apparently, it might therefore not be completely irrelevant what happens in the other state, because the Court would not have examined the justification if it would exclude them to be prima facie selective in the first place. For the application of transfer pricing rules which are based on the arm's length principle, this might mean that the State aid rules could require to double-check whether the profits adjusted downwards are actually included somewhere else.

Even though the *Magnetrol International* decision concerns national transfer pricing legislations and not directly situations of mismatches (as discussed in respect of the *Engie* and, potentially, *Huhtamäki* cases), it could still allow to derive some implications for the latter as well. The situation as described by the Court resembles a lot a scenario of mismatches in which the state accepts the taxable treatment in the other state, or the existence of double (non-)taxation of profits. Perhaps the Court found a deliberate mismatch due to the fact that the domestic legislation attached the domestic tax treatment to the tax treatment in another country. If the rules as such were rendering the national tax treatment dependent on the tax treatment in another state – at least this should supposedly be the objective of these rules. This solution can then be reconciled with the Commission's approach in the *McDonald's* case, in which the tax treatment in Luxembourg was not dependent on the treatment in the US since the taxing right was allocated to the US and it was up to the other state to tax the income or not. The *Huhtamäki* case might be a borderline case concerning mismatches, as it should be confirmed by the Commission whether the deduction of interest in one state should also be deemed to be depending on the inclusion in another state. In this respect, it remains to be seen whether the Courts will confirm this view in the other pending cases. For the future, a mismatch situation like in the *Huhtamäki* case might be subject to secondary EU legislation, because the ATAD requires the implementation of anti-mismatch mechanisms in national laws.[102]

§4.05 CONCLUSIONS

Mismatches can occur in various forms, either within one state or due to the interplay of rules laid down in different jurisdictions. In the course of its latest decision-making practice, the Commission has started investigating both intra-state as well as inter-state mismatches.

An analysis of the *Engie* case, which concerns a classic example of an intra-state mismatch, shows the difficulties that arise in establishing properly the selectivity of the rules. Two rules which both analysed separately from each other are not in risk of being contradictory to State aid law, might lead to a selective advantage when applied

102. In particular, Art 9 on Hybrid mismatches of the ATAD I, Council Directive (EU) 2016/1164 of 12 July 2016 laying down rules against tax avoidance practices that directly affect the functioning of the internal market, OJ L 193/1; and ATAD II, Council Directive (EU) of 29 May 2017 amending Directive (EU) 2016/1164 as regards hybrid mismatches with third countries. According to Art 11 para 5a of the ATAD I (concerning Art 9 thereof), the rules on hybrid mismatches have to be implemented by the MS until the end of 2019. Pursuant to Art 2 para 1 of the ATAD II, the implementation of rules on reverse hybrids has to be effected until yearend 2021.

simultaneously. The selectivity of the rules therefore results from the concurrent application which favours certain undertakings to the detriment of others. The existence of an intra-state mismatch could be due to a side-effect of rules generally pursuing a legitimate objective of the tax system concerned, like the avoidance of economic double-taxation. Therefore, it could potentially be open for justification. However, it is questionable whether the measure can be considered proportionate if another intrinsic objective of the system is, for example, the avoidance of abuse. This argument should not be underestimated considering the growing importance of the prohibition of abusive practices in the case law of the Courts.[103] Thus, MSs should be careful when there is a chance of application of national anti-abuse legislation, particularly in cases of mismatches.

Concerning inter-state mismatches, it has to be distinguished between genuine and deliberate mismatches. Disparities or genuine mismatches which arise due to the parallel application of the law in different jurisdictions are considered outside the scope of State aid law. As a result of the autonomy of the MSs and their tax sovereignty, they are free to establish their own tax systems and must not necessarily take into consideration how their rules interrelate with the provisions ins other states. This might also be the reason why the Commission has not further pushed forward in the *McDonald's* case.

However, with regard to deliberate mismatches a nuanced view must be taken. Such a mismatch can be characterized, for instance, by the fact that the state disregards connecting factors it has established on its own. This could be the case, if the rules are intended to apply a legal consequence depending on the treatment in the other state, but the treatment there is not taken into consideration in the assessment. Thus, if a state chooses to attach its legal consequences to another one, it has to do so correctly and in a way which does not lead to a selective advantage for particular undertakings. At least this is what the General Court seemed to have indicated when it held in the *Magnetrol International* case that transfer pricing legislation – leading to a selective preferential treatment of undertakings because it is not taking into account the tax treatment in the other state – could potentially not be justified by having the intrinsic objective of avoiding double taxation. Deliberate mismatches occurring on the basis of linking factors implemented in one state might be difficult to establish as it requires thorough investigation to trace back which of the states involved acted in contradiction with the State aid rules. With opening investigations in the *Huhtamäki* case, the Commission has an opportunity to dig deeper into the substance of the matter and this 'grey area' of State aid law.

103. For example, it was only recently that the general principle of avoidance of abuse was applied by the Court in the field of direct taxation. In the Judgement of the CJEU, Joined cases C-115/16, C-118/16, C-119/16 and C-299/16, *N Luxembourg 1*, para. 101, the Court held that 'the principle that abusive practices are prohibited [...] constitutes a general principle of EU law which applies irrespective of whether the rights and advantages that are abused have their basis in the Treaties, in a regulation or in a directive'; *see also* Judgement of the CJEU, Joined cases C-116/16 and C-117/16, *T Danmark*, para. 75 and 76; in both decisions the Court referred to its case law in the field of VAT, in which it also acknowledged the existence of the general principle, *see* Judgement of the CJEU, C-251/16, *Cussens*, paras. 30 and 31.

However, the Commission did not take the chance to further develop this area of State aid in its opening decision. Problematic part of the Commission's investigations remains the fact that it applies a one-sided approach with a very broad reference system, which may be labelled as a uniform 'hypothetical' tax system. Such a system that assumes equality principle and neglects the existence of special national provisions for taxing MNEs could not be considered by the tax authorities and governments at the moment when rulings in the scope of these investigations were granted.

As the analysis has shown, establishing selectivity in terms of deliberate mismatches might be challenging, one solution could be the opening of investigations in both MSs concerned. This would allow a precise analysis of the national law in each of the states and the interplay of the rules. Additionally, it would be recommendable to focus not only on the effect at the level of the individual group company. The structure established by the group to which the individual undertaking belongs should not be disregarded and therefore, as the Commission did in *Engie*, the effects at the group level should be taken into account as well.

In the event that both states, seen from each country-perspective, should be involved in the grant of State aid, recovery could cause another issue. As it is not excluded that the advantage could in theory be conferred by collaborating states, the illegal aid would have to be recovered by both of them. Since it would not correspond to the purpose of recovery of restoring the competitive situation that would exist without the conferral of aid, it would not be reasonable to recover the same amount in each state. A proportional recovery could be an option to solve this issue. In the future, many problematic areas that could create deliberate and genuine mismatches most probably will be resolved by the ATAD I and ATAD II which include anti-hybrid rules. Yet, transfer pricing legislation is not harmonized within the EU and an agreement will probably not be reached in the near future either for the MSs are still quite reluctant to accept the Commission's proposals on the CCCTB.[104] Thus, if the Court should share the view that transfer pricing rules are apt to cause deliberate mismatches, they could continue to remain in this grey area of State aid.

104. In the CCCTB proposal, the Commission submits a profit allocation method based on a predefined formula which would apply throughout the EU see Proposal for a Council Directive on a Common Consolidated Corporate Tax Base (CCCTB), COM(2016) 683 final of 25 October 2016.

CHAPTER 5

State Aid and Domestic Anti-tax Avoidance Rules: Who Is in Charge? – A Preliminary Analysis

Daniël S. Smit

§5.01 INTRODUCTION

The current public attention for business taxation of multinationals has created mounting pressure on government's international tax policies. In February 2013, the Organisation for Economic Co-operation and Development (OECD), with the political support of the countries of the G20, launched its ambitious project on Base Erosion and Profit Shifting (BEPS).[1] With the BEPS project, the OECD and G20 seek to create one single set of consensus-based, international tax rules to protect tax bases of countries. The BEPS project was finalized in October 2015 by releasing the so-called BEPS-package. This package contains fifteen Actions that should provide governments the domestic and international instruments that are needed to tackle BEPS. Currently, the OECD focuses on supporting and monitoring the implementation of the BEPS package in both OECD and non-OECD countries. As a result, the existing international tax rules are currently being reassessed and reformed in a way that we have not seen before.

Within the European Union (EU), the European Commission (EC) has strongly reaffirmed the OECD's work on BEPS. In fact, the EU has taken the role of front-runner. Shortly after the release of the BEPS package in 2015, the EC has released a number of new legislative proposals.[2] These proposals seek to implement, on a harmonized basis, parts of the BEPS-package throughout the EU. In addition, in the wake of the above international tax policy developments, the EC has decided to start combating certain

1. OECD (2013), *Action Plan on Base Erosion and Profit Shifting*, OECD Publishing.
2. *See, e.g.*, Council Directive (EU) 2016/1164 of 12 July 2016 laying down rules against tax avoidance practices that directly affect the functioning of the internal market (ATAD 1).

international tax planning strategies on the basis of the EU State aid rules. For example, Algirdas Semeta (former Commissioner for Taxation and Customs) confirmed in a speech of 11 February 2014, that the EC 'is gathering information on tax planning strategies under State aid rules'.[3] Margrethe Vestager (current Commissioner for Competition) reaffirmed on 2 October 2014 that she is going 'to continue the work that [Joaquín] Almunia started in order to throw light on some of these [tax] arrangements if possible'.[4] To sum up, combating tax avoidance 'is in the air' and the EU State aid rules are currently used by the EC as a tool to that end.

It is widely acknowledged that Member States must comply with their obligations stemming from EU law when designing and applying anti-tax avoidance measures. In this respect, the focus is traditionally on the question whether such measures are compatible with the economic freedoms included in the Treaty on the Functioning of the European Union (TFEU).[5] A question that has deserved much lesser attention in scholarly literature until date is to what extent Member States are restricted under the EU State aid rules in their choice how to design anti-tax avoidance measures.[6] This chapter provides for a preliminary analysis which could serve as an upbeat to more in-depth research on this matter. The relation between anti-tax avoidance measurses that follow from an EU Directive and the EU State aid rules does not form part of this chapter.[7]

The outline of this chapter is as follows. First, a brief overview of the EU State aid rules is provided (section §5.02). Next, based on a number of non-exhaustive concrete case examples, the research question is further explored (section §5.03). The focus will be on anti-tax avoidance measures as such, overkill in anti-tax avoidance measures, underkill in anti-tax avoidance measures and safe harbour rules under anti-tax avoidance measures. The final section (section §5.04) provides for the main conclusions of this chapter. It is concluded that Member States are restricted to some extent in their choice how to design anti-tax avoidance measures under the EU State aid rules, but it is currently unclear to which extent.

§5.02 THE STATE AID FRAMEWORK IN A NUTSHELL

The TFEU provides for a prohibition on unlawful State aid. This prohibition aims at removing or abolishing State aid incompatible with the European internal market. The

3. Speech by Algirdas Šemeta dated 11 Feb. 2014, http://europa.eu/rapid/press-release_SPEECH-14-117_en.htm (retrieved at 1 Apr. 2019).
4. Hearing of Margrethe Vestager by the Committee on Economic and Monetary Affairs dated 2 October 2014, http://www.europarl.europa.eu/hearings-2014/resources/library/media/20141022RES75845/20141022RES75845.pdf (retrieved at 1 Apr. 2019).
5. Recently, for example, CJ 20 Dec. 2017, C-504/16 en C-613/16 (*Juhler Holding/Deister Holding*) and CJ 26 Feb. 2019, C-115/16 (N Luxembourg). In scholarly literature, *see, e.g.*, D.M. Weber, *Tax Avoidance and the EC Treaty Freedoms*. Alphen aan den Rijn: Kluwer Law International, 2005.
6. Until date, the focus in scholarly literature is on the compatibility with the EU State aid rules of tax rulings in the context of international tax planning structures; *see, e.g.*, P. Rossi-Maccanico, *Fiscal Aid, Tax Competition, and BEPS*, Tax Notes Intl. 857 et seq. (2014) and R.H.C. Luja, *Will the EU's State Aid Regime Survive BEPS?*, British Tax Rev. 3, 379–390 (2015).
7. *See* on this relationship: ECJ 23 Apr. 2009, C-460/07 (*Puffer*).

EC is the exclusive administrative body competent to assess whether a State aid measure is incompatible with the European internal market, subject to legal supervision by the General Court (GC) and the Court of Justice of the European Union (CJEU). A procedure of prior notification applies in this regard.[8] The EU State aid provisions also aim at restoring to a situation where State aid has not been granted. To that end, the beneficiary of the aid is, in principle, required to repay the aid received, including interest, unless such would be contrary to the general EU principle of legitimate expectations, i.e., legitimate expectations raised by European institutions.[9] The recovery of the aid is subject to a limitation period of ten years.

A tax measure constitutes state aid when the following four criteria are met. First of all, there must be an advantage to the recipient.[10] This test not only governs positive benefits, such as subsidies, but also carries advantages in the form of a reduction in the tax burden of a taxpayer.[11] Second, the advantage must be granted by the intervention of a state or through state resources. An actual transfer of state resources is, however, not required. Also a loss of tax revenue by a Member State qualifies.[12] Third, the advantage is liable to affect trade between the Member States. This requirement is generally met if the beneficiary carries on an economic activity involving trade between Member States. Finally, the advantage distorts or threatens to distort competition by favouring certain undertakings or the production of certain goods. A tax measure is selective if it deviates from the common tax system applied by a Member State. In order for a tax measure to confer a selective advantage, it must favour certain undertakings compared with others which are in a comparable legal and factual situation in the light of the objectives of the tax system in question. Essentially, the selectivity test therefore boils down to a question of discrimination and comparability.[13] The selectivity assessment is conducted by means of a three-step test: (i) the identification of the reference system, which constitutes the framework against which the selectivity of a measure is assessed; (ii) the assessment as to whether the measure at stake derogates from the reference system, as identified under the first step and (iii) assessment as to whether the selectivity of the measure can be justified.[14] A measure constituting State aid may be justified, but only on the basis of the grounds listed in Article 107(2) or 107(3) TFEU or by the nature or general scheme of the tax system, provided that the

8. Art. 108(3) TFEU, except for the cases where aid can be considered 'existing aid'.
9. Art. 14(1) of Council Regulation (EC) No 659/1999 of 22 Mar. 1999 laying down detailed rules for the application of Art. 93 of the EC Treaty, *OJ* 1999 L 83, 1.
10. *See, e.g.*, 2007/256/EC: Commission Decision of 20 Dec. 2006 on the aid scheme implemented by France under Art. 39 CA of the General Tax Code — State aid C 46/2004 (ex NN 65/2004), OJ 2007 L 112, 41 et seq., para. 100.
11. For example, ECJ 10 Jan. 2006, C-222/04, *Cassa di Risparmio di Firenze and others* [2006] ECR I-289, para. 113 and the case law cited there.
12. For example, 2006/269/EC: Commission Decision of 8 Feb. 2006 — State aid C 22/2004 (ex N 648/2001) on tax deductions for professional fishermen (Sweden), *OJ* 2006 L 99, 21 et seq., para. 30.
13. *See also*, for example, M. Lang, Selectivity as a Criterion to Determine Whether a Tax Measure Constitutes State Aid, in *Legal Remedies in European Tax Law* 270 (P. Pistone ed., Amsterdam: IBFD Publications, 2009).
14. The landmark case where this notion of justification was introduced was the Italian textile case (Case 173/73 *Italy v. Commission*, para. 33).

requirement of proportionality is met and that the measure does not go beyond what is necessary.[15] According to the CJ, a distinction must be made in this respect between the objectives attributed to a particular tax scheme which are extrinsic to it, on the one hand (which are not permissible) and the mechanisms inherent in the tax system itself which are necessary for the achievement of such objectives, on the other (which may be permissible).[16]

Tax measures which are effectively open to all economic agents operating within a Member State, by contrast, are in principle regarded as general measures. However, in exceptional cases the mere application of the general tax system may still result in selectivity. In a case regarding the proposed Gibraltar corporate tax regime, the CJ found that the reference system as defined by Gibraltar was founded on criteria that were of a general nature, but it discriminated factually between companies which were in a comparable situation, resulting in a selective advantage being given to offshore companies.[17] Hence, under circumstances, the application of the reference system itself may boil down to de facto selectivity.[18]

§5.03 ANTI-TAX AVOIDANCE RULES IN THE LIGHT OF THE STATE AID RULES

[A] Anti-tax Avoidance Rules as Such

It is commonly accepted that anti-tax avoidance rules must comply with the obligations stemming from the TFEU freedoms. This means for example that non-rebuttable presumptions of abuse may be incompatible.[19] The question is whether anti-tax avoidance rules, as such, may be scrutinzed under the State aid rules as well. This question comes up because typically, some enterprises (the targeted bonafide cases) will not fall under the scope of a given anti-tax avoidance measure while others (the targeted non-bonafide cases) will. Hence, one could argue, at least at first glance, that there is an advantage being granted to the first group of enterprises.

The EC answers the above question, at least implicitly, in the affirmative. In its 2016 Notice, the EC mentions that '[t]he provision of anti-abuse rules may be justified as measures to prevent tax avoidance by taxpayers'.[20] This implies that anti-tax avoidance rules may give rise to selectivity (otherwise, a justification would not be needed) and that such rules may, but not necessarily are by definition, justified.

The same reasoning can be found in the CJ's case law. In this respect, the *GIL Insurance* is relevant. In this case a specific insurance premium tax (IPT) applied by the

---

15. CJEU 8 Sep. 2011, Joined Cases C-78/08 to C-80/08 *Paint Graphos and others* [2011] ECR I-7611, para. 75.
16. CJEU 8 Sep. 2011, Joined Cases C-78/08 to C-80/08 *Paint Graphos and others* [2011] ECR I-7611, para. 69.
17. CJEU, 15 Nov. 2011, Gibraltar, joined cases C-106/09 P and C-107/09 P.
18. *See* in more detail §3.03.
19. Recently, for example, CJ 20 Dec. 2017, C-504/16 en C-613/16 (*Juhler Holding/Deister Holding*).
20. Commission Notice on the notion of State aid as referred to in Art. 107(1) of the Treaty on the Functioning of the European Union, C/2016/2946, OJ C 262, 19.7.2016, p. 1 et seq., para. 183.

United Kingdom was at stake. This tax aimed to stop a certain trend in practice whereby service contracts for the repair and maintenance of domestic appliances (e.g., fridges, laundry machines, cars) sold or rented (VAT = 17.5%) were being replaced by contracts of insurance ancillary to the sale or rental contracts (Value-Added Tax [VAT] exempt). The reason was that services contracts would be subject to 17.5% VAT whereas insurance contracts were VAT exempt. To stop this practice, the said general IPT was introduced. This tax provided for two different tax rates: 17.5% for insurance premiums relating to domestic appliances and 4% for all other insurance premiums. The taxpayer at stake argued before the CJ that the difference between the 4% and 17.5% tax rate constituted State aid. The CJ rejected this claim. The CJ held that 'the application of the higher rate of IPT to a specific part of the insurance contracts previously subject to the standard rate must be regarded as justified by the nature and the general scheme of the national system of taxation of insurance'.[21] The CJ's core within its reasoning seems to be that the rate 'was introduced to counteract the practice of taking advantage (...) by manipulating the prices of rental or sale of appliances and of the associated insurance'[22] and that 'the higher rate of IPT has the appearance of a regulatory charge intended specifically as a deterrent to the conclusion of connected insurance contracts [and that [t] he introduction of a higher rate of IPT on certain contracts was not intended to confer an advantage on all operators who offer contracts of insurance subject to the standard rate of IPT, in application of the general system of taxation of insurance'.[23]

In more recent decision in A-Brauerei, the CJ once again accepted the need to combat tax avoidance as a justification within the context of an alleged State aid scheme. This case concerned a reorganisation exemption in the German transfer tax. This facility was in principle open to certain legal conversions - including mergers or divisions - within a group of companies. The requirement was that the companies concerned had to be linked with each other through a shareholding relationship of at least 95%. In addition, this 95% ownership requirement had to be met for a period of five years prior and for a period five-year following the conversion in order to prevent abuse of the facility. The exemption was introduced in 2009 and appeared to have a dual purpose: to facilitate the restructuring of companies and to increase their competitiveness in response to the financial crisis that Germany has been experiencing since 2008. The essential question was whether the facility could give rise to State aid concerns vis-à-vis enterprises that could rely on the exemption, given that enterprises that do not meet all specified requirements would not be entitled to the exemption. With respect to the 5-year minimum shareholdholding period, being of an anti-avoidance nature, the CJ established, under reference to its earlier decision in *GIL Insurance* that 'such a shareholding appears justified by the intention of excluding

21. CJ 29 Apr. 2004, C-308/01 (*GIL Insurance Ltd and Others v. Commissioners of Customs & Excise*), para. 78.
22. CJ 29 Apr. 2004, C-308/01 (*GIL Insurance Ltd and Others v. Commissioners of Customs & Excise*), para. 74.
23. CJ 29 Apr. 2004, C-308/01 (*GIL Insurance Ltd and Others v. Commissioners of Customs & Excise*), para. 75.

undesirable windfall effects and, therefore, of preventing abuse, by precluding shareholdings of that level, which will come to an end once the restructuring has been concluded, from being acquired for a short period for the sole purposes of benefiting from that tax exemption'.[24] The CJ concluded that '[t]he prevention of abuse may constitute a justification linked to the nature or general scheme of the system concerned'.[25]

In my view, however, putting the prevention of abuse in the context of justification grounds is conceptually less logical then it may seem at first glance. This is because it implies that the group of bona fide taxpayers, that do not fall under the anti-tax avoidance rule, would receive a selective advantage, implying that this group is subject to a deviating set of rules. This is, however, not the case; the latter group is subject to the normally applicable tax regime. It is true that the application of an anti-tax avoidance rule constitutes a deviation, but that deviation does not confer an advantage, but a disadvantage to the group of non-bona fide taxpayers. A simple example may illustrate this. Assume a Member State has an interest limitation rule in force that is fully proportionate in that it only applies to abusive situations (hence the measure does not involve overkill nor underkill). As a result, the group of bona fide taxpayers does not fall within the scope of the interest limitation rule, as a result of which interest is deductible. Assuming that the Member State taxes business profits on a net rather than on a gross basis, interest deduction would constitute part of the normal reference system, and not an exception. There is an exception being made for non-bonafide taxpayers, but as said, this exception results in a disadvantage rather than in an advantage. In my view, therefore, the application of anti-tax avoidance legislation is not about granting an advantage to the group of bona fide taxpayers who after all follow the standard, the normally applicable tax rules, but about creating a disadvantage for the group of abusers who want to deviate from the standard, to circumvent the normally applicable tax rules. Hence, there should be no selective advantage under the EU State aid rules in this case; at most there could be a disadvantage that may be incompatible with the TFEU freedoms. The question whether the interest limitation measure can be justified under the State aid rules should thus no longer come into play.

[B] Anti-tax Avoidance Rule and Overkill

[1] Overkill in Anti-tax Avoidance Rules

Related to the previous question is the question to what extent *overkill* in an anti-tax avoidance measure may constitute State aid. From the analysis made in the previous section it follows that the EC and the CJ appear to assess anti-tax avoidance rules under the State aid rules in the context of justification grounds. This implies that *overkill* could be scrutinized by the EC under reference to the principle of proportionality, for example where an enterprise that *ratione legis* falls outside the scope of the said rule

24. CJ 19 Dec. 2018, C-374/17 (A-Brauerei), para. 51.
25. CJ 19 Dec. 2018, C-374/17 (A-Brauerei), para. 51.

would nonetheless be hit by that rule while other enterprises that similarly fall outside the scope of the said rule *ratione legis* are actually - correctly - excluded from that rule based on its actual scope and wording.

In this respect, it is relevant to notice that in the case of A-Brauerei, the CJ did not question the proportionality of the German anti-tax avoidance rule. In this case, the five-year minimum holding period was apparently accepted as a means to combat tax avoidance, without questioning whether this period was proportionate. The question therefore comes up under which circumstances the EC actually would or could call the proportionality of an anti-tax avoidance measures into question. Notwithstanding the analysis made below, the EC should in my view make use of that power only in exceptional circumstances for the sake of legal certainty. This means that as long as the set threshold is not manifestly arbitrary or unreasonable, it should in my view remain within the Member States' margin of appreciation to determine the thresholds of an anti-avoidance rule, even if these thresholds may contain overkill.

This said, in my view, the existence of overkill in an anti-tax avoidance measure should not constitute State aid in the first place for the same reasons as set out in the previous section. As a result, the principle of proportionality should insofar not come into play anymore. A simple example may illustrate this. Assume a Member State has an interest limitation rule in force that is not proportionate as it applies mechanically, irrespective of whether the actual taxpayer is bona fide or not (hence overkill). This means that some bona fide taxpayers will not be entitled to deduct their interest expenses whereas other bona fide taxpayers are. In my view, again, the latter group is not treated more favourably, but simply falls within the generally applicable rule of net taxation. In other words, there is no selective advantage being made to this group of taxpayers. It is the first group that is hit by an exception (no interest deduction), but this exception confers a disadvantage rather than an advantage to this group. Hence, also in the case of overkill, there should in my view be no selective advantage under the EU State aid rules; at most there is a disadvantage that may be incompatible with the TFEU freedoms.

[2] Reduction of Overkill in Anti-tax Avoidance Rules

A related question is what holds, or should hold, if a Member State *reduces* overkill contained in an anti-tax avoidance measure, but does so only partially. This would mean that between the same group of enterprise that *ratione legis* falls outside the scope of the said anti-tax avoidance rule, some enterprises would no longer be hit by that rule, while others would continue to fall under the scope of that rule. Here, the recent German case Heitkamp sheds some light on this question. This case is about the German general restriction on the right to loss relief if there is a takeover of at least 25% of the shares in the taxpayer. Under the so-called 'Sanierungsklausel', however, this general restriction is removed, and loss relief remains possible, in the case of a takeover of an ailing company. The German measure entered into force (with retroactive effect) on 1 January 2008. In 2011, the EC decided that the German scheme constitutes prohibited State aid.[26] According to the EC, there was a deviation from the main rule that in case of substantial take-overs, the right to loss relief vaporized. In appeal, the taxpayer argued that the objective of the German legislation is to prevent abuse of loss relief (as a result of trading in shell companies). Since that abuse will not occur in the case of ailing companies, that group is not comparable from the point of view of the said objective. The General Court, however, dismissed this argument. In brief, it held that the right to loss relief vaporized automatically, regardless of whether there was any abuse.[27] The aim of the scheme is therefore not to prevent abuse, but simply to reduce the right to loss relief in the event of a significant change in the company's interests. The CJ, however, overruled the General Court's decision. It held that 'the selectivity of a tax measure cannot be precisely assessed on the basis of a reference framework consisting of some provisions that have been artificially taken from a broader legislative framework'.[28] It went on by ruling that 'by (...) excluding from the relevant reference framework in the present case the general rule of loss carry-forward, manifestly the General Court defined it too narrowly'.[29] This would imply, in my view, that the German provision for ailing companies must not be seen as an exception, but as a part of the main rule that says that, in principle, losses can be offset against (future) profits. Under the German Sanierungsklausel, the main rule thus 'revives'. It is noted, however, that a final decision has not been taken yet in this case and that the CJ's ruling may be open to different interpretations.[30]

In my view, this decision gives support for the position that Member States are free to reduce *overkill* in their anti-tax avoidance measures, even if they do so in a selective fashion. And in my view, that is logical. A simple example may illustrate this. Assume a Member State has an interest limitation rule in force that is not proportionate as it applies mechanically, irrespective of whether the actual taxpayer is bona fide or not (hence overkill). At some stage, a possibility for the taxpayer to provide some proof to the contrary is introduced. This possibility is, however, restricted and the overkill is therefore not fully withdrawn. This means that some bona fide taxpayers will still not be entitled to deduct their interest expenses (although this group becomes smaller) whereas an increased group of other bona fide taxpayers are. In my view, the State aid analysis should be the same as depicted in the previous section. This means that there is, again, no selective advantage granted to the latter group, but a disadvantage to the former. Allowing deduction of interest expenses constitutes the general rule, and not the exception. On top of that, the view to the contrary would mean that it would be a matter of all-or-nothing for the Member States when reducing overkill in their domestic

26. Commission Decision 2011/527/EU of 26 Jan. 2011 on State aid C 7/10 (ex CP 250/09 and NN 5/10) implemented by Germany – Scheme for the carry-forward of tax losses in the case of restructuring of companies in difficulty (Sanierungsklausel), 2011/527/EU, Pb. L 235, p. 26.
27. General Court 4 Feb. 2016, T-287/11 (*Heitkamp BauHolding v. Commission*), para. 133.
28. CJ 28 June 2018, Case C-203/16 P (Dirk Andres, acting as liquidator in the insolvency of Heitkamp BauHolding GmbH), para. 103.
29. CJ 28 June 2018, Case C-203/16 P (Dirk Andres, acting as liquidator in the insolvency of Heitkamp BauHolding GmbH), para. 103.
30. *See, e.g.*, L. De Broe, The State Aid Selectivity-Test in Corporate Tax Matters: CJEU Applies Common Sense in Its Judgments on the German 'Sanierungs' - clause, but Do We Have All Pieces of the Puzzle Now?, EC Tax Review 2018/06.

anti-tax avoidance rules. Member States could then be prevented from *gradually* reducing the adverse effects of *overkill* at all, which would leave all bona fide taxpayers in a worse off overkill situation. Bringing an anti-tax avoidance measure more in line with its rationale, albeit not completely, should in my view thus be permissible under the EU State aid rules and could, at most, constitute an issue under the TFEU freedoms.

[C] Anti-tax Avoidance Rule Contains Underkill

Opposite to the question dealt with in the previous section, the question comes up to what extent *underkill* in anti-tax avoidance rules may give rise to State aid concerns. In its 2016 Notice, the EC takes the position in this respect that '[a]nti-abuse rules might be selective if they provide for a derogation (non-application of the anti-abuse rules) to specific undertakings or transactions, which would not be consistent with the logic underlying the anti-abuse rules in question'.[31] The EC does not further elaborate, so the question is what this statement precisely means. A distinction could be made between 'weaknesses' in a particular tax system and underkill an a particular anti-tax avoidance rule. Both are discussed below.

[1] Weaknesses in a Particular Tax System

An example of features of underkill generally included in a tax system was at state in the recent Gibraltar 3 case. When assessing the tax system operated in Gibraltar, the EC discovered 'certain weaknesses' in that tax system. First, it found that the territorial system of taxation operated in Gibraltar could create opportunities for cross-border tax planning with a significant risk of non-taxation of the relevant companies' profits in both Gibraltar and the countries where the activities are actually performed.[32] Second, it discovered some weaknesses in the procedure for the granting of tax rulings, in particular the absence of any designated procedure providing clear requirements for both the applicant and the tax authorities and the absence of adequate ex ante and ex post control procedures.[33] Finally, weaknesses were also identified in relation to the general anti-avoidance provision, including the transfer pricing rules, since application of this provision is conditional on the existence of an 'artificial arrangement'.[34] The EC stated that '[n]one of those weaknesses constitutes State aid in their own right'.[35] However, the EC also stated that 'in the absence of appropriate measures to address those weaknesses, the tax authorities may enjoy an excessive level of discretion in the enforcement of the rules, which may increase the risk of State aid being granted'.[36] Eventually, the EC refrained from a formal decision on this point, seemingly because

31. Commission Notice on the notion of State aid as referred to in Art. 107(1) of the Treaty on the Functioning of the European Union, C/2016/2946, OJ C 262, 19 July 2016, p. 1 et seq., para. 183.
32. Commission Decision of 19 Dec. 2018 on the State Aid SA.34914 (2013/C), implemented by the United Kingdom as regards the Gibraltar Corporate Income Tax Regime, para. 238.
33. *Ibid.*, para. 239.
34. *Ibid.*, para. 240.
35. *Ibid.*, para 241.
36. *Ibid.*, para. 241.

Gibraltar's government had agreed to introduce legislative and regulatory changes with a view to addressing those weaknesses. In my view, this is understandable. Accepting that weaknesses in a tax system could, by itself, give rise to State aid would give the EC potentially a tool under the State aid rules that would reach much further than merely scrutinizing selective tax treatment. Under this approach, the EC potentially could start dictating how Member States' tax systems should look like, with the existence of a domestic reference framework no longer being necessary. The EC would autonomously decide what constitutes a weakness in a particular tax system, and what would not. In my view, that would go beyond the scope of the EU State aid rules.

[2] Exception Clauses in an Anti-tax Avoidance Rule

A more concrete example of *underkill* constitutes the EC's decision of the full and partial exemption for group financing activities under the UK controlled foreign company (CFC) rules. Under these rules, low-taxed passive income from (inter alia) non-trading financing activities can constitute chargeable CFC profits which are 'picked-up' at the level of the controlling UK parent. Chargeable profits of a CFC are defined as profits that have been artificially diverted from the UK. As a general rule, a CFC charge applies to non-trading finance profits to the extent they are derived from assets and risks in relation to which any relevant significant people functions are carried out in the UK (the so-called *UK activities-test*).[37] Non-trading finance profits will also be captured if the CFC has earned the profits from loans that are funded from relevant UK funds (the so-called *UK connected capital test*).[38] An exception to the above tests is made for intra-group financing activities (so called non-trading finance profits from qualifying loan relationships). The basic rule here is that only 25% of the CFC's profits will be included in the CFC charge (75%-exemption). In addition, a 100% exemption can be claimed for a loan to a non-UK resident group company to the extent this loan was funded either (a) out of certain assets of the CFC (those that have arisen in the territory to which the qualifying loan is made) or (b) out of newly issued group capital, i.e., funds raised by issuing shares from the group's top company (the *qualifying resources rule*).[39] Furthermore, the full exemption can be claimed to the extent that on a consolidated basis the net interest income of all UK resident members of the multinational group exceeds their net interest borrowings (the 'matched interest' *rule*).[40]

The UK Government takes the position that the exemption for group financing simply covers circumstances that present a low risk of artificial diversion and thus

37. European Commission 26 Oct. 2017, State Aid SA.44896 (2017/C ex 2017/NN) – United Kingdom CFC Group Financing Exemption, OJ 2017/C 400/03, p. 10 et seq. para. 16.
38. *Ibid.*, para. 17. Subject to a specific motive test, the CFC charge also applies if non-trading finance profits directly or indirectly arise from an arrangement with a UK corporate taxpayer connected with the CFC and if non-trading finance income arises from a relevant finance lease made by the CFC (in)directly to a connected UK corporate taxpayer. These exceptions are not subject to the EC's state aid investigation and are not further discussed here.
39. *Ibid.*, para. 29.
40. *Ibid*, para. 29.

avoidance and is to be seen as an integral part of that reference system, and not as a derogation.[41] With respect to the 75%-exemption, the UK Government states that this rule constitutes a proportionate and reasonable response measuring the extent to which the CFC is overcapitalized with capital sourced from UK borrowings. This is because it would be very difficult to trace or otherwise establish precisely the extent to which an equity investment in a CFC has been sourced from borrowings incurred by a UK member of a group.[42] The full exemption addresses, according to the UK government, circumstances where the underlying facts indicate that there has been no diversion of profits from the UK, either by the (near) absence of UK funding of the CFC or by the (near) absence of any net UK borrowing costs.[43]

In its opening decision, the EC takes the position that the above exemptions constitute a selective derogation that cannot be justified. Although the EC acknowledges that there may be good reasons to differentiate between the criteria within a CFC-scheme, such 'objective criteria must be applied consistently and equally to similar types of non-trading finance profits [and that] [a]pplying more lenient criteria or exemptions to some situations and stricter criteria to other similar ones has the effect of treating some operators that are in a legally and factually comparable situation in view of the objective of the reference system concerned better than other operators'.[44] Put differently, 'introducing anti-avoidance rules while including only some operators or transactions in these rules and not others that are in a legally and factually comparable situation is contrary to State aid rules if there is no valid justification within the internal logic of the reference system'.[45]

On 2 April 2019, the EC took its final decision in this case. Based on the press release issued on the same date[46], the EC decided that in situations where financing income from a foreign group company, channelled through an offshore subsidiary, is financed with UK connected capital and with no UK activities being involved in generating the finance profits, the group financing exemption is justified and does not constitute State aid under EU rules. This is because 'such an exemption avoids complex and disproportionately burdensome intra-group tracing exercises that would be required to assess the exact percentage of profits funded with UK assets'. The EC therefore acknowledged that 'the Group Financing Exemption in these cases provides for a clear proxy that is justified to ensure the proper functioning and effectiveness of the CFC rules'. On the other hand, the EC decided that when financing income from a foreign group company, channelled through an offshore subsidiary, derives from UK activities, the group financing exemption is not justified and constitutes State aid under EU rules. This is because 'the exercise required to assess to what extent the financing income of a company derives from UK activities is not particularly burdensome or complex'. In addition, the exemption 'does not seek to address any possible complexity related to the allocation of financing income to UK activities'.

41. *Ibid.*, paras 39–40.
42. *Ibid.*, para. 42.
43. *Ibid.*, para. 45.
44. *Ibid.*, paras 81–82.
45. *Ibid.*, para. 115.
46. *See* http://europa.eu/rapid/press-release_IP-19-1948_en.htm (retrieved at 2 Apr. 2019).

Although the final decision has not yet been published, a more fundamental question lies behind the EC's decision. The EC's decision learns that an exception to an anti-tax avoidance rule may give rise to selectivity meaning that a tax-related policy goal must be available to justify such an exception. However, an opposite perspective (e.g., taken by the UK Government) could be taken as well under reference to the Heitkamp case (discussed in section §5.03[B][2]) under which the exceptions to the CFC rule should be seen as part of the general reference framework according to which overseas CFC profits that fall outside the CFC rules are not picked up in the UK. In other words, an exception being made to an anti-tax avoidance rule would not be considered as an advantage, but as the application of the normal reference framework. When it comes to underkill and State aid, the crucial question is which approach is correct. The decision in Heitkamp is not conclusive, so further CJ case law is needed.

[3] Approval of Exploiting Legal Gaps Within a Tax System

A case that balances somewhere between the previously discussed two situations is the Engie-case. Despite the decision in the Gibraltar-3 case, the EC seems to go one step further in this case which concerns a domestic, complex financing structure. The tax feature of this domestic structure was that the remuneration by a Luxembourg debtor in Luxembourg would be tax-deductible, whereas the corresponding receivable would be tax-exempt at the level of the Luxembourg recipient under the Luxembourg participation exemption. In other words, there was an internal 'mismatch', as a result of which part of the profits of Engie in Luxembourg was ultimately not taxed. According to the Luxembourg tax authorities, the financing structure, as well as its tax consequences, stood within the limits of the Luxembourg tax law. That is why the tax authorities issued a ruling to Engie confirming the Luxembourg tax consequences.

According to the EC, however, the Engie ruling constitutes State aid. The EC uses a number of separate arguments in this respect. The ruling is, according to the EC, contrary to the Luxembourg general prohibition of abuse of rights.[47] As there was no double tax, the participation exemption should furthermore have been left out of the application on the basis of its objective.[48] And, last but not the least, the result of non-taxation is contrary to the purpose of the Luxembourg corporate income tax act.[49] This latter argument is most relevant for purposes of this chapter. This is because the EC essentially seems to say that there is tax avoidance that Luxembourg should have put a stop to. Put more sharply, there should have been no gap in the Luxembourg tax legislation. The EC's approach implies that there is apparently a European minimum standard for combating abuse hidden in the European State aid rules. In my view, this is quite something, especially if one consides that this hidden norm would effectively

47. Commission Decision of 20 June 2018, SA.44888 (2016/C) (ex 2016/NN) implemented by Luxembourg in favour of ENGIE, para. 314.
48. *Ibid.*, paras 236–237.
49. *Ibid.*, para. 190 and paras 198–200.

apply with a retroactive effect of ten years. One may therefore legitimately wonder whether the EC isn't stretching the State aid rules too much here.[50]

[D] Anti-tax Avoidance Rules and Safe Harbour Rules

[1] Safe Harbour Rules and Underkill

Closely connected to the previous issue of underkill in anti-tax avoidance rules is the phenomenon of safe harbour rules included in domestic anti-tax avoidance rules. Typically, safe harbour rules may aim at providing legal certainty and to reduce complexity and administrative burden in favour of enterprises that *ratione legis* should fall outside the scope of an anti-tax avoidance rule.

The EC's decision in the UK CFC rules (see section §5.03[C][2]) learns that fixed proxies under anti-tax avoidance rules may be permissible, provided that the objective behind the said proxy is inherent to the tax system at stake. In my view, this is understandable. Otherwise, the EC could start introducing its own thresholds (e.g., the EC could replace the 75%-exemption by, for example, a 65%-exemption) which would, once again, raise legal certainty concerns. As concluded in section §5.03[B][1] in the context of overkill, it should in my view remain within the Member States' margin of appreciation to determine the thresholds of an anti-avoidance rule, even if these thresholds may contain underkill, as long as the set threshold is not manifestly arbitrary or unreasonable in the view of the objective pursued.

[2] Safe Harbour Rules and De Facto Selectivity

In the context of safe harbour rules the question can furthermore be raised whether safe harbour rule could, by itself, give rise to selectivity if they de facto give rise to differential treatment. In this regard, reference is made to the Gibraltar-2 case.[51] In brief, this case regarded the proposed Gibraltar corporate tax regime. The main contemplated criteria for corporate tax liability, however, did not consist of income, but of premises and employees. The CJ concluded that offshore companies would not be taxed under the proposed regime, which was not a random consequence of the regime at issue, but followed precisely from the contemplated criteria for corporate tax liability.[52] The CJ consequently ruled that although the reference system as defined by Gibraltar was founded on criteria that were of a general nature, it nonetheless discriminated factually between companies that were in a comparable situation,

50. For a critical view *see also* S.C.W. Douma, Staatssteunpraatjes vullen geen gaatjes!, *NTFR* 2018/2105 and Jérôme Monsenego, The Engie case: some open questions on the EU State aid rules and the prevention of tax avoidance, 10 Sep. 2018, http://competitionlawblog.kluwercompetitionlaw.com/2018/09/10/engie-case-open-questions-eu-state-aid-rules-prevention-tax-avoidance, (retrieved at 1 Apr. 2019).
51. CJEU 15 Nov. 2011, Joined Cases C-106/09 P and C-107/09 P *Commission and Spain v. Government of Gibraltar and United Kingdom*).
52. *Ibid.*, para. 106.

resulting in a selective advantage being given to offshore companies.[53] Apparently, the benchmark for selectivity in this case no longer was whether there was an exception to the main rule. The mere application of the main rule factually resulted in selectivity.

Although intuitively one could endorse the CJ's decision given the peculiarities of this case, the CJ's approach nonetheless raises important conceptual difficulties. After all, how should one calculate the advantage (difference between main rule and deviation) if it is already the main rule that results in selectivity? This decision implies that the EC could set its own benchmark in such a case, e.g., a (minimum) norm as to how a corporate income tax system should at least look like. This means that selectivity might arise not only in cases of a deviation from the domestic general system, but also in case of a deviation from certain higher European (unwritten) norms.

A second case that is relevant in this context is the ANGED-case. In brief, and as far as relevant, this case concerns a number of Spanish local environmental taxes on large individual retailers to contribute to the protection of the environment and town and country planning. The threshold for these taxes is whether the retailer's sales area is 2,500 m^2 or more. The question is whether this threshold constitutes prohibited State aid as it distinguishes between small and large retailers. The CJ rules that this is not the case.[54] From the point of view of the objective of the lcoal Spanish scheme (protection of the environment and town and country planning), large and small retailers are objectively not comparable and different treatment is therefore permitted.[55]

In my view, the mere fact that in the majority of cases large companies are affected by a tax-avoidance rule should not be sufficient to accept the existence of de facto selectivity. The fact that, more or less by chance, persons affected by the introduction of a tax consist to a large extent of one particular group of enterprises should in my view, by itself, not give rise to selectivity.[56] The answer to this question might be different, however, if it can be established that the parameters set-out under the anti-tax avoidance rule appear to be 'linked' to a specific group of enterprises.[57] This would imply that precisely due to choice that a Member State made for setting the parameters, a specific group of enterprises is affected intrinsically and not as a random consequence.[58]

§5.04 CONCLUSION

In this chapter the question has been explored as to what extent are the Member States restricted in their choice of how to design anti-tax avoidance measures under the EU

53. *Ibid.*, para. 107.
54. CJ 26 Apr. 2018, C-233/16 (Asociación Nacional de Grandes Empresas de Distribución (ANGED)), para.
55. *Ibid.*, para. 55.
56. *See* by analogy Opinion Advocate General Kokott dated 9 Nov. 2018, C-233/16 (Asociación Nacional de Grandes Empresas de Distribución (ANGED)), para. 35.
57. By analogy CJ 5 Feb. 2014, C-385/12 (Hervis Sport), paras 39 et seq.
58. *See* by analogy Opinion Advocate General Kokott dated 9 Nov. 2018, C-233/16 (Asociación Nacional de Grandes Empresas de Distribución (ANGED)), point 38 and CJ 15 Nov. 2011, Joined Cases C-106/09 P and C-107/09 P *Commission and Spain v. Government of Gibraltar and United Kingdom*), para. 106.

State aid rules. The answer to this question is one the one hand clear: Member States are restricted. At the same time, it is currently unclear to say to what extent; further case-law must be awaited. In my view the impact should be limited for the sake of legal certainty.

CHAPTER 6

The EU Notion of Legitimate Expectations in the Context of State Aid Law: What Role for National Judges?

Carla De Pietro

§6.01 INTRODUCTION: DEFINING LIMITATIONS AND UNCERTAINTIES AFFECTING THE PROTECTION OF LEGITIMATE EXPECTATIONS BY NATIONAL JUDGES

Protection of legitimate expectations in the field of European Union (EU) State aid law has a particularly important function as it aims at preserving the rights of individuals within the Internal Market. Very significantly, in the context of State aid, protection of legitimate expectations is based on a central role of national judges. In fact, only national judges can preserve the legitimate expectations of beneficiaries of unlawful aid during the period that precedes the decision of the Commission, and - even after that period - when the measure is considered by the Commission to be compatible with the Internal Market.

Accordingly, an effective protection of legitimate expectations necessarily implies the autonomy of national judges. Unfortunately, this is not completely the case. As will be shown below in this chapter, although the enforcement of State aid law at national level is governed by the principle of procedural autonomy, the power of national judges has been substantially limited through the case law of the Court of Justice. According to Advocate General Cosmas, ' precisely because of the particular nature of State aid and the need to safeguard the imperative Community interest in rectifying the conditions of competition, the Court has the tendency to restrict the legal autonomy of the national legal orders, by laying down itself the substantive requirements for recognizing that legitimate expectations are entertained'.[1] In fact, the Court of Justice has developed a very stringent notion of legitimate expectations,[2] which not only substantially limits the application of the corresponding national concepts, but – at the same time, as will be shown below – makes national judges actually dependent on the preliminary rulings of the Court of Justice.

In addition, it is clear that autonomy of national judges is concretely guaranteed only when they are actually able to decide on the basis of clear rules. This clarity has certainly been undermined through the judgments of the Court of Justice in the (Centre d'exportation du livre français) CELF cases.[3]

These decisions represent a turning point in the case law of the Court of Justice. As will be explained below, with these judgments the Court has – in fact – limited the scope of the standstill clause to the need of avoiding the introduction of incompatible aid within the Internal Market. It is submitted that this position has had an impact on the protection of legitimate expectations by national judges that has not been enough appreciated in literature. With an innovative stance, this chapter argues that through these judgments – and mainly through the CELF II judgment – the Court – coherently with the modified scope of the standstill clause – has extended the scope of the notion of legitimate expectations also to the compatibility of the aid. However, this result has very problematic effects for national judges. In fact, it remains uncertain how the application of this broader notion of legitimate expectations should be reconciled with the previous case law of the Court of Justice which, as will be explained below, has developed the notion of legitimate expectations exclusively on the basis of the concept of unlawfulness (i.e., lack of notification and/or breach of the standstill clause). According to this author, instead of clarifying the power of national judges when applying the notion of legitimate expectations, with the CELF decisions – and especially the CELF II judgment – the Court of Justice has rendered this power more uncertain.

Thus, the purpose of this chapter is to critically analyze the role of national judges, and especially the effectiveness of their powers, when legitimate expectations are at issue. As a consequence, this chapter represents an important contribution to the academic research concerning the notion of legitimate expectations as applicable in the field of State aid law. The chapter makes the significant contribution of linking the interpretation of the case law about legitimate expectations to the desirable autonomy of national judges in the institutional framework of EU State aid control. In fact, it seems that – for the benefit of a uniform application of State aid law – the Court of

1. Opinion of Advocate General Cosmas, delivered on 23 Nov. 1999 in case C-83/98 P, *France v. Ladbroke Racing and Commission*, para. 58.
2. Also the European Commission emphasizes that '[t]he standard which the Community courts apply in this respect is very strict'. *See*, European Commission, *Commission Notice on the Enforcement of State Aid Law by National Courts*, (2009/C 85/01), 2009, para. 32.
3. Court of Justice of the European Union (CJEU), C-199/06, *Judgment of 12 Feb. 2008, CELF and ministre de la Culture et de la Communication (C-199/06, ECR 2008 p. I-469)*; CJEU, C-1/09, *Judgment of 11 Mar. 2010, CELF and ministre de la Culture and de la Communication (C-1/09, ECR 2010 p. I-2099)*.

Justice has limited the autonomy of national judges in cases where legitimate expectations are at issue to an undesirable level. Consequently, with an innovative perspective, this chapter has the ultimate purpose of establishing, in the context of legitimate expectations, how to find the right balance between the need to guarantee a uniform application of State aid law and the need to assure that national judges have a degree of autonomy which guarantees an effective enforcement of State aid law at national level.

§6.02 LEGITIMATE EXPECTATIONS AND THE COMPETENCE OF NATIONAL JUDGES

The legislative point of reference for the application of the EU notion of legitimate expectations in matter of State aid is Article 16(1) of the Procedural Regulation.[4] According to this provision, '[t]he Commission shall not require recovery of the aid if this would be contrary to a general principle of Union law'. As is well known, protection of legitimate expectations is recognized as a general principle of Union Law.[5]

In the case *Commission v. Germany*,[6] the Court of Justice specified that when a beneficiary claims legitimate expectations on the lawfulness of the aid before a national court, it is up to this court to evaluate the concrete circumstances of the case. In the case *SFEI (Syndicat Français de l'Express International and others)* and others the Court further explained that 'a national court requested to order the repayment of aid must grant that application if it finds that the aid was not notified to the Commission, unless by reason of exceptional circumstances repayment is inappropriate'.[7] In light of this position of the Court of Justice, the Commission stated that '[t]he legal standard to be applied in this context should be similar to the one applicable under Articles 14 and 15 [now 16 and 17] of the Procedural Regulation. In other words, circumstances which would not stand in the way of a recovery order by the Commission cannot justify a national court refraining from ordering full recovery under Article 88(3) [now 108(3)] of the Treaty'.[8]

The competence of national judges in matter of legitimate expectations derives from the direct effect of the last sentence of Article 108(3) of the Treaty on the Functioning of the European Union (TFEU), within the framework of recovery proceedings.[9] As is well known, the direct applicability of this provision was already

4. Council Regulation (EU) 2015/1589 of 13 July 2015 laying down detailed rules for the application of Art. 108 of the Treaty on the Functioning of the European Union.
5. *See*, CJEU, Cases 205/82 to 215/82, *Judgment of 21 Sept. 1983, Deutsche Milchkontor GmbH (205 to 215/82, ECR 1983 p. 2633), para. 30.*
6. CJEU, C-5/89, *Judgment of 20 Sep. 1990, Commission v. Germany (C-5/89, ECR 1990 p. I-3437)*, para 16.
7. CJEU, C-39/94, *Judgment of 11 July 1996, SFEI and others (C-39/94, ECR 1996 p. I-3547)*, para. 71.
8. European Commission, *supra* n. 2, para. 32.
9. European Commission, *supra* n. 2, paras 30–33; Denis Jouve, *Recovering Unlawful and Incompatible Aids by National Courts: CELF and Scoot/Kimberly Clark Cases*, 3 EStAL 367, 367 (2017); B. Brandtner, T. Beranger and C. Lessenich, *Private State Aid Enforcement*, 1 EStAL 23, 25 (2010).

clarified by the Court of Justice in the *Costa v. E.N.E.L.* case.[10] However, in the case *Lorenz v. Germany* the Court has specified that 'the immediately applicable nature of this prohibition extends to the whole of the period to which it applies. Thus the direct effect of the prohibition extends to all aid which has been implemented without being notified and, in the event of notification, operates during the preliminary period, and where the Commission sets in motion the contentious procedure, up to the final decision'.[11]

The EU notion of legitimate expectations, as applicable in matters of State aid, has been developed by the Court of Justice in connection with the scope and function of Article 108(3) TFEU, which - as is well known - establishes an obligation for Member States of notifying the Commission of any plan to introduce new aid measures. As a consequence, new aid measures cannot be implemented until the Commission has approved them. Thus, very significantly, in the case *Commission v. Germany* the Court stated that 'in view of the mandatory nature of the supervision of State aid by the Commission under Article 93 [now 108] of the Treaty, undertakings to which an aid has been granted may not, in principle, entertain a legitimate expectation that the aid is lawful unless it has been granted in compliance with the procedure laid down in that article. A diligent businessman should normally be able to determine whether that procedure has been followed'.[12]

This passage has to be connected with what explained by the Court of Justice in the case *Steinike und Weinlig v. Germany*: 'the intention of the Treaty, in providing through Article 93 [now 108] for aid to be kept under constant review and supervised by the Commission, is that the finding that an aid may be incompatible with the common market is to be determined, subject to review by the Court, by means of an appropriate procedure which it is the Commission's responsibility to set in motion'.[13]

Commission and national courts have distinct competences. As emphasized by the Court of Justice in the Federation Nationale du Commerce Extérieur des Produits Alimentaires (FNCE) judgement, 'the principal and exclusive role conferred on the Commission by Articles 92 and 93 [now 107 and 108] of the Treaty, which is to hold aid to be incompatible with the common market where this is appropriate, is fundamentally different from the role of national courts in safeguarding rights which individuals enjoy as a result of the direct effect of the prohibition laid down in the last sentence of Article 93(3) of the Treaty. Whilst the Commission must examine the compatibility of the proposed aid with the common market, even where the Member State has acted in breach of the prohibition on giving effect to aid, national courts do no more than preserve, until the final decision of the Commission, the rights of individuals faced with a possible breach by State authorities of the prohibition laid down by the last sentence of Article 93(3) of the Treaty. When those courts make a ruling in such a matter, they

10. CJEU, C-6/64, *Judgment of 15 July 1964, Costa v. E.N.E.L. (6-64, ECR 1964 p. 585)*; *see also*, M. L. Struys and H. *Abbott, The Role of National Courts in State Aid Litigation*, 28 E.L. Rev. 172, (2003).
11. CJEU, C-120/73, *Judgment of 11 Dec. 1973, Lorenz GmbH v. Bundesrepublik Deutschland and others (120/73, ECR 1973 p. 1471)*, para. 8.
12. CJEU, C-5/89, *supra* n. 6, para. 14.
13. CJEU, C-78/76, *Judgment of 22 Mar. 1977, Steinike & Weinlig (78/76, ECR 1977 p. 595)*, para. 9.

do not thereby decide on the compatibility of the aid with the common market, the final determination on that matter being the exclusive responsibility of the Commission, subject to the supervision of the Court of Justice'.[14]

In the FNCE judgement, the Court of Justice has ruled that the breach of the last sentence of (now) Article 108(3) TFEU determines the invalidity of national measures implementing unlawful aid. As a consequence, '[n]ational courts must offer to individuals in a position to rely on such breach the certain prospect that all the necessary inferences will be drawn, in accordance with their national law, as regards the validity of measures giving effect to the aid, the recovery of financial support granted in disregard of that provision and possible interim measures'.[15]

Very importantly, in the same judgment, the Court ruled that a subsequent final positive decision of the Commission does not have the effect of regularizing ex post facto the invalidity of the national measures implementing an unlawful aid. According to the Court, '[a]ny other interpretation would have the effect of according a favourable outcome to the non-observance by the Member State concerned of the last sentence of Article 93(3) [now 108(3)] and would deprive that provision of its effectiveness'.[16]

In the case *SFEI and others*, the Court ruled that, in case of infringement of (now) Article 108(3) TFEU, national courts are not required under EU law to declare that they lack jurisdiction or to stay the proceedings if the Commission has not released its decision yet.[17] On the contrary, the fact that the Commission has started the preliminary examination procedure or the formal investigation procedure 'cannot release' national judges from the obligation of protecting individuals affected by a breach of (now) Article 108(3) TFEU.[18] Thus, the Court expressly emphasized that '[a]ny other interpretation would have the effect of encouraging the Member States to disregard the prohibition on implementation of planned aid'.[19]

Finally, in the *Transalpine* case the Court of Justice expressly stated that 'it is of little consequence whether an application [before a national court] is made before or after adoption of the decision declaring the aid compatible with the common market, since the application relates to the unlawful situation resulting from the lack of notification'.[20]

Two important conclusions can be drawn from the analysis above:

(1) The competence of national judges in matters of State aid is very significant. This is especially true when legitimate expectations are at issue. In fact, only national judges can preserve the legitimate expectations of beneficiaries of unlawful aid during the period that precedes the decision of the Commission,

14. *CJEU*, C-354/90, *Judgment of 21 Nov. 1991, Fédération nationale du commerce extérieur des produits alimentaires and others v. France (C-354/90, ECR 1991 p. I-5505)*, para.14.
15. CJEU, C-354/90, *supra* n. 14, para. 12.
16. CJEU, C-354/90, supra n. 14, para. 16.
17. CJEU, C-39/94, *supra* n. 7, para. 53.
18. CJEU, C-39/94, *supra* n. 7, para. 44.
19. CJEU, C-39/94, *supra* n. 7, para. 45.
20. CJEU, C-368/04, *Judgment of 5 Oct. 2006, Transalpine Ölleitung in Österreich (C-368/04, ECR 2006 p. I-9957), para. 55.*

and - even after that period - when the measure is considered by the Commission to be compatible with the Internal Market.

(2) The above-mentioned case law of the Court of Justice emphasises that Article 108(3) TFEU is essentially aimed at guaranteeing the assessment of the European Commission.[21] Consequently, the powers of national judges are conceived as functional at guaranteeing the effectiveness of this provision.[22]

§6.03 THE EU NOTION OF LEGITIMATE EXPECTATIONS IN THE CONTEXT OF STATE AID LAW

As already emphasized in the previous paragraph, the EU notion of legitimate expectations has been developed by the Court of Justice in the context of State aid law in connection with the provision, now contained in Article 108(3) TFEU, according to which new aid measures must be notified to the European Commission and they cannot be implemented before the assessment of the Commission has been completed. In case of unlawful aid, a national judge can avoid ordering recovery if the beneficiary legitimately expected the aid to be lawful or that the measure was not a State aid under Article 107(1) TFEU.

Generally speaking, the EU notion of legitimate expectations has been developed by the Court of Justice in order to protect individuals against the retroactive effects of measures (including legislation) taken by the EU Institutions. In this context, the Court of Justice has expressly ruled that no legitimate expectations can be entertained in case of violation of EU law. Thus, in the case *Sideradria v. Commission* the Court ruled: '[t]he applicant's final submission must ... be rejected since it is wrongly based on the principle of the protection of legitimate expectations. That principle may not be relied upon by an undertaking which has committed a manifest infringement of the rules in force'.[23]

This is the starting point for a correct understanding of the notion of legitimate expectations[24] as specifically developed by the Court of Justice in matter of State aid. In fact, the State aid notion of legitimate expectations assumes relevance precisely in case

21. Cf. B. Cheynel and A. Giraud, *New Paradigm for Recovery of Unlawful Aid in the EU – National Judges and the 'Exception of Compatibility'*, 31 World Competition 557, 564 (2008).
22. *See also*, Opinion of Advocate General Mazák delivered on 24 May 2007 in Case C-199/06, paras 22–37.
23. CJEU, C-67/84, *Judgment of 12 Dec. 1985, Sideradria v. Commission (67/84, ECR 1985 p. 3983)*, para. 21. *See also*, CJEU, C-96/89, *Judgment of 16 May 1991, Commission v. Netherlands (C-96/89, ECR 1991 p. I-2461), para. 30.*
24. M. Weisbrot, *Application of the Principle of Protection of Legitimate Expectations in Recovery of Unduly Paid Subsidies in the Context of Judicial Coherence in the European Union*, 8 REALaw 347, 368–373 (2015); E. Fink, *The Possibility of Protection of Legitimate Expectations in Recovery of Unlawful State Aid*, 20 Juridica Int'l 133 (2013); M. Rzotkiewicz, *The General Principles of EU Law and Their Role in the Review of State Aid Put into Effect by Member States*, 3 EStAL 464, 467–470 (2013); A. Giraud, *A Study of the Notion of Legitimate Expectations in State Aid Recovery Proceedings: 'Abandon All Hope, Ye Who Enter Here?'*, 45 CML Rev. 1399 (2008); K. Jaros and N. Ritter, *Pleading Legitimate Expectations in the Procedure for the Recovery of State Aid*, 4 EStAL 573 (2004).

of a breach of Article 108(3) TFEU.[25] As a consequence, the notion of legitimate expectations has been developed very strictly. As the Court of Justice constantly emphasizes, legitimate expectations in the field of State aid can be invoked only in exceptional circumstances. Thus, every time there is a breach of Article 108(3) TFEU - in principle - the relevance of legitimate expectations is excluded, unless the beneficiary is able to prove that - due to exceptional circumstances - it legitimately expected the measure to be lawful.[26] This, indeed, results in a very strict burden of proof for the beneficiary. In practical terms, the Court of Justice has only very rarely acknowledged the occurrence of legitimate expectations.

In the case *RSV v. Commission*,[27] the Court of Justice decided that a period of more than twenty-six months in order for the Commission to make a decision gave rise to the legitimate expectations of the beneficiary that 'the Commission's doubts no longer existed and that the aid would encounter no objections'.[28]

According to the Court of Justice, only a delay that is 'unreasonable' can give rise to legitimate expectations.[29]

Thus, in the case *Germany v. Commission*,[30] the Court of Justice denied the occurrence of legitimate expectations and emphasized that the circumstances in *RSV v. Commission* were 'exceptional'[31]:

- Already for some years the concerned sector was receiving aid approved by the Commission.
- The contested Commission's decision concerned new aid to cover additional costs connected to the same operation, for which the Commission had already authorized previous aid.

According to the Court of Justice, legitimate expectations arise when beneficiaries have received precise assurances by a EU Institution.[32] Thus, in *Belgium and Forum 187 v. Commission* the Court of Justice broadened the recognition of legitimate

25. Cf. Giraud, *supra* n. 24, at 1405–1406.
26. *See*, CJEU, C-5/89, *supra* n. 6, para. 16: '[i]t is true that a recipient of illegally granted aid is not precluded from relying on exceptional circumstances on the basis of which it had legitimately assumed the aid to be lawful and thus declining to refund that aid. If such a case is brought before a national court, it is for that court to assess the material circumstances, if necessary after obtaining a preliminary ruling on interpretation from the Court of Justice'. This paragraph has to be read in connection with para. 14 of the same judgement. *See*, *supra* n. 12. The mentioned paragraphs express the constant case law of the Court of Justice in matters of legitimate expectations.
27. CJEU, C-223/85, *Judgment of 24 Nov. 1987, RSV v. Commission* (223/85, ECR 1987 p. 4617).
28. CJEU, C-223/85, *supra* n. 27, para. 16.
29. *See*, CJEU, C-346/03, *Judgment of 23 Feb. 2006, Atzeni and others (C-346/03 and C-529/03, ECR 2006 p. I-1875)*, para. 67. *See also*, GC, Case T-109/01, *Judgment of 14 January 2004, Fleuren Compost v. Commission (T-109/01, ECR 2004 p. II-127)*, para. 146.
30. CJEU, C-334/99, *Judgment of 28 Jan. 2003, Germany v. Commission (C-334/99, ECR 2003 p. I-1139)*.
31. CJEU, C-334/99, *supra* n. 30, para. 44. *See also*, CGEU, C-298/00 P, *Judgment of 29 Apr. 2004, Italy v. Commission (C-298/00 P, ECR 2004 p. I-4087)*, para. 90; CJEU, C-372/97, *Judgment of 29 April 2004, Italy v. Commission (C-372/97, ECR 2004 p. I-3679)*, para. 117.
32. *See*, CJEU, joined cases C-182/03 and 217/03, *Judgment of 22 June 2006, Belgium and Forum 187 v. Commission (C-182/03 and C-217/03, ECR 2006 p. I-5479)*, para. 147.

expectations, already acknowledged in the contested decision of the Commission, exactly on the basis of previous assurances given by the Commission itself on the absence of aid element characterizing the Belgian tax regime for coordination centres.[33]

In any case, according to the Court, legitimate expectations can be acknowledged only if there are no overriding public interests, which must prevail over the interests of the beneficiaries.[34]

By defining the concept of legitimate expectations, including the concept of exceptional circumstances, in its substantive elements, the Court of Justice has very much limited the autonomy of national judges in applying the respective national notions under the principle of procedural autonomy. Most importantly, it is clear that a notion of legitimate expectations that is based on the 'exceptional' nature of the circumstances at issue results as very difficult to apply in concrete terms. Indeed, the need to define circumstances which are 'exceptional' excludes to a big extent the possibility to apply by analogy the case law of the Court of Justice. In fact, the Court constantly emphasizes the possibility for national judges, when requested to evaluate the occurrence of exceptional circumstances which give rise to legitimate expectations, to ask for a preliminary ruling.[35]

The position of Advocate General Cosmas on this attitude of the Court of Justice is very critical: 'national courts are in a difficult position. First, they do not feel secure when they rely on the specific provisions of national law ... Second, the Court of Justice ... is giving them strong encouragement to refer questions to it for a preliminary ruling on a systematic basis'.[36]

§6.04 THE CELF CASES AND THE DELICATE BALANCE BETWEEN THE UNLAWFULNESS OF THE AID AND ITS EXPECTED COMPATIBILITY

Further uncertainties affecting the application of the notion of legitimate expectations by national judges have derived from the position taken by the Court of Justice in the two judgements issued within the context of the CELF cases.[37]

CELF (Centre d'exportation du livre français) was a public limited company operating as an export agent with the aim of disseminating the French culture abroad. In order to help CELF to offset the extra costs connected to small orders of books, from 1980 until 2002 France granted CELF subsidies. SIDE (Société internationale de diffusion et d'édition), being a competitor of CELF, in 1992 asked the European Commission whether these subsidies had been notified by the French State. As the Commission was, in fact, not aware of the granting of these subsidies to CELF, more information was required to France. Consequently, the European Commission confirmed to SIDE the existence of aid that must had been notified. In 1993, the

33. CJEU, joined cases C-182/03 and 217/03, *supra* n. 32, paras 147–167.
34. *See*, CJEU, joined cases C-182/03 and 217/03, *supra* n. 32, para 148.
35. *See*, *supra* n. 26.
36. Opinion of Advocate General Cosmas, *supra* n. 1, para. 68.
37. CJEU, C-199/06 and C-1/09, *supra* n. 3.

Commission adopted a decision[38] in which it considered the aid to be compatible with the Internal Market on the basis of Article 92(3)(d) of the EC Treaty (now Article 107(3)(d) TFEU).

SIDE appealed this decision before the Court of First Instance (now General Court), which in 1995 annulled the decision of the European Commission.[39] Thus, in 1996 the Commission opened a formal investigation procedure and in 1998 adopted a decision[40] in which the subsidies were considered as unlawful State aid, but, again, compatible with the Internal Market under Article 92(3)(d) of the EC Treaty (now Article 107(3)(d) TFEU).

This decision was also appealed by SIDE before the Court of First Instance (now General Court), which in 2002, again, annulled[41] the decision of the Commission to the extent that the aid was considered compatible with the Internal Market. However, for the third time, in 2004 the Commission adopted a positive decision.[42]

When the CELF I judgment was issued by the Court of Justice, SIDE had already appealed this third decision of the Commission before the Court of First Instance (now General Court).[43]

After the first annulment of the Court of First Instance in 1995, SIDE requested the French Minister for Culture and Communication to stop granting the subsidies to CELF and recover the sums already paid. Upon the rejection of this request, proceedings started before national administrative judges. Within the context of these proceedings, the French Conseil d'État (Council of State) referred to the Court of Justice two questions, the first of which, relevant for the purposes of this chapter, reads as follows:

> 1. Is it permissible under Article 88 [EC] [now 108 TFEU] for a State which has granted to an undertaking aid which is unlawful, and which the courts of that State have found to be unlawful on the ground that it had not previously been notified to the ... Commission as required under Article 88(3) EC, not to recover that aid from the economic operator which received it on the ground that, after receiving a complaint from a third party, the Commission declared that aid to be compatible with the rules of the common market, thus effectively exercising its exclusive right to determine such compatibility?[44]

Clearly, this question does not directly concern legitimate expectations. However, the analysis of the position of the Court of Justice is very important for the purposes of this chapter because it has determined a shift in the case law of the Court that directly affects the applicable notion of legitimate expectations.

---

38. Commission Decision NN 127/92 of 18 May 1993, OJ 1993 C 174, p. 6.
39. GC, T-49/93, *Judgment of 18 Sep. 1995, SIDE v. Commission (T-49/93, ECR 1995 p. II-2501).*
40. Commission Decision 1999/133/EC of 10 June 1998, OJ 1999 L 44, p. 37.
41. GC, T-155/98, *Judgment of 28 Feb. 2002, SIDE v. Commission (T-155/98, ECR 2002 p. II-1179).*
42. Commission Decision 2005/262/EC of 20 Apr. 2004, OJ 2005 L 85, p. 27.
43. GC, Case T-348/04, *Judgment of 15 Apr. 2008, SIDE v. Commission (T-348/04, ECR 2008 p. II-625).*
44. The second preliminary question reads as follows: '2. If that obligation to repay the aid is confirmed, must the periods during which the aid in question was declared by the ... Commission to be compatible with the rules of the common market, before those decisions were annulled by the Court of First Instance of the European Communities, be taken into account for the purpose of calculating the sums to be repaid?'

On the basis of the case law analysed in Paragraph 2 above, one would have expected the Court of Justice to emphasize the need of guaranteeing full recovery of unlawful aid even after a final positive decision of the Commission.[45] However, the Court held that the essential objective of the last sentence of (now) Article 108(3) TFEU is to avoid that incompatible State aid is introduced in the Internal Market. Therefore, if the European Commission has already issued a final positive decision at the moment when a national judge is required to decide, there is no obligation for this judge to order the recovery of the capital amount. More precisely, the Court of Justice ruled that UE law 'does not impose an obligation of full recovery of the unlawful aid'.[46] In these circumstances, the national judge is only obliged to order the recovery of the interests for the period of unlawfulness. This is because, in order to have the same amount available while pending the decision of the Commission, the beneficiary would have borrowed it on the market. Therefore, according to the Court the only advantage given to the beneficiary by granting an unlawful aid which is compatible with the Internal Market consists of not paying interests on the received sum.[47]

It is important to note that the conclusion of the Court of Justice according to which, in case of a previous final positive decision of the Commission, EU law does not impose to national judges the recovery of the capital amount derives from the aim of the last sentence of (now) Article 108(3) TFEU.[48]As emphasized by the Court, '[t]he last sentence of Article 88(3) EC [now 108(3) TFEU] is based on the preservative purpose of ensuring that an incompatible aid will never be implemented. That purpose is achieved first, provisionally, by means of the prohibition which it lays down, and, later, definitively, by means of the Commission's final decision, which, if negative, precludes for the future the implementation of the notified aid plan'.[49] The Court of Justice has, in fact, modified the scope of the standstill clause, which is now essentially aimed at avoiding the introduction of incompatible aid within the Internal Market rather than guaranteeing, as such, the assessment of the Commission.[50]

After the CELF I judgment of the Court of Justice, the Conseil d'État ordered the recovery of the interests. However, as far as the recovery of the capital amount was concerned, the Conseil d'État considered it necessary to refer new questions to the Court of Justice. According to the French court, this was necessary in light of the fact that, after the CELF I judgment, even the third positive decision of the Commission was annulled by the Court of First Instance (now General Court).[51]

As far as legitimate expectations are concerned, the Conseil d'État asked whether the fact that three decisions of the European Commission, subsequently annulled by the Court of First Instance (now General Court), considered the aid at issue compatible

45. Cf. Cheynel and Giraud, *supra* n. 21, at 559.
46. CJEU, C-199/06, *supra* n. 3, para. 46.
47. CJEU, C-199/06, *supra* n. 3, paras 45–55.
48. Cf. P. Adriaanse, *Appropriate Measures to Remedy the Consequences of Unlawful State Aid*, 2 REALaw 73, 80 (2009).
49. CJEU, C-199/06, *supra* n. 3, para. 47.
50. T. Jaeger, *The CELF-Judgement: A Precarious Conception of the Standstill Obligation* (in *SIDE v. CELF* Case Law and Notes), 2 EStAL 259, 285–286 (2008).
51. GC, Case T-348/04, *supra* n. 43.

with the Internal Market represents an exceptional circumstance which allows national judges to avoid recovery.[52,53]

In the CELF II judgement,[54] the Court of Justice excluded that the situation at issue could give rise to legitimate expectations. According to the Court, the fact that the Commission adopted three positive decisions, which were subsequently annulled by the Court of First Instance (now General Court), as rare as may be, is the consequence of the functioning of the EU system.

The author of the present chapter agrees with this interpretative position of the Court of Justice. However, there is another aspect of the CELF II judgement that cannot be underestimated. In fact, on the basis of this judgment, the Court of Justice has extended the scope of legitimate expectations, which in the previous case law exclusively concerned the lawfulness of the aid, to the compatibility of the aid.

Actually, in the case at issue there are no doubts that the aid is unlawful. The fact that the subsidies granted to CELF were unlawful State aid was stated as from the beginning by the Commission and never put into question by the involved parties. Therefore, legitimate expectations stemming from the three positive decisions of the Commission could only concern the compatibility of the measure. This is indirectly confirmed by the Court of Justice, which in the case at issue stated: '[s]uch an event [the annulment of the third positive decision of the Commission] is not, in itself, liable to give rise to a legitimate expectation and to constitute an exceptional circumstance. The unusual succession of three annulments reflects, *a priori*, the difficulty of the case and, far from giving rise to a legitimate expectation, would rather appear likely to increase the recipient's doubts as to the *compatibility* of the disputed aid' '(emphasis added)'.[55]

When answering the question concerning legitimate expectations, the Court of Justice significantly relied on the CELF I decision. In that judgment the Court expressly recalled the case *Italy v. Commission* and stated: '[t]he Court has ... held that, so long as the Commission has not taken a decision approving aid, and so long as the period for bringing an action against such a decision has not expired, the recipient cannot be sure as to the *lawfulness* of the proposed aid which alone is capable of giving rise to a legitimate expectation on his part' '(emphasis added)'.[56]

In this passage the term 'lawfulness' is clearly not used in its strictly technical meaning (which implies notification of the measure and compliance with the standstill clause). In the case *Italy v. Commission*, the measure had been notified and considered as incompatible by the Commission. Therefore, considering that in this case there are no doubts on the aid nature of the measure, legitimate expectations could exclusively

52. CJEU, C-1/09, *supra* n. 3, para. 22.
53. The first question referred to the Court of Justice reads as follows: '(1) May the national court stay proceedings concerning the obligation to recover State aid until the Commission ... has ruled, by way of a final decision, on the compatibility of the aid with the rules of the common market, where a first decision of the Commission declaring that aid to be compatible has been annulled by the Community judicature?' *See*, CJEU, C-1/09, *supra* n. 3, para. 22.
54. CJEU, C-1/09, *supra* n. 3.
55. CJEU, C-1/09, *supra* n. 3, para. 51.
56. CJEU, C-199/06, *supra* n. 3, para. 67.

concern its compatibility. In fact, as reported by the Court of Justice, Italy based its plea concerning legitimate expectations on the argument that a certain definition of SMEs created 'an expectation among the enterprises concerned ... that their application for increased aid would be approved [by the Commission]'.[57] Considering that – as said above – the measure had been notified by Italy, the 'approval' in this context could only concern its compatibility.

In literature, Cheynel and Giraud also expressed doubts on the use of the term 'lawfulness' in the above-mentioned passage of the CELF I judgment. Very interestingly, these authors argued: '[i]t is possible that the Court intended to limit the scope of this statement [i.e., the reference to 'unlawfulness' in paragraph 67 of the CELF I judgment] to cases in which the recipient of the aid entertains legitimate expectations as to the validity of the compatibility decision(s) issued by the Commission as opposed to the national measures adopted by the Member State to grant the aid'.[58]

However, legitimate expectations 'as to the validity of the compatibility decision(s)' in substance amount to legitimate expectations as to the compatibility of the measures.

Thus, the analysis above shows that the judgments issued by the Court of Justice in the context of the CELF cases, instead of clarifying the powers of national judges when applying the notion of legitimate expectations, have given rise to important uncertainties. It is arguable that through these judgments – and mainly through the CELF II judgment – the Court has extended the scope of the notion of legitimate expectations also to the compatibility of the aid. In fact, this result is coherent with the limitation of the scope of the standstill clause to avoid the introduction of incompatible aid within the Internal Market. However, it remains completely uncertain how this reconstruction of the notion of legitimate expectations can be reconciled with the features of this notion (including the very strict burden of proof) as developed by the Court of Justice in its previous case law and exclusively based on the unlawfulness of the aid.

At the moment, national judges have no parameters on the basis of which the evaluation of the legitimate expectations on the compatibility of the measure should be conducted. In this situation, judges can only request preliminary rulings from the Court of Justice. However, according to the author, an approach based on the need of systematically requesting preliminary rulings, by deeply undermining the autonomy of national judges, necessarily damages the effectiveness of State aid law.

§6.05 CONCLUSIONS: WHAT ROLE FOR NATIONAL JUDGES?

The EU notion of legitimate expectations has the fundamental function of protecting individuals against the retroactive effects of measures taken by the EU Institutions. More specifically, in the field of State aid, the notion of legitimate expectations is aimed

57. CJEU, C-91/01, *Judgment of 29 Apr. 2004, Italy v. Commission (C-91/01, ECR 2004 p. I-4355), para. 62.*
58. Cheynel and Giraud, *supra* n. 21, at 570.

at protecting the beneficiary of an aid measure which had legitimately expected this measure to be lawful.

Thus, the State aid notion of legitimate expectations has been developed by the Court of Justice in connection with the scope and function of (now) Article 108(3) TFEU. Very significantly, in the *Commission v. Germany* case the Court stated that 'in view of the mandatory nature of the supervision of State aid by the Commission under Article 93 [now 108] of the Treaty, undertakings to which an aid has been granted may not, in principle, entertain a legitimate expectation that the aid is lawful unless it has been granted in compliance with the procedure laid down in that article. A diligent businessman should normally be able to determine whether that procedure has been followed'.[59]

The State aid notion of legitimate expectations has been developed very strictly. In fact, this notion assumes relevance only in case of violation of Article 108(3) TFEU. Therefore, according to the case law of the Court of Justice, in case of unlawful aid, in principle, the existence of legitimate expectations is excluded, unless - due to exceptional circumstances - the beneficiary had legitimately expected the aid to be lawful.

Only national judges can preserve the legitimate expectations of beneficiaries of unlawful aid during the period that precedes the decision of the Commission, and, even after that period, when the measure is considered by the Commission to be compatible with the Internal Market.

In light of this significant role of national judges, their autonomy - as functional to an effective enforcement of State aid law - should be fully guaranteed. However, notwithstanding the enforcement of State aid law at national level is governed by the principle of procedural autonomy, the Court of Justice - through its case law - has considerably restricted the role of national judges.

In fact, the Court of Justice, by defining the notion of legitimate expectations in its substantive elements, has considerably limited the possibility for national judges of applying national law. Most importantly, by founding the notion of legitimate expectations on the 'exceptional' nature of the relevant circumstances, the Court has made it concretely difficult for national judges to apply by analogy its case law. In this respect, national judges are substantially dependent on the preliminary rulings of the Court of Justice.

Further uncertainties that undermine the autonomy of national judges when applying the notion of legitimate expectations have derived from the decisions of the Court of Justice in the CELF cases. Very importantly, this chapter has shown that, by modifying the scope of the standstill clause, the Court of Justice has extended the notion of legitimate expectations also to the compatibility of the measure. In fact, this solution is coherent with the new position of the Court of Justice according to which the purpose of the last sentence of (now) Article 108(3) TFEU essentially consists in avoiding that incompatible State aid is introduced in the Internal Market.

59. CJEU, C-5/89, *supra* n. 6, para. 14.

However, it remains completely uncertain how to reconcile the application of this broader notion of legitimate expectations with the previous case law of the Court of Justice which has developed the notion of legitimate expectations exclusively on the basis of the concept of unlawfulness.

The approach of the Court of Justice defining the notion of legitimate expectations at EU level has indeed the purpose of guaranteeing a uniform application of State aid law within the Internal Market. However, in the opinion of this author, in order to assure an effective enforcement of State aid law at national level it is necessary to guarantee a certain degree of autonomy to national judges.

In light of this position, it becomes critical to find a point of balance between the need to guarantee a uniform application of State aid law and the need to assure that national judges have a degree of autonomy which guarantees an effective enforcement of State aid law at national level.

More precisely, this autonomy is actually granted only when national judges are concretely in the position of adopting decisions on the basis of rules that are clear and do not constantly require preliminary rulings of the Court of Justice.

Therefore, according to the author, the results of the analysis conducted in this chapter require to clarify – through EU law – both the proper application of the notion of legitimate expectations on the compatibility of the measures and the concept of exceptional circumstances. According to this author, it is essential that these clarifications are given with the aim of guaranteeing a substantial level of autonomy to national judges. In the view of this author, guaranteeing autonomy necessarily implies the development of a system in which the request for a preliminary ruling is confined to very specific and difficult issues and do not represent a constant need. Regardless of the formal attribution of powers, the matters within the competence of national judges should be regulated by clear rules guaranteeing the actual exercise of these powers.

CHAPTER 7

Ex-Officio Application of EU State Aid Rules by National Courts

Marc Fierstra

§7.01 INTRODUCTION

The increased interest in the enforcement of European Union (EU) State aid rules, triggered by the State Aid Modernisation project,[1] renewed the attention for the role of national courts as being pivotal to the effective application of the obligation of Article 108, paragraph 3, Treaty on the Functioning of the European Union (TFEU). This attention also includes the question whether national courts should apply Article 108, paragraph 3, TFEU on their own motion. The qualification of a state measure as State aid requires a complex economic and legal assessment[2] so one could argue that if this analysis was left to the initiative of parties, the hurdle for them to apply Article 108, paragraph 3, TFEU would be too high. Moreover, the national procedural framework might imply that none of the parties to a case submitted to a national court, has an interest in relying on Article 108, paragraph 3, TFEU because neither of them is able to gain profit of the non-application of the measure that might be qualified as a State aid rule. Tax litigation provides an example. The taxable person intends to pay less tax than the charge imposed while the government will not demand a higher amount than it imposed. The use of tax incentives to foster specific economic development - and recent actions by the European Commission[3] in this regard illustrates the pertinence of the topic of ex-officio application.

1. Communication from the Commission EU State Aid Modernisation (SAM), Com/2012/0209 final.
2. See the extensive Notice on the notion of the State aid as referred to in Art. 107(1) of the Treaty on the Functioning of the European Union, OJ 2016 C 262.
3. E.g., state aid implemented by Ireland to Apple, SA.3873; *see also* DG Competition Working Paper on State aid and Tax Rulings, June 2016.

§7.02 THE CONCEPT OF EX-OFFICIO APPLICATION

The question if European law requires national courts to apply (rules of) European law on their own motion often provokes anxious emotions. The ever increasing body of European law, many times relating to complicated issues, suggests that such an obligation, that supplements their obligations to apply national law, is a task with a Herculean dimension. Moreover this question raises fundamental issues relating to the role of courts in disputes submitted to them. It touches upon the division of roles in general between the parties to a dispute and the judiciary. If a court only decides on the pleas raised by parties, the judgement in identical cases may differ according to the expertise of the parties (or their lawyers).[4] The answer to the question has a direct bearing on the balance struck in legal systems between the participants involved in the administration of justice. An ex-officio obligation reflects the responsibility of the judiciary for the application of the law with surpassing the general division of roles in legal proceedings. Every legal system contains some ex-officio obligation for courts, albeit a limited one. However when discussing the extent of an ex-officio obligation, it should be borne in mind that the role of a court is to settle a dispute submitted by parties. Deciding a dispute is quite different from finding a right solution to a case study, especially if only part of that case study is submitted to the court.

In order to avoid misunderstanding it is necessary to differentiate between types of ex-officio obligations. All types of ex-officio obligations involve judicial activism: the court and not the parties, has to take an initiative. The first type of ex-officio application is an expression of the principle: curia jus novit. The court knows the law and should therefore determine which rules of (national) law are applicable to the submissions of the parties and should apply those rules. The parties should state the arguments that could support the conclusion that the court should decide in their favour, but if the parties do not express them in legal terms it is for the court to do so. The first type of ex-officio application relates to the obligation of the court to qualify in legal terms the pleas raised by parties. The legal qualification by the court should have a basis in the (factual supported) submissions by the parties.

The second type of ex-officio obligation is less common. This type relates to an obligation to supplement the pleas by the parties with the relevant facts. The obligation to supplement relevant facts is based on the idea that the decisions of the court should be based on the objective and true facts and not on the facts as they are (mis)understood and presented by parties. In this type of ex-officio obligation the court verifies facts even if they are not challenged by the other party to the litigation, and explores the existence of facts not relied upon by either party insofar as relevant to decide on the dispute that the parties submitted to the court to be decided.

The third type of ex-officio obligation requires the court to rule on relevant pleas on which the parties did not rely. The court ensures the objective enforcement of the

4. Compare the national cases that give rise to ECJ 15 June 2006, Dokter, C-28/05, ECLI:EU:C:2006:408 and ECJ 7 June 2007, Van der Weerd a.o., C-222/05, ECLI:EU:C:2007:318. From a substantive point of view the cases are identical but only in one case the applicant raised the claim that the decision was contrary to provisions of a directive.

law and is thereby not dependent on or restricted by the parties. The court is not bound by the ambit of the dispute as determined by the parties. It is common that this type of ex-officio obligation is limited to the application of specific rules of which the application is mandatory and fundamental. Sometimes, rules to which the third type of ex-officio obligation applies are in literature denoted as public policy rules.

Whatever type of ex-officio obligation is applicable, one should keep in mind that however important the full and effective application of certain rules is, and the application of EU law is no exception, a court is not able to do anything if parties refrain from starting legal proceedings, or if parties refrain from legal remedies if a judgement might be contrary to the law or is based on an factual misunderstanding. Whatever ex-officio obligation might rest on a court, it will always remain dependent on at least the initiative of the parties to bring the case to the court.

These three basic types of ex-officio application by courts have in common that they involve some degree of judicial activism. Apart from the differentiation of the types of ex-officio application it is essential to distinguish between the legal basis of each type of ex-officio obligation. The legal basis of these obligations can be found either in the character of the substantive rule to be applied or in the role of the judiciary in the legal proceedings vis à vis the parties.[5]

An ex-officio obligation that arises from the nature of a rule will be applicable regardless of whether the case will adjudicated by a EU court or by a court of one of the member states. An example of an obligation to apply rules ex-officio based on the nature of the rules can be found in the field of European consumer protection.[6] Ex-officio application of Type 3 is usually founded in the nature of the rule.

If the judicial task is regarded as the foundation of the obligation to carry out ex-officio activities, the existence of an ex-officio obligation will vary according to the applicable legal system. On the other hand, the nature of the substantive rule to be applied will usually not be relevant. If an ex-officio obligation of Type 1 or 2 exists, it will in most cases be inherent to the judicial function.

The ex-officio activities by the Court of Justice of the European Union (ECJ) that can be based on the scope of the judicial function are, in direct actions, limited in number. Infringement of essential procedural requirements is viewed as a matter that must be raised by the ECJ of its own motion. The ex-officio activities with regard to the legality of an act under this heading are limited to lack of competence and absence of reasons.[7] The French legal concept of 'la légalité externe' provides a useful parallel. For the sake of completeness it is mentioned that the ECJ examines ex-officio if an action brought to it, is admissible.

Judicial activism of the ECJ in the context of the procedure for a preliminary ruling is limited. The ECJ will not limit its decision to the provisions of EU law explicitly

5. Compare: ECJ 2 April 1998, Sytraval, C-367/95P, ECLI:EU:C:1998:154, para. 67.
6. ECJ 27 June 2000, Oceano, joined cases C-240/98 to C-244/98, ECLI:EU:C:2000:346; ECJ 26 October 2006, Mostaza Clara, C-168/05, ECLI:EU:C:2006:675; ECJ 9 November 2010, Penzugyi Lizing, C-137/08, ECLI:EU:C:2010:659.
7. ECJ 2 April 1998, Sytraval, C-367/95P, ECLI:EU:C:1998:154, para. 67; ECJ 30 Mar. 2000, Florimex, C-265/97P, ECLI:EU:C:2000:170, para. 114; ECJ (Grand Chamber) 16 Dec. 2013, C-272/12P, ECLI:EU:C:2016:812, para. 28.

mentioned by the referring court but will extract from all the information provided by the referring court, in particular from the grounds of the decision referring the questions, the points of EU law which require interpretation, having regard the subject matter of the dispute.[8] The activism practiced by the ECJ in the application of Article 267 TFEU can be compared to ex-officio application of type 1.

The question how much judicial activism is required will not be decided by every legal system in the same way. Moreover, even within one specific legal system the extent of an ex-officio obligation may differ according to the field of law. E.g., in the field of civil law parties will be free to agree on their relationship and accordingly free to determine which part of their conflict they want to have decided by a court.[9] This illustrates that the line between the two different foundations of an ex-officio obligation is sometimes blurred.

Moreover it is conceivable that the extent of an ex-officio obligation is more limited for an appellate or court of cassation than for a court of first instance. It might be that an appellate court or a court of cassation will not review ex-officio whether a court of first instance has (fully) complied with its ex-officio obligations. Usually the review by courts of cassation is limited to the correct interpretation of law; review of facts is excluded or very limited. Legal review by a court of cassation will therefore not include an ex-officio obligation of the second type.[10]

§7.03 RELATED ISSUES

Several topics are closely related to the topic of ex-officio application because they relate to limitations of the power of courts to apply rules of law anyhow. In the preceding paragraph it was already mentioned that the initiative of a party to submit a dispute to the court is indispensable.

The first related concept is that of public policy rules. Usually, fundamental mandatory rules are qualified as public policy rules. The application or non-application of such a rule may not be dependent on the pleas raised by either party to the dispute submitted to the court. However, the expression public policy rule is also used in other contexts. In the EcoSwiss judgment the ECJ had to decide whether an arbitral award in which EU competition rules had not been applied could be enforced in the member states of the EU. The ECJ ruled that such an arbitral award infringed public order and could therefore not be enforced.[11] This judgment applied the public order concept in the specific context of the enforcement of arbitral awards, in context in which the term public order has a well-defined meaning.[12]

8. ECJ 27 Oct. 2009, CEZ, C-115/08, ECLI:EU:C:2009:660, para. 81; ECJ 10 May 2017, Chavez-Vilchez, C-133/15, ECLI:EU:C:2017:354, para. 48: ECJ 30 Jan. 2018, Amersfoort, joined cases C-360/15 and C-31/16, ECLI:EU:C:2018:44, paras 55–59.
9. ECJ 14 Dec. 1995, Van Schijndel, joined cases C-430/93 and C-431/93, ECLI:EU:C:1995:441.
10. Compare the limitation in Art. 256, first paragraph, last sentence, TFEU to review by the ECJ of judgments of the General Court of the EU.
11. ECJ 1 June 1999, EcoSwiss, C-126/97, ECLI:EU:C:1999:269.
12. *See* New York Convention of 10 June 1958 on the Recognition and Enforcement of Arbitral Awards.

The ECJ repeated its qualification of EU competition rules as rules of public order also outside the context of arbitration. In the Manfredi judgment, the ECJ ruled that Article 101 TFEU was a matter of public policy and national courts should apply the competition rules 'automatically'.[13] This judgment induced speculation that the ECJ ruled that Article 101 TFEU and Article 102 TFEU should be applied ex-officio (type 3) because this legal effect is in many member states usually attached to the legal qualification of a rule as a rule of public order. However, the ECJ did not elaborate what it meant by this 'automatically'. Nor can it be deduced from the judgment what type of ex-officio application the ECJ had in mind. If it can be accepted that the qualification of a rule as a rule of legal order is dependent on the inherent nature of that rule, the qualification should have the same legal effect regardless whether the rule is applied by the ECJ or by national courts. If this hypothesis holds true, the practice with regard to adjudicating cases brought by private parties against decisions by the Commission applying the EU competition rules, indicates that the ECJ had certainly not the third type ex-officio application in mind and most probably not even the second type.[14] In procedures before the General Court of the EU parties are required to state their claims and pleas in the application. Only in exceptional cases, new pleas and evidence are accepted in a later stage and declared inadmissible without considering them ex-officio. It can therefore not be excluded that the legal effect of the qualification of competition rules as rule of public policy is limited to ex-officio application of type 1 and, outside the specific context of arbitration, is limited to the legal qualification of pleas raised by one of the parties.

The second related concept is the principle of res judicata. A judgement becomes final if no legal remedies are being used or if all legal remedies are exhausted. The ECJ stresses the importance of the stability of the law and legal relations and the sound administration of justice for every legal order. Therefore the principle of res judicata remains applicable even if that judgement appears to be contrary to EU law.[15] However, if certain conditions are being met, the state could be held liable according to the Köbler case law.[16] This case law provides for *compensation* instead of *application* of EU law.

In the third place the ECJ accepts procedural limitations of the application of EU law by national courts. A procedural limitation implying that pleas should be raised before the court that hears the case in first instance and excluding that such a plea could be raised for the first time in appellate proceedings is, although it might result in the non-application of EU law by a national court, accepted by the ECJ.[17] In the same line of reasoning, the ECJ held compatible with EU law a national rule according to which a redundant worker was not allowed to challenge the due observance by an

13. ECJ 13 July 2006, Manfredi, C-295/04, C-269/04, C-297/04 and C-298/04, ECLI:EU:C:2006:461.
14. Compare ECJ 14 Nov. 2017, British Airways, C-122/16P, ECLI:EU:C:2017:861.
15. ECJ 6 Oct. 2015, Tarsia, C-69/14, ECLI:EU:C:2015:662.
16. ECJ 30 Sep. 2003, Köbler, C-224/01, ECLI:EU:C:2003:513, para. 103; ECJ 8 Dec. 2011, Chalkor/Commission, C-386/10P, ECLI:EU:C:2011:815, para. 66.
17. ECJ 17 Mar. 2017, Benallal, C-161/15, ECLI:EU:C:2017:175.

employer to inform and to consult the staff representatives within a workers council according to Directive 75/129/EEC relating to collective redundancy.[18]

In the fourth place, it should be mentioned that the ECJ accepts on obligation to reopen administrative proceedings if an administrative decision that became final, appears to be contrary to EU law. This EU obligation for administrative review of decision is not a general one but is limited to well-defined situations. In the Kühne & Heitz judgment the ECJ found an obligation to review a final administrative decision if an application for review as made to it, in order to take account of judgment of the ECJ when the administrative body has the power to reopen that decision according to national law and the decision has become final as result of a judgment based on a misinterpretation of EU without a question being referred to the ECJ under Article 267, paragraph 3, TFEU. The application should be made immediately after the person concerned became aware of that judgment of the ECJ.[19]

§7.04 THE CONTEXT: STATE AID RULES

It should be recalled that the role of national courts with regard to State aid, is relatively limited. Only Article 108, paragraph 3, TFEU is directly applicable. The provision prohibits states to implement a state aid measure before notification of that measure to the European Commission and after notification, before the Commission has undertaken its preliminary investigation and after the Commission has started a formal investigation procedure.

The application of State aid rules in the field of tax law is one that encounters a peculiar problem. It is common practice that it is a competitor of the beneficiary who raises the claim, that a specific state measure constitutes State aid that is prohibited by the TFEU. Competitors are however not party in a tax procedure in which that tax law is applied. Moreover, it is standing case law that those who are liable to pay tax cannot rely on the argument that a fiscal measure enjoyed by other businesses constitutes State aid in order to avoid payment of that tax.[20] The taxpayer however has no interest in claiming that an applied tax facility constitutes prohibited State aid. Such a claim could only result in paying more tax. The tax inspector has no interest in claiming that rules enacted by his own government should be set aside. So both parties to the litigation have basically no interest in claiming the incompatibility of national tax provisions with Article 108, paragraph 3 TFEU. Only in specific circumstances this will

18. ECJ 16 July 2009, C-12/08, ECLI:EU:C:209:466, para. 49.
19. ECJ 13 Jan. 2004, Kühne and Heitz (poultry meat parts), C-453/00, ECLI:EU:C:2004:17.
20. ECJ 15 June 2006, Air Liquide Industries Belgium, C-393/04 and C-41/05, ECLI:EU:C:2006:403, para. 43; ECJ 6 Oct. 2015, Finanzamt Linz/IFN Holding, C-66/14, ECLI:EU:C:2015:661, para. 21.

be different[21] and will the government rely on non-compliance with the obligation of Article 108, paragraph 3, TFEU.[22]

A situation in which the parties only rarely have an interest in (correct) application is not unique to tax cases in relation to Article 108, paragraph 3, TFEU. In the case Heemskerk and Schaap, the College van Beroep voor het bedrijfsleven (a Dutch specialized court) asked the ECJ if an ex-office obligation (type 3) exits if the exporter of calves claimed more EU export refunds than granted by the competent agency while this court found no entitlement at all existed to export refunds. The ECJ, unlike the Advocate-General, rejected an ex-officio obligation because such obligation would be contrary to the rights of defence, legal certainty and legal expectations.[23] This judgment provides support for the view that a limited interest of parties to rely on (correct) application of a provision of EU law does not call for a special treatment by a national court, like ex-officio application.

§7.05 SHOULD EU LAW BE APPLIED BY NATIONAL COURTS MORE RIGOROUSLY THAN NATIONAL LAW?

It could be argued that EU law is special compared to national law and should be applied by national courts more rigorously. Some support for this submission can be found in case law. In the landmark judgment Costa/ENEL it was being held that EU law could not be overridden by domestic legal provisions without being deprived of its character as EU law and without the legal basis of the EU itself being called into question.[24] National courts must apply EU law in its entirety and set aside national legislative provisions which might prevent EU rules from having full force and effect.[25] This case law, however, reflects a substantive law approach while an ex-officio obligation belongs to the domain of procedural rules that are unlike substantive rules not subject of European legislation, and therefore, comes within the scope of the principle of national procedural autonomy.

21. E.g., ECJ 27 June 2017, Congregación de Escuelas Pías Provincia Betania, C-74/16, ECLI: EU:C:2017:496 were a local authority opposed to an exemption of local tax by virtue of national legislation, see my detailed analysis in Nederlands Tijdschrift voor Europees Recht (NtER), 2017, pp. 181–189.
22. Tacitly it is assumed that a state can rely on its shortcomings vis à vis private individuals, ECJ 8 Dec. 2011, Residex Capital IV, C-275/10, ECLI:EU:C:2011:814 however ground to support the claim that the state cannot rely on its wrongdoing can be found in ECJ 26 Feb., Marshall, 152/84, ECLI:EU:C:1986:84, para. 49; ECJ 12 July 1990, Foster, C-188/89, ECLI:EU:C:1990:313, para. 17; ECJ 25 July 1991, Theresa Emott, C-208/90, ECLI:EU:C:1991:333, para. 23; ECJ 14 Sep. 2000, Collino and Chiappero, C-343/98, ECLI:EU:C:2000:441, para. 22; ECJ 24 Jan. 2012, Dominguez, C-282/10, ECLI:EU:C:2010:33, para. 38; ECJ 6 Nov. 2018, Bauer and Willmeroth, C-569/16, C-570/16, ECLI:EU:C:2018:871, para. 70.
23. ECJ 15 Nov. 2008, Heemskerk and Schaap/Productschap Vee en Vlees, C-455/06, ECLI:EU: C:2008:650; conclusion by Advocate-General Y. Bot, ECLI:EU:C:2008:258.
24. ECJ 15 July 1964, Costa/ENEL, 6/64, ECLI:EU:C:1964:66.
25. ECJ 9 Mar. 1978, Simmenthal, 106/77, ECLI:EU:C:1978:49.

§7.06 PROCEDURAL AUTONOMY

Notwithstanding the direct effect of provisions of EU law, the decentralized system of enforcement of EU law implies that it is the national courts that are entrusted with ensuring the legal protection that citizens derive from the direct effect. According to well-established case law by the ECJ it is for the domestic legal system of each member state to designate the courts having jurisdiction and to determine the procedural conditions governing actions at law intended to ensure the rights citizens derive from EU law. This principle of procedural autonomy is limited by a procedural non-discrimination rule according to which EU law should not be applied with procedural rules that are different or less favourable than the procedural rules applicable to similar national claims. The principal of procedural autonomy is moreover limited by the effectiveness rule according to which the effective application of EU law may not be virtually impossible or excessively difficult.[26]

The principle of procedural autonomy does not preclude that in EU legislation in relation to specific substantive, rules procedural rules may be adopted. Article 2 of Regulation 1/2003,[27]contains for instance, rules relating to the burden of proof in relation to the application of EU competition rules. In the field of public procurement law, the remedies directives set minimum national standards to ensure that rapid and effective means of redress are available.[28]

It is clear from the case law that EU law does not preclude a court from assessing on its own motion whether national rules are in conformity with EU law.[29] Nevertheless, this competence might be limited by Article 47 of the EU Charter of Fundamental Rights. This provision does not preclude a national court from examining the facts of a case on its own motion on the condition that the court does not substitute itself for the competent authorities.[30] Also the principle of the prohibition of reformation in peius, which implies that an individual bringing court action must not be placed in a less favourable position than if he had not brought that action, might restrict national ex-officio competence. Although in the judgment Heemskerk and Schaap this principle was enshrined in national law - and therefore the question to be answered by the ECJ was in essence whether this principle was contrary to the effectiveness rule - the reference in the judgment to rights of the defence, legal certainty and protection of legitimate interests suggests that these general principles of EU law will have the same effect.[31]

26. ECJ 16 Dec. 1976, Rewe, 33/76, ECLI:EU:C:1976:188.
27. Council Regulation (EC) 1/2003 of 16 Dec. 2002 on the implementation of the rules on competition laid down in Arts 81 and 82 of he Treaty, OJ 2003 L1.
28. Directive 89/665/EEC on the coordination of the laws, regulations and administrative provisions relating to the application of review procedures to the award of public supply and public works contracts, OJ 1989, L 665; Directive 92/13/EEC coordinating the laws, regulations and administrative provisions relating to the application of Community rules on procurement procedures of entities operating in the water, energy, transport and telecommunications sectors, OJ 1993, L13; as amended by Directive 2007/66/EC, OJ 2007, L 335.
29. ECJ 11 July 1991, A. Verholen, joined cases C-87/90, C-88/90 and C-89/90, ECLI:EU:C:1991:314.
30. ECJ 14 June 2017, Online Games Handels GmbH, C-685/15, ECLI:EU:C:2017:452.
31. ECJ 15 Nov. 2008, Heemskerk and Schaap, C-455/06, ECLI:EU:C:2008:650.

The effectiveness rule does not require national courts to raise on their own motion an issue concerning the breach of provisions of EU law where such examination would oblige them to abandon the (passive) role assigned to them by going beyond the ambit of the dispute defined by the parties themselves and relying on facts and circumstances other than those on which the party with an interest in those provisions based its claim.[32]

The ECJ applied this case law also to administrative law courts. In the judgment Van der Weerd the ECJ ruled that EU law does not entail a general obligation to apply EU law if the parties do not raise an EU plea. This judgment provides moreover a fine example of the possible consequences of this approach. The issue at stake - whether a national measure to suppress an breakout of foot and mouth was compatible with Directive 85/511/EEC introducing Community measures for the control of foot-and-mouth disease - was explicitly raised only in another case dealt with by the referring court at almost the same time. In that case the substantive issue was subject of a request for a preliminary ruling.[33] The referring court therefore was fully aware of the EU issues but could only deal with them - and could only prevent that the national decisions were incompatible with the directive (dependent on the interpretation of the provisions of the Directive), possible conflicting judgments - if it was under an EU obligation to raise the issue ex-officio.

The ECJ confirmed its approach that EU law does not contain a general obligation to apply substantive EU rules ex-officio in a judgment relating to the application of the VAT Directive. The ECJ stressed moreover that only in exceptional cases the public interest requires an ex-officio intervention by national courts.[34] All the cases mentioned concern the existence of a type 3 ex-officio obligation. According to the same line of reasoning the ECJ confirmed that EU law does not require that member states provide for an ex-officio examination of measures restricting fundamental freedoms.[35]

The ECJ did also accept limitations on the full application of EU law caused by limitations on the role of national courts. In the Benallal judgment, the ECJ held compatible with EU law a national rule implying that a point of law that was raised for the first time before the appeal court is inadmissible.[36] The ECJ consequently accepted limitations to the full application of EU law and did not require the appeal court to apply the EU rule ex-officio. In the same line of reasoning is the Mono Car Styling judgment in which the ECJ held compatible with EU law a national rule according to which a redundant worker was not allowed to challenge the due observance by an employer to inform and consult the staff representatives within the workers council, an obligation laid down in directive 75/129/EEC relating to collective redundancy.[37]

32. ECJ 14 Dec. 1995, Van Schijndel, joined cases C-430/93 and C-431/93, ECLI:EU:C:1995:441.
33. ECJ 7 June 2007, Van der Weerd, joined cases C-222/05 to C-225/05, ECLI:EU:C:2007:318.
34. ECJ 26 Apr. 2017, Farkas, C-564/15, ECLI:EU:C:2017:302, paras 31–33.
35. ECJ 28 Feb. 2018, Sporting Odds, C-3/17, ECLI:EU:C:2017:130, para. 56.
36. ECJ 17 Mar. 2016, Benallal, C-161/15, ECLI:EU:C:2016:175.
37. ECJ 16 July 2009, Mono Car Styling, C-12/08, ECLI:EU:C:2009:466, para. 49.

The non-discrimination rule implies that an obligation to raise mandatory rules of national law on its own motion by virtue of national law entails an obligation to raise EU rules of the same nature on its own motion.[38]

§7.07 EX-OFFICIO APPLICATION OF EU STATE AID RULES

The ECJ did not rule explicitly on the existence of an obligation for national courts to apply Article 108, paragraph 3, TFEU on their own motion. This issue did arise in the main proceedings leading to the Finanzamt Linz judgment. The referring court requested Article 107 TFEU in relation to Article 108, paragraph 3, TFEU to be interpreted. The admissibility of the request for a preliminary ruling was contested because none of the parties to the dispute in the main proceeding had introduced a claim on the basis of Article 108, paragraph 3, TFEU and the sole task of the national court is to safeguard the rights of individuals until a final decision is taken by the Commission, pursuant to Article 108, paragraph 3, TFEU. Even the Commission contended that the company involved, to which the national provision was beneficial, could not rely on non-observance of Article 108, paragraph 3, TFEU. Because the order for reference did not contain information from which it could be inferred that, despite it being impossible for the company to draw any benefit from a possible breach of the State aid rules, the answer would nonetheless be necessary for the referring court in order to be able to resolve the dispute before it. Therefore, the ECJ decided that the question relating to the interpretation of the State aid rules was inadmissible.[39] Although this reasoning relates to the obligation of a referring court to provide reasons why it needs a preliminary ruling to decide the main proceeding, and did not address explicitly the obligation to apply Article 108, paragraph 3, TFEU ex-officio, it suggests that the ECJ is not willing to accept such an obligation. If the ECJ was of the opinion that national courts ought to apply Article 108, paragraph 3, TFEU on their own motion, no reasoning is required to argue why an answer to the question relating to the interpretation of the notion of State aid was needed be the referring court to decide the main proceeding. From a logical point of view the judgement does leave room to conclude that the ECJ only excluded the possibility of an ex-officio application of Article 108, paragraph 3, TFEU if it were in the interest of one of the parties to the main proceeding. It is doubtful however such a limited reading of the Finanzamt Linz judgement is justified. Because the effective enforcement of Article 108, paragraph 3, TFEU is mainly in the interest of competitors and, as already indicated in this contribution, they are only rarely party to a tax case in which they are able to raise this claim. Finanzamt Linz would have been an excellent opportunity to rule that a national court should apply Article 108, paragraph 3, TFU ex-officio if the ECJ wished to protect competitors that only had rare opportunities to be party to tax litigation. Therefore, the Finanzamt Linz judgement supports the view the EU state aid rules do not require from national courts any ex-officio activity.

38. ECJ 14 Dec. 1995, Van Schijndel, joined cases C-430/93 and C-431/93, ECLI:EU:C:1995:441, paras 13–14.
39. ECJ 6 Oct. 2015, Finanzamt Linz/IFN Holding, C-66/14, ECLI:EU:C:2015:661, paras 16–24.

Support for this interpretation of the Finanzamt Linz judgment can be found in earlier case law. In the Markmann judgment, the ECJ ruled in general terms that it is for the internal legal system of every member state to determine the legal procedure for the direct application of Article 108, paragraph 3, TFEU.[40] The Markmann judgment implies that neither the terms nor the nature of Article 108, paragraph 3, TFEU entail any ex-officio obligation for national courts. This ruling seems to be confirmed by the Sytraval judgement in which the ECJ held that the Commission is not obliged to examine certain objections with regard to national measures that were subject of an investigation procedure under Article 108, paragraph 2, TFEU, of its own motion if these objections were not raised by the complainant.[41] In its judgment with regard to exemptions of excise duty on mineral oils, the ECJ stressed upon exceptional nature of an ex-officio obligation and ruled that a plea based on infringement of Article 107, paragraph 1, TFEU because of the non-attributability of the measure to the member state cannot be raised by a court on its own motion.[42] This judgment confirms that the nature of the notion of state aid in Article 107, paragraph 1, TFEU is not such that it implies an ex-officio obligation. Therefore, neither the ECJ or General Court nor the national courts seems to derive from the EU state aid law provisions an ex-officio obligation.

§7.08 ALTERNATIVES TO EX-OFFICIO APPLICATION OF STATE AID RULES

Although the analysis of the Finanzamt Linz judgment as well as other case law mentioned support the finding that (national) courts are not obliged to apply Article 108, paragraph 3, TFEU on their own motion, the significance of this interpretation should not be overrated for three reasons. The first reason is that the case law of the ECJ tends to limit the authority of judgments by national courts in which Article 108, paragraph 3, TFEU is applied incorrectly. A leading case is the Lucchini judgment.[43] Lucchini applied to the competent national authorities for aid for modernization of steel plants. National authorities failed to take a decision and Lucchine brought proceedings to establish its right to the aid claimed. Both the court in first instance and the appellate court ordered the competent authorities to pay the amount claimed. The competent authorities did not lodge an appeal in cassation. Upon notification of the aid the Commission decided, prior to the judgment of the court of first instance, that the aid intended for Lucchini was incompatible with the common market. The decision by the national authorities to revoke the decision granting aid to Lucchini was successfully challenged in court because the judgment ordering the aid to be paid had acquired the

40. ECJ 11 Dec. 1973, Markmann, 121/71, ECLI:EU:C:1973:153, para. 9.
41. ECJ 2 Apr. 1998, Sytraval, C-367/95P, ECLI:EU:C:1998:154, para. 60; *see also* CFI 14 Jan. 2004, Fleuren Compost, T-109/01, ECLI:EU:T:2004:4, para. 49, General Court 16 Mar. 2016, Frucona, T-103/14, ECLI:EU:T:2016:152, para. 140.
42. ECJ (Grand Chamber) 10 Dec. 2013, Commission/Ireland, C-272/12P, ECLI:EU:C:2013:812, paras 28–29.
43. ECJ (Grand Chamber) 18 July 2007, Lucchini, C-119/05, ECLI:EU:C:2007:434.

authority of res judicata since the authorities abstained from challenging the judgment at the court of cassation. The ECJ ruled that the principle of res judicata cannot be invoked to prevent the recovery of aid granted in breach of EU law which has been found to be incompatible with the common market in a decision by the Commission which has become final. This similar strict line of reasoning, though not based on the division of competences which is characteristic for the state aid mechanism in the treaty, has also been applied to a rule according to which findings relating to a specific period have force of res judicata for a later period, if those findings were contrary to EU law, in this specific case contrary to the VAT Directive.[44] In the Klausner Holz judgment the ECJ ruled that a declaratory judgment stating that an agreement between Klausner Holz and public authorities for the sale of wood was valid, could not be used to prevent a court in another procedure between the same parties to rule on the question whether the agreement could be qualified as State aid for the application of Article 108, paragraph 3, TFEU. The ECJ however stressed that the dispute that gave rise to the declaratory judgement did not concern, either principally or incidentally, the State aid characteristics of the agreement at issue, so that this question was not examined by that court.[45]

The second reason that promotes the effective application of the EU State aid regime notwithstanding that national courts are not obliged to apply Article 108, paragraph 3, TFEU on their own motion, is case law by which a Court decision in itself can be qualified as state aid.[46]

The third reason that put into perspective the role of national court in the enforcement of Article 108, paragraph 3, TFEU is that the Commission is always competent to investigate existing aid and may prohibit this type of aid.

§7.09 CONCLUSION

Ex-officio application of EU law in itself is a complicated topic. The concept of ex-officio application and the legal base of such an obligation is not as clear as it might appear at first sight. In order to understand the case law of the ECJ it is nevertheless necessary to distinguish these different aspects related to the ex-officio application of rules of law. Although a strong argument can be made to advocate an obligation for national courts to apply Article 108, paragraph 3, TFEU on their own motion, the case law of the ECJ does not seem to be in favour of such application. The ECJ did rule without any ambiguity that ex-officio application can only be required in exceptional cases. The ECJ accepted an obligation to apply provisions of directives relating to consumer protection ex-officio in order to restore the equilibrium between seller and consumer. This aim was decided upon by the European legislator. State aid rules as such don't seem to be such an exceptional case. The analysis of the Finanzamt Linz judgment indicates that national courts are not required to apply Article 108, paragraph 3, TFEU on their own

44. ECJ 3 Sep. 2009, Fallimento Olimpiclub, C-2/08, ECLI:EU:C:2009:506.
45. ECJ 11 Nov. 2015, Klausner Holz Niedersachsen, C-505/14, ECLI:EU:C:2015:742.
46. ECJ 26 Oct. 2016, DEI, C-590/16P, ECLI:EU:C:2016:979.

motion. Several other judgements seem to confirm this reading. The ECJ however indicated in its case law through several ways to remedy the non-application of Article 108, paragraph 3, TFEU by national court that counterbalance the lack of a requirement to apply Article 108, paragraph 3, TFEU ex-officio.

CHAPTER 8

National Courts as 'Guardians' of Commission Recovery Decisions

Anne Van de Vijver

§8.01 INTRODUCTION

The European Commission has a central role in the enforcement of State aid rules. It keeps under review all systems of aid existing in the Member States. If the Commission finds that aid is not compatible with the internal market, it will decide that the State concerned must abolish or alter such aid.[1] In 1973 the Court of Justice has held that accordingly, the Commission is also entitled to require repayment of such aid.[2] This jurisdiction is now explicitly confirmed in Community law.[3]

The recovery of State aid, however, faces a lot of hurdles. The European Commission repeatedly highlighted the need for better targeted enforcement and monitoring.[4] In 2005, it adopted a road map for State aid reform, the State Aid Action Plan ('the SAAP'), to improve the effectiveness, transparency, credibility and predictability of the State aid regime under Community law. Recent years the role of national courts in the enforcement of State aid rules has become increasingly important. First, the SAAP stresses that private litigation before national courts could contribute to a better enforcement. Private litigation refers to beneficiaries' competitors (or others)

1. Art. 108(2) of the Treaty on the Functioning of the European Union (TFEU).
2. Case 70/72, Commission v. Germany, [1973] ECR 813, para. 13.
3. Art. 16 (1) Council Regulation (EU) 2015/1589 of 13 July 2015 laying down detailed rules for the application of Art. 108 of the Treaty on the Functioning of the European Union (codification) ('Procedural Regulation').
4. State Aid Action Plan: Less and better targeted State aid: a roadmap for State aid reform 2005–2009, COM(2005) 107 final; Notice from the Commission Towards an effective implementation of Commission decisions ordering Member States to recover unlawful and incompatible State aid (2007/C 272/05).

challenging the grant of unlawful aid before national courts.[5] The research of the European Commission shows that this private enforcement is still very (too) limited.[6] Second, national courts also play an important role in the enforcement of Commission recovery decisions. Since recovery of aid must in principle take place in accordance with national procedural law (*infra* §8.02[B]), such enforcement is subject to review by the national courts.[7] This contribution examines the role of the national courts as the 'guardians' of Commission recovery decisions.

The involvement of national courts usually arises from actions brought by beneficiaries for review of the legality of repayment orders issued by national authorities. Depending on national procedural law, other types of legal action may be possible, such as actions by national authorities against the beneficiary aimed at the full implementation of a Commission recovery decision.[8] The responsibility of the national courts is high since their decision may result in a failure to recover State aid, for instance when they impede recovery due to national procedural law (e.g., national limitation periods, *infra* §8.03[A][5]).[9] In that case the Commission can introduce infringement proceedings with the Court of Justice against the Member State, and the latter may face (high) penalties. Consequently, it is important to know the obligations and prohibitions that are part of the role of the national courts as 'guardians' of Commission recovery decisions. The scope of such role is not regulated in Community law but has been developed in the case law of the Court of Justice.[10]

§8.02 OBLIGATION TO ENFORCE THE COMMISSION RECOVERY DECISION

[A] Prohibition to Rule on the Validity of the Commission Recovery Decision

The validity of a Commission recovery decision is sometimes challenged before a national court. Beneficiaries may for instance challenge a repayment order issued by national authorities based on the argument that the underlying Commission decision is not valid.

5. See also Jose Louis Buendia Sierra and Miguel Angel Bolsa Ferruz, 'State Aid Assessment: What National Courts Can Do and What They Must Do' (2017). EStAL 3, 408–417; Phedon Nicolaides, 'Are National Courts Becoming an Extension of the Commission' (2014). EStAL 3, 409–413.
6. Available at http://ec.europa.eu/comm/competition/state_aid/studies_reports/studies_reports.cfm.
7. Denis Jouve, 'Recovering Unlawful and Incompatible Aids by National Courts: CELF and Scott/Kimberly Clark Cases' (2017). EStAL 3, 367–376.
8. Commission notice 2009/C 85/01 on the enforcement of state aid by national courts ('Commission Notice on National Courts'), para 21.
9. Case C-224/01, *Köbler*, [2003] ECR I-10239; Case C-173/03, *Traghetti del Mediterraneo*, [2003] ECR I-5177. See also David Ordonez-Solis, 'Waiting for National Judges in Infringement Proceedings on State Aid' (2017). EStAL 3, 377–394.
10. Denis Jouve, 'Recovering Unlawful and Incompatible Aids by National Courts: CELF and Scott/Kimberly Clark Cases' (2017). EStAL 3, 367–376.

However, the Court of Justice has repeatedly held that national court actions cannot challenge the validity of the underlying Commission decision where the claimant could have challenged this decision directly before the Community courts.[11] The right to a fair trial is in principle guaranteed by the European Union (EU) procedures.[12] If the validity of the Commission decision is not challenged by means of a direct appeal before Community courts within the prescribed period, it is to be considered as final. This also means that the national courts may not suspend the execution of the recovery decision on grounds linked to the validity of the Commission decision.[13] The lodging of appeals for annulment against the recovery decision before the Community courts is not a justification to suspend the execution of the recovery.[14] In *Commission v. France* the Court of Justice considered that 'the decision at issue is presumed to be lawful and [...] despite the existence of the action for annulment, it remains binding in all aspects on the French Republic'.[15]

Where it is not clear that the claimant can bring an annulment action before Community courts, for example where the measure was an aid scheme with a wide coverage for which the claimant may not be able to demonstrate an individual concern, the national courts remain competent to offer legal protection. In this case, however, national courts have no jurisdiction themselves to declare the Commission decision invalid.[16] They must request a preliminary ruling from the Court of Justice.[17] In this context national courts can suspend the execution of the recovery decision but only subject to the very strict legal requirements as determined by the Court of Justice in the *Zuckerfabrik*[18] and *Atlanta*[19] jurisprudence (*infra* §8.03[B]).

[B] Procedural Autonomy

Community law does not prescribe how recovery should take place or which organ of the Member State should be in charge of the practical implementation of a recovery decision. The recovery must in principle take place in accordance with national procedural law.[20] This also explains why the enforcement of the Commission decision is subject to review by the national courts. The applicable procedure is normally determined by nature of the measure underlying the granting of the aid.[21] National

11. Case C-188/92, TWD Textilwerke Deggendorf *v.* Germany, [1994] ECR I-833, para. 17, 25 1 26. See also Joined Cases C-346/03 and C-529/03, Atzeni and Others, [2006] ECR I-1875, para. 31; Case C-232/05, Commission *v.* France, [2006] ECR I-10071, para. 59.
12. Case C-232/05, Commission *v.* France, [2006] ECR I-10071.
13. Case C-232/05, Commission *v.* France, [2006] ECR I-10071, paras 59 and 60.
14. Case C-261/99, *Commission v. France,* [2001] ECR I-2537.
15. Case C-261/99, *Commission v. France,* [2001] ECR I-2537, para. 26.
16. Case C-119/05, *Lucchini,* [2007] ECR 1-6199; Case 314/85, *Foto-Frost,* [1987] ECR *04199.*
17. Case C-346/03, *Atenzi,* [2006] ECR I-1875; Case C-119/05, *Lucchini,* [2007] ECR 1-6199, para. 53; Case C-274/12P, *Telefonica,* [2013] ECLI:EU:C:2013:852.
18. Joined Cases C-143/88 and C-92/89, Zuckerfabrik Süderdithmarschen and Zuckerfabrik Soest *v.* Hauptzollamt Itzehoe and Hauptzollamt Paderborn, [1991] ECR I-415, para. 33.
19. Case C-465/93, Atlanta Fruchthandelsgesellschaft and Others *v.* Bundesamt für Ernährung und Forstwirtschaft, [1995] ECR I-3761, para. 51.
20. Case C-24/95, *AlcanII,* [1997] ECR 1997, p. I-1591.
21. Commission Notice 2007, para. 51.

procedural law also determines which national court is competent. Depending on the case the administrative, civil, commercial or even constitutional courts will have to take decisions in State aid cases.

[C] Obligation to Identify Beneficiaries and Determine Aid to Be Recovered

The purpose of the recovery is to re-establish the situation that existed in the market prior to the granting of the aid. The recovery of unlawful and incompatible aid is not a penalty,[22] but the logical consequence of the finding that it is unlawful. In order to re-establish the situation, the full amount of the aid, including interest, has to be recovered from the beneficiaries.[23] The Commission cannot and is legally not required to identify the beneficiaries of the State aid or to fix the exact amount to be recovered. It is sufficient for the Commission to include in its decision information enabling the Member State to determine the beneficiaries and the amount, without too much difficulty.[24] The absence of individual amounts to be recovered cannot justify non-recovery.[25]

The national authorities, subject to review by the national courts, have the obligation to identify the beneficiaries and the individual amounts to be recovered. This task can be very difficult. *Commission v. France* illustrates that the beneficiaries of an exemption may be unknown because they were not required to report to the tax authorities.[26] Also the calculation of the amount to be recovered can be very complex.[27] For instance, in *Maribel bis/ter* the State aid was granted in the form of a reduction of social security contributions. To calculate the State aid, it was necessary to determine, in more than 2000 enterprises and for each quarter, the number of manual workers employed at precise periods.[28] The Court of Justice has ruled that the guidelines in the Commission decision are binding for the national courts, but subsequent correspondence between Commission and authorities on the calculation of individual amounts to be recovered is not. Nevertheless, based on the principle of loyal cooperation, national courts cannot completely ignore such correspondence.[29] In *Mediaset* the Court of Justice has confirmed that it is not excluded that aid to be recovered amounts to zero.[30]

22. Case C-75/97, Belgium v. Commission, [1999] ECR I-03671, para. 65.
23. Case C-183/91, Commission v. Greece, [1993] ECR I-3131, para 16; Case C-419/06, *Olympic Airways*, [2008] ECR I-27; Case C-169/95, *Spain v. Commission*, [1997] ECR I-135.
24. Case C-480/98, Spain v. Commission, [2000] ECR I 8717, para. 25; Joint Cases C-67/85, C-68/85 and C-70/85, Kwekerij van der Kooy BV and others v. Commission, [1988] ECR 219.
25. Case C-243/10, *Commission v. Italy* [2012] ECLI:EU:C:2012:182.
26. Case C-214/07 *Commission v. France* [2008] ECR I-8357, para. 13.
27. A. Maitrot de la Motte, 'The Recovery of the Illegal Fiscal State Aids: Tax Less to Tax More' (2017). EC Tax Review 2, 75–88.
28. Case C-75/97, *Belgium v. Commission*, [1999] ECR I-3671, para. 85.
29. Case C-69/13, *Mediaset*, [2014] ECLI:EU:C:2014:71.
30. Case C-69/13, *Mediaset*, [2014] ECLI:EU:C:2014:71, para. 37.

§8.03 OBLIGATION TO ENSURE IMMEDIATE AND EFFECTIVE RECOVERY

[A] Obligation to Leave National Procedural Law That Prevents Immediate and Effective Recovery, Unapplied

[1] General

As 'guardians' of the Commission recovery decision, national courts are obliged to ensure immediate and effective recovery of the State aid. The Court of Justice has repeatedly decided that national courts must leave national procedural law that prevents immediate and effective recovery, unapplied.[31] For example, to the extent that immediate and effective recovery is impeded, the national courts must in principle ignore the absence or the irregularity of recovery title under national law (B), the principle res judicata (C), provisions of national insolvency/bankruptcy laws (D), the national limitation periods and suspension rules (E).

[2] Absence or Irregularity of Recovery Title

The Court of Justice has decided that Community law does not require recovery of aid to be effected on the basis of the Commission recovery decision alone.[32] The Commission decision as such is not an enforceable instrument (*titre exécutoire*) vis à vis the beneficiary of the aid. The right to a fair hearing, including the rights of defence, requires that an individual enforceable instrument is issued according to national procedural law, subject to review of national courts (*supra* §8.02[B]).[33]

In the past beneficiaries have argued that such individual enforceable instrument in the form of an administrative repayment order cannot be based on the Commission decision, but also requires a *domestic legal basis*. For instance, in *Commission v. Italy* the Italian Republic argued that under the Italian Constitution, only a legislative measure is appropriate for regulating administrative activity of recovery and the amounts to be repaid in this context. However, the Court of Justice did not accept this argument.[34] Also in *Commission v. Germany* the Court of Justice repeated that if the ordinary rules are not feasible for the effective recovery of the State aid, it may be necessary to have recourse to 'other measures, since such measures cannot be excluded on the grounds relating to national law'.[35] The Court of Justice does not further explain what is meant by 'other measures'. In this procedure recovery was not successful yet because of long procedures before the civil courts. The Commission

31. Case C-232/05, Commission *v.* France, [2006] ECR I-10071, paras 49 to 53; Commission Notice on National Courts, para. 64.
32. Case C-527/12, *Commission v. Germany* [2014], EU:C:2014:2193, para. 39.
33. Case C-527/12, *Commission v. Germany*, [2014] EU:C:2014:2193, paras 39 & 45.
34. Case C-304/09, *Commission v. Italy*, [2010] ECR I-0000.
35. Case C-527/12, *Commission v. Germany*, [2014], EU:C:2014:2193, para. 55.

suggested that, since apparently this procedure was not feasible, the 'national procedural law should have given way to EU law and the defendant was itself under a duty to provide for a means of enforcement by the adoption of an administrative measure under EU law ordering the recovery of the aid in question'.[36] Probably such administrative measure is also what the Court of Justice had in mind.

In *Scott SA & Kimberly Clark SAS* the beneficiary opposed against the repayment order issued by the national authorities since it showed an irregularity. More specifically, it did not mention the names of the signatories, which is an obligatory formality under French law. The Court of Justice decided that the annulment of the repayment order is only possible if such annulment is 'devoid of real consequences',[37] i.e., if regularization of the order is possible and if it does not result in the beneficiaries having use of the sums. The irregularity cannot impede effective and immediate recovery. Jouve claims that this case shows that in fact the national courts have very little or even no procedural autonomy.[38]

[3] Res Judicata

Another argument invoked before national courts to oppose against a repayment order is based on the principle of res judicata. In *Lucchini* for example the Commission stated in 1990 that the aid granted to an Italian company was incompatible with the common market. After this decision the Italian civil court decided that the aid, which had actually not been paid yet, must nevertheless be paid by the Italian authorities to the company. The decision of the Italian court was based on the fact that under Italian law the aid had been granted and that, accordingly, the Italian authorities were liable to pay the debt. After some appeal procedures eventually the aid was paid to Lucchini in 1996. The Commission then ordered recovery of the aid, since it had been declared incompatible. Such recovery was challenged by Lucchini. The Italian administrative court agreed with the arguments of the company and decided that the repayment was not possible based on the principle of res judicata. The Italian civil court had already decided that Lucchini was entitled to the aid. The Court of Justice decided, however, that the principle of res judicata was not applicable here since the decision of the Italian civil court did not concern the State aid question. National courts have no jurisdiction to give a decision on whether State aid is compatible with the common market, so the decision of the Italian civil court could not have dealt with this question.[39]

In *Commission v. Slovak Republik*[40] the Court of Justice took another approach. The case concerns a bankruptcy procedure in which the Slovak tax authorities had agreed to write off the major part of a tax liability of a Slovak company. This agreement had been approved by the competent Slovak court in 2004. Only after that decision the

36. Case C-527/12, *Commission v. Germany*, [2014], EU:C:2014:2193, para. 27.
37. Case C-210/09, *Scott SA & Kimberly Clark SAS*, [2010] ECR I-04613, 26–32, para. 58.
38. Denis Jouve, 'Recovering Unlawful and Incompatible Aids by National Courts: CELF and Scott/Kimberly Clark Cases' (2017). EStAL 3, 367–376.
39. Case C-119/05, *Lucchini*, [2007] ECR 1-6199.
40. Case C-507/08, *Commission v. Slovak Republic*, [2010] ECR I-13489.

European Commission investigated the matter and ordered recovery of State aid in 2006. Here also the Slovak courts dismissed the action of the Slovak tax authorities to order repayment of the unlawful aid on the ground that the agreement approved by the Slovak court had acquired the force of res judicata. The Court of Justice explained that this case differs from the *Lucchini* case since the court judgement possessed of the force of res judicata precedes the decision of Commission.[41] Furthermore, the Court of Justice acknowledged the importance of the principle res judicata both at EU level and at the level of the Member State: 'In order to ensure stability of the law and legal relations, as well as the sound administration of justice, it is important that judicial decisions which have become definitive after all rights of appeal have been exhausted or after expiry of the time-limits provided to exercise those rights can no longer be called into question'.[42] However, since Slovak procedural law provided the possibility for an 'extraordinary appeal' against the 2004 decision of the Slovak court, the Court of Justice decided that in this specific case the principle res judicata did not set limits to the recovery obligation.

The question is what would have been the decision of the Court of Justice in the absence of such alternative. Birnstiel claims that the outcome would probably have been the same. He submits that in such scenario a Member State would most probably face blame for not having provided a procedural framework which allows for recovery.[43] However, the fact that the Court of Justice explicitly confirmed that 'European Union law does not in all circumstances require a national court to disapply domestic rules of procedure conferring the force of res judicata on a judgement, even if to do so would make it possible to remedy an infringement of European Union was by the judgment in question'[44] seems an indication that it may have decided otherwise.

[4] Provisions of National Insolvency/Bankruptcy Laws

Also the argument that a beneficiary is insolvent or subject to bankruptcy proceedings has not been accepted by the Court of Justice to justify non-compliance with a recovery decision. The financial situation of the beneficiary has no effect on the obligation to recover unlawful and incompatible aid.[45] If the assets of the beneficiary are insufficient to satisfy all creditors' claims, the Commission decision may be considered to be properly executed in case of partial recovery when the company is liquidated and its assets are sold under market conditions.[46] However, as long as the aid has not been fully recovered, the Member State should oppose to any transfer of assets that is not carried out on market terms and/or that is organized so as to circumvent the recovery decision.[47]

41. Case C-507/08, *Commission v. Slovak Republic*, [2010] ECR I-13489, para. 57.
42. Case C-507/08, *Commission v. Slovak Republic*, [2010] ECR I-13489, para. 59.
43. Alexander Birnstiel, 'Recovery of Unlawful State Aid: The Role of Member State Courts in State Aid Recovery Scenarios' (2012). EStAL 3, 645–650.
44. Case C-507/08, *Commission v. Slovak Republic*, [2010] ECR I-13489, para. 60.
45. Case C-42-93, Spain v. Commission, [1994] ECR I-4175.
46. Case C-52/84, Commission v. Belgium, [1986] ECR p. 89.
47. Case C-277/00, Germany v. Commission ('SMI'), [2004] ECR I-3925.

The Court of Justice has repeatedly stressed that when implementing recovery decisions against insolvent beneficiaries, Member State authorities should ensure that due account is taken throughout the insolvency proceedings of the Community interest.[48] Also Member States should immediately register recovery claims in the bankruptcy proceedings.[49] National courts should not allow continuation of activities in the absence of full recovery.[50]

[5] National Limitation Periods and National Suspension Rules

Community law provides a limitation period of ten years for the recovery of State aid.[51] The limitation period begins on the day on which the unlawful aid is awarded to the beneficiary[52] and may be interrupted by any action taken by the Commission or the national authorities at the request of the Commission.[53] The Court of Justice had decided that national judges must leave shorter national limitation periods unapplied.[54]

National procedural law may also provide automatic suspension of national acts ordering the recovery in case of appeal before national courts. National courts must also leave such legislation unapplied.[55] More specifically, courts must ignore such rules at each appeal and take any provision to guarantee the execution of the Commission decision.[56]

[B] Prohibition to Suspend Execution of the Commission Decision

The obligation to ensure immediate and effective recovery of the State aid also means that national court actions may, in principle, not suspend the execution of the Commission recovery decision. The Court of Justice allows exceptions to this rule but only subject to the very strict legal requirements as defined in the *Zuckerfabrik*[57] and *Atlanta*[58] jurisprudence. A national court may only suspend recovery orders under the following conditions: (i) the court has serious doubts as regards the validity of the Community act. If the validity of the contested act is not already in issue before the Court of Justice, it must itself refer the question to the Court; (ii) there must be urgency

48. Commission Notice 2007, para. 62.
49. Case C-277/00, Germany v. Commission ('SMI'), [2004] ECR I-3925; case C-499/99, Commission v. Spain [2002], ECR I-603, paras 28–44.
50. Commission Notice 2007, para. 66.
51. Art. 17(1) Procedural Regulation.
52. C-81/10P *France Télécom v. Commission*, [2011] ECLI_811? 81.
53. Art. 17(2) Procedural Regulation.
54. Case C-24/95, *AlcanII*, [1997] ECR 1997, p. I-1591.
55. Case C-232/05, Commission *v.* France, [2006] ECR I-10071.
56. Denis Jouve, 'Recovering Unlawful and Incompatible Aids by National Courts: CELF and Scott/Kimberly Clark Cases' (2017). EStAL 3, 367–376.
57. Joined Cases C-143/88 and C-92/89, Zuckerfabrik Süderdithmarschen and Zuckerfabrik Soest *v.* Hauptzollamt Itzehoe and Hauptzollamt Paderborn, [1991] ECR I-415, para. 33.
58. Case C-465/93, Atlanta Fruchthandelsgesellschaft and Others *v.* Bundesamt für Ernährung und Forstwirtschaft, [1995] ECR I-3761, para. 51.

in the sense that the interim relief is necessary to avoid serious and irreparable damage to the party seeking relief and (iii) the court has to take due account of the Community interest. In its assessment of all those conditions, the national court must respect any ruling by the Community courts on the lawfulness of the Commission decision or on an application for interim relief at Community level.[59]

Applications before the Community courts to suspend the recovery are rarely successful. In this context it is interesting to note that in one case the President of the General Court accepted the urgency of the case based on the consideration that the Greek authorities should better focus on combating tax avoidance than on the recovery of small sums of State aid from more than 800.000 Greek farmers:it is easy to foresee that a significant proportion of the hundreds of thousands of beneficiaries would refuse to pay the sums demanded, necessitating massive intervention on the part of the tax authorities' staff, who have not, however, increased in number. It is evident that such forcible large-scale collection of tax would prevent the tax authorities to an appreciable extent from devoting themselves to one of their priorities, namely, combating tax avoidance and colleting sums eluding tax that are nearly 50 times greater than the contested payments.[60]

[C] Absolute Impossibility

While the previous sections show that the procedural autonomy of the national courts is largely reduced, the recovery obligation for the national courts is not absolute. However, only the absolute impossibility to implement a recovery decision can justify non-compliance. This exception is extremely narrow. The Court of Justice has repeatedly confirmed that 'legal, political or practical difficulties [...] without taking any real steps [...] and without proposing any alternative arrangements' cannot be taken into account.[61] The following arguments for instance were rejected by the Court of Justice: the risk of double repayment resulting from concurrence of State aid rules and insolvency procedures,[62] the fact that refund may cause a risk of social unrest,[63] the fact that the beneficiary is insolvent or subject to bankruptcy proceedings.[64] *Commission v. France* is a rare example of a case in which the Court of Justice accepted that recovery was not possible. In this case France did not have the information required to identify the beneficiaries since there was no reporting obligation.[65]

The length of national litigations cannot be accepted either as an absolute impossibility for effective and immediate recovery. Still, to overcome this problem the Commission may accept a provisional implementation of the decision when it is

59. See also C-302/09, *Commission v. Italy*, [2011] ECLI:EU:C:2011:634.
60. Order in case T-52/12R, *Greece v. Commission*, [2012] ECLI:EU:T:2012:447, para. 47. See also Leigh Hancher, 'State Aid Recovery – A New Public Order?' (2013). EStAL 1, 1–4.
61. Case C-63/14, *Commission v. France*, [2015] EU:C:2015:458, para. 49.
62. Case C-331/09, *Commission v. Poland*, [2011] I-02933.
63. Case C-63/14, *Commission v. France*, [2015] EU:C:2015:458.
64. Case C-529/09, *Commission v. Spain*, [2013] ECLI:EU:C:2013:31; Case C-42/93, *Spain v. Commission*, [1994] ECR I-4175.
65. Case C-214/07, *Commission v. France*, [2008] ECR I-8357, para. 13.

subject to litigation before a national court (e.g., the payment of the full amount of unlawful and incompatible aid into a blocked account. The Member State must ensure that the advantage linked to the unlawful and incompatible aid leaves the company. The Member State should submit, for approval by the Commission, a justification for the adoption of such provisional measures and a full description of the provisional measure envisaged. Contrary to the constitution of a blocked account, the use of bank guarantees may not be considered as an adequate provisional measure since the total amount of the aid is still at the recipient's disposal.[66]

§8.04 OBLIGATION TO GUARANTEE BENEFICIARIES' FUNDAMENTAL RIGHTS, BUT ALSO TO LEAVE NATIONAL FUNDAMENTAL PRINCIPLES UNAPPLIED

The Court of Justice has acknowledged that it is also the role of national courts to guarantee the beneficiaries' fundamental rights such as the principle of protection of legitimate expectations.[67]

At several occasions beneficiaries of State aid have invoked that the Commission decision was contrary to their legitimate expectations. As mentioned above, however, national courts have no jurisdiction themselves to declare the Commission decision invalid.[68] They must request a preliminary ruling from the Court of Justice.[69] In this context the Court of Justice has given a very restrictive interpretation to the protection of legitimate expectations.[70] First, the beneficiary of State aid can only plead legitimate expectations against a Commission recovery decision if that aid had been duly notified to the Commission. According to the Court of Justice a 'diligent businessman' would have been able to verify whether the aid was notified or not.[71] Jouve submits that this restrictive interpretation seems severe for beneficiaries of a modest size such as SMEs, which may not have the structures to be familiar with Community law. He submits that leaving somewhat more autonomy to national courts could allow them to consider the situation on a case-by-case basis in order to rule on acts of real negligence.[72] Second, the Commission itself must have given specific assurances that the measure in question does not constitute State aid, or that it is not covered by the standstill obligation.[73] In

66. Commission Notice 2007, para. 70.
67. On the principle of the protection of the legitimate expectations: Case C-24/95, Alcan, [1997] ECR I-1591, para. 25, Case C-5/89, BUG-Alutechnik, [1990] ECR I-3437, paras 13 & 14. For an example where the ECJ recognised the existence of legitimate expectations on the side of the beneficiary: Case C-223/85, RSV, [1987] ECR 4617.
68. Case C-119/05, *Lucchini*, [2007] ECR 1-6199; Case 314/85, *Foto-Frost*, [1987] ECR *04199*.
69. See Case C-346/03, *Atenzi*, [2006] ECR I-1875; Case C-119/05, *Lucchini*, [2007] ECR 1-6199, para. 53; Case C-274/12P, *Telefonica*, [2013] ECLI:EU:C:2013:852.
70. David Ordonez-Solis, 'Waiting for National Judges in Infringement Proceedings on State Aid' (2017). EStAL 3, 377–394.
71. C-81/10P *France Télécom v. Commission*, [2011] ECLI_811? 81; Case C-5/89, BUG-Alutechnik, [1990] ECR I-3437; Commission Notice on National Courts, para. 32.
72. Denis Jouve, 'Recovering Unlawful and Incompatible Aids by National Courts: CELF and Scott/Kimberly Clark Cases' (2017). EStAL 3, 367–376.
73. Case C-182/03 & C-217/03, *Belgium and Forum 187 v. Commisson*, [2006] I-05479; Case C-223/85, RSV, [1987] ECR 4617; Case T-129/96, *Preussag Stahl*, ECR 1998 II-00609.

RSV for instance by waiting twenty-six months before making the recovery decision, the Court of Justice decided that the Commission disregarded the requirements of legal certainty.[74] Assurance by an EU official who is acting outside the scope of his mandate cannot be taken into account.[75] Third, misconduct of the granting authority cannot give rise to legitimate expectations either.[76]

National courts were also asked by beneficiaries to annul the national repayment order based on the argument that it was contrary to their legitimate expectations. The question then is to what extent national courts can rely on the *national* principle of protection of legitimate expectations. According to the Court of Justice full respect of the principle of effectiveness requires that also the national principle of protection of legitimate expectations is left unapplied when the State aid has not been duly notified to the Commission.[77] There seems to be one exception to this principle. According to the Court of Justice a beneficiary can invoke 'exceptional circumstances' that justify its legitimate expectations even when the aid has not been notified. The national courts must assess these exceptional circumstances.[78] It is not clear what circumstances could be accepted. Literature suggests for instance situations in which State aid is granted in an atypical form and in which the beneficiary could, consequently, not have known that the aid should have been notified.[79]

§8.05 OBLIGATION TO DIALOGUE AND TO COOPERATE

The Procedural regulation provides dialogue and cooperation between the national courts and the European Commission.[80] The national courts may ask the Commission to transmit to them information in its possession or its opinion on questions concerning the application of State aid rules. Also, the Commission, acting on its own initiative, may submit written observations to the courts of the Member States that are responsible for applying the State aid rules. It may, with the permission of the court in question, also make oral observations. Conversely, for the exclusive purpose of preparing its observations, the Commission may request the relevant court of the Member State to transmit documents at the disposal of the court, necessary for the Commission's assessment of the matter.[81]

74. Case C-223/85, RSV, [1987] ECR 4617, para. 12.
75. Case T-129/96, *Preussag Stahl*, ECR 1998 II-00609.
76. Case C-39/06, *Commission v. Germany*, [2008] ECLI:EU:C:2008:349.
77. Case C-24/95, *AlcanII*, [1997] ECR 1997, p. I-1591.
78. Case C-5/89, BUG-Alutechnik, [1990] ECR I-3437.
79. Aline De Vos, 'De Rol van het Europese en het Belgische vertrouwensbeginsel bij terugvordering van Europese subsidies en staatssteun' (2012–2013). Rechtskundig Weekblad 4, 122–135.
80. See also Adam Scott, 'Cooperation and Good Faith: State Aid Rules and National Courts – Procedural and Interpretive Consequences' (2017). EStAL 3, 354–366.
81. Art. 29 Procedural Regulation.

§8.06 CONCLUSION

This contribution shows that the role of the national courts as 'guardians' of the Commission recovery decision is arduous. The national courts have to stay within very strict boundaries set by Community law, and very often must leave national procedural law and national fundamental principles unapplied. The room for manoeuvre to find a balance between Community law and national law is narrow, and the risk is high since to the extent that effective and immediate recovery is impeded, the national courts' judgements may eventually trigger penalties for the Member States. Also, the examples illustrate that the implementation of the recovery of unlawful State aid is very complex. Since the number of cases is rather limited, national courts have little opportunity to specialize in this matter.

The national courts can find help and support through the dialogue and cooperation as provided for in the Procedural regulation. Also the European Commission started to organize several training programs on State aid.[82] Finally, we suggest that also national legislators should take up their responsibility and assist the national courts to partly overcome these challenges by introducing feasible recovery legislation. Such recovery legislation can for instance designate the competent national court, provide detailed rules to identify the beneficiaries and to determine the amount to be recovered, explicitly provide a domestic legal basis for administrative repayment orders, and align national limitations periods with the Community limitation period of ten years.

82. For example, this book results from the project 'Fiscal State Aid and the Role of National Judges within the EU Commission's Modernization Programme'. This project co-financed by the European Commission and organized by Tilburg University in cooperation with University of Bologna, University of Antwerp, and Vienna University of Economics and Business had the aim of increasing awareness on the importance of the role of national judges to guarantee an effective enforcement of EU State aid law and the possibilities of guaranteeing a more effective enforcement of state aid law at national level. *See also* Erika Szyszcak, 'National Judges and Training in EU State Aid Law' (2017). EStAL 3, 470–475.

CHAPTER 9

Recovery Procedures and National Issues: The Belgian 'Excess Profit Exemption' Scheme

Bruno Peeters

§9.01 INTRODUCTION

The European Commission decided on 11 January 2016 that the selective tax benefits granted by Belgium in the context of its excess profit exemption scheme (the so-called excess profit rulings) are not in line with the European rules on state aid.[1] This excess profit exemption scheme was introduced in 2004 but was never notified to the Commission as possible State aid. As a result of the publicity that the Belgian government itself gave to the existence of this specific tax regime, the European Commission launched an in-depth investigation in February 2015. The Commission came to the conclusion that the Belgian excess profit exemption scheme differs from the normal practice under Belgian corporate tax and is contrary to the European rules on State aid.

The European Commission then ordered the Belgian State to take all possible measures with a view to recovering this State aid from its beneficiaries. The European Commission estimated the total amount to be recovered at around EUR 700 million.[2]

1. Art. 1 of the Decision (EU) 2016/1699 of 11 January 2016 on the excess profit exemption State aid scheme SA.37667 (2015/C) (ex 2015/NN) implemented by Belgium *OJ L* 260/61, 27 September 2016. Hereafter called 'Decision'. https://eur-lex.europa.eu/legal-content/EN/TXT/PDF/?uri=OJ:L:2016:260:FULL&from=EN (assessed 14 July 2018).
2. European Commission – Press release, *IP/16/42*.

The Belgian State still tried unsuccessfully to suspend the obligation to repay by means of an interlocutory procedure before the Court.[3] An appeal has also been made on the merits.[4] However, this appeal does not suspend the obligation to repay.

The companies that had obtained an advanced ruling that allowed them to exempt the so-called excess profits, and actually applied this advanced ruling, were required to refund the benefits granted.[5]

This contribution discusses in detail the way in which Belgium has complied with this recovery obligation (Chapter 4). First, brief explanations are given on the disputed excess profit exemption scheme (Chapter 2) and on the decision to recover by the European Commission (Chapter 3). For more details on this scheme and this decision, reference is made to the aforementioned decision of the European Commission of 11 January 2016.[6]

The substance of the case itself and the validity of the European Commission Decision are not discussed. In this respect it must however be noticed that in its judgment of 14 February 2019, the General Court has in two cases annulled the aforementioned Commission decision (European Union [EU]) 2016/1699.[7] According to the General Court the Commission has erroneously considered that the Belgian excess profit system at issue, constituted an aid scheme.[8]

---

3. Order of the President of the General Court of 19 July 2016 – *Belgium v. Commission* 19 July 2016, T-131/16. https://eur-lex.europa.eu/legal-content/en/TXT/PDF/?uri=uriserv%3AOJ.C_.2016.326.01.0028.01.ENG (assessed 14 July 2018).
4. Belgium (case T-131/16) as well as 29 concerned companies have appealed against the Decision. For an overview we refer to the website of the Commission: http://ec.europa.eu/competition/elojade/isef/case_details.cfm?proc_code=3_SA_37667 (assessed 25 March 2019).
5. The annex to the Decision of the European Commission provides a (non-exhaustive) overview of the concerned companies.
6. Decision (EU) 2016/1699 of 11 January 2016 on the excess profit exemption State aid scheme SA.37667 (2015/C) (ex 2015/NN) implemented by Belgium *OJ L* 260/61, 27 September 2016. Hereafter called 'Decision'. https://eur-lex.europa.eu/legal-content/EN/TXT/PDF/?uri=OJ:L:2016:260:FULL&from=EN (assessed 25 March 2019).
7. GC, 14/2/2019, T-131/16 and T-263/16, Belgium and Magnetrol/Commission, numbers 135 and 136.
8. Unlike most State aid cases in tax matters, the Belgian excess profit ruling cases are not about individual aid but about an aid scheme. The judgement of the General Court regarding the absence of a scheme is based on the fact that the essential elements of the excess profit rulings did not feature in the relevant Belgian underlying tax provisions and that the Belgian Ruling Commission, which issued these rulings, did more than just technically applying these provisions without discretion.

   The judgment also confirmed that Member States' measures of direct taxation are subject to State aid review, which allows the EU Commission to investigate these measures (number 67). The Court did however not consider the existence of a selective advantage which is at the core of all related appeals. This judgement thus has limited predictive value for the pending State aid cases which are not about aid schemes but about individual aid.

   At the moment this contribution was finalized it was unclear whether the Commission will accept the Court's judgement or whether it will appeal it before the Court of Justice. Even if the Commission accepts the judgement, it is, however, not excluded that it continues an investigation into individual excess profit rulings so as to determine whether these rulings, while not being part of a State aid scheme, could nevertheless constitute individual State aid.

§9.02 THE CONTESTED EXCESS PROFIT EXEMPTION SCHEME

[A] Legal Framework

The excess profit exemption scheme was based on Article 185, paragraph 2, b) of the Belgian Income Tax Code 92 (hereafter: ITC 92). This scheme offered Belgian resident companies that are part of a multinational group and Belgian permanent establishments of companies established abroad that are part of a multinational group, the possibility of reducing their taxable base in Belgium by deducting a so-called 'excess profit' from their actual profits. This excess was determined by estimating the hypothetical average profit that a stand-alone company with comparable activities can expect to make in similar circumstances and by deducting this amount (tax) from the profit that the concerned Belgian group entity has actually booked.[9]

[B] *Ratio Legis* of the Excess Profit Exemption Scheme

The excess profit exemption meant that a Belgian group entity would only be taxed on its business (arm's length) profit. To this end, an exemption from tax was granted for the profit booked that is greater than the business profit. More specifically, it concerns an exemption from taxation of profits resulting from synergies, economies of scale or other benefits due to the entity's membership of a multinational group.[10]

[C] Excess Profit Ruling

On the basis of Article 185, par. 2, b) ITC, an advanced decision (hereafter: ruling) by the Belgian tax administration is required to qualify for the exemption of this surplus. According to that provision, a ruling could only be obtained for cross-border relations of entities belonging to a multinational group of affiliated companies.[11]

[D] Application of the Scheme in Belgium

The excess profit exemption scheme had been in existence since 2004 and had gradually gained in importance. It is said that sixty-six rulings for fifty-five companies have been issued.[12]

9. Decision, number 13.
10. Decision, number 14.
11. Decision, number 20.
12. Decision, number 59.

§9.03 UNLAWFUL STATE AID

In its decision of 11 January 2016, the European Commission[13] concludes that the system of excess profit exemption constitutes a State aid scheme within the meaning of Article 1(d) of Regulation (EU) 2015/1589.[14] It is a state-funded measure (reduction of the taxable base)[15] which adversely affects EU trade and involves a distortion of competition.[16]

According to the Commission, a selective advantage is granted to the beneficiaries under the excess profit exemption scheme. The exemption scheme differs from the normal corporate tax system that is used as a reference scheme.[17] Furthermore, this derogation cannot be justified by the nature and the design of the tax system.[18]

The beneficiaries of the scheme are the Belgian entities which are part of a multinational group and which have requested and received a tax ruling under Article 185, paragraph 2, (b) ITC 92 and for which, with a view to determining their taxable income in the framework of the general Belgian corporate tax system, a unilateral downward adjustment has been applied to the profit actually booked in their accounts.[19]

The controversial scheme is, according to the European Commission, a scheme with which operating aid is granted.[20] Such aid cannot as a rule be regarded as compatible aid.[21] Moreover, Belgium has not invoked any of the grounds for a finding of compatibility of the State aid scheme.[22] It had also not informed the Commission of any intention to grant aid under the contested scheme nor had it complied with the standstill obligation laid down in Article 108(3) of the TFEU. Therefore, according to the Commission, the system of excess profit exemption constitutes an unlawful aid scheme which has been implemented in breach of Article 108(3) of the Treaty.[23]

13. Decision, number 94.
14. Council Regulation (EU) 2015/1589 of 13 July 2015 laying down detailed rules for the application of Art. 108 of the Treaty on the Functioning of the European Union (codification), *OJ. L.* 24 September 2015, vol. 248, 9. (hereafter: Council Regulation (EU) 2015/1589).
15. Decision, numbers 112–114.
16. Decision, number 115–116.
17. Decision, number 121, 124–128, 169.
18. Decision, number 171, 181.
19. Decision, number 183.
20. Decision, number 188.
21. Decision, number 191.
22. Decision, number 190.
23. Decision, numbers 193–194.

§9.04 CONSEQUENCES OF THE ASSESSMENT AS UNLAWFUL STATE AID: RECOVERY

[A] Legal Basis for Recovery

Article 16(1) of Regulation (EU) 2015/1589[24] requires the Commission to order the recovery of unlawful and incompatible aid. According to that provision, the Member State concerned must also take all necessary measures to recover the aid which has proved to be incompatible with the internal market. Article 16(2) of the same Regulation provides that the aid to be recovered shall include interest from the date on which the unlawful aid was available to the beneficiary up to the date of actual recovery of the aid. Regulation (EC) No 794/2004 specifies the methods for calculating recovery interest rates.[25] Finally, Article 16(3) of Regulation (EU) 2015/1589[26] provides that 'recovery shall be effected without delay and in accordance with the procedures under the national law of the Member State concerned, provided that they allow the immediate and effective execution of the Commission's decision'.

Recovery of the aid in violation of a general legal principle is not possible.[27] In this context, Belgium had argued that both the principles of respect for legitimate expectations and legal certainty, as well as the difficulties in quantifying the amount of aid and the risk of double taxation, prevent the recovery of the aid.[28] However, these arguments were rejected by the Commission.[29]

[B] Methodology for Recovery Imposed by the European Commission

[1] General Principle: Restoring the Situation Ex Ante

The removal of the aid measure aims at restoring the former situation. That objective is achieved if *each* beneficiary has repaid the sums granted on the basis of unlawful aid - thereby losing the market advantage which it enjoyed vis-à-vis its competitors - thus restoring the situation prior to the granting of aid.[30]

[2] Calculation of the Amount to Be Recovered

It is not for the Commission to determine the exact amount of the aid to be repaid. It is sufficient that the Commission's decision contains the information enabling the

24. Council Regulation (EU) 2015/1589, p. 9.
25. Commission Regulation (EC) No 794/2004 of 21 April 2004 implementing Council Regulation (EC) No 659/1999 laying down detailed rules for the application of Art. 93 of the EC Treaty, *OJ. L* 30 April 2004, vol. 140, 1.
26. Council Regulation (EU) 2015/1589, 9.
27. Council Regulation (EU) 2015/1589, 9.
28. Decision, number 197.
29. Decision, numbers 198–199, 201–203.
30. Decision, number 205.

addressee of the decision to determine this amount on its own without undue difficulty.[31]

The Commission notice on direct business taxation[32] stipulates that the amount to be recovered must be calculated on the basis of a comparison between the actual tax paid and the tax that would have been due if the generally applicable rule had been applied. To this end, the Belgian tax authorities must make a new assessment of the tax liabilities of the entities that have benefited from the controversial scheme for each year in which they benefited from the scheme. The following must be taken into account for each beneficiary of the aid measure:[33]

- the amount of tax saved as a result of all rulings issued to that beneficiary; and
- the cumulative interest on that amount, calculated from the time the aid was granted to the current reimbursement.[34]

The amount of tax saved in a given year by a given ruling is equal to the profit actually deducted from a positive taxable basis, multiplied by the corporate tax rate that applied in the fiscal year concerned.[35]

The aid is deemed to have been granted on the day that the tax saved would have been due in any fiscal year if the ruling had not been issued.[36] If the deduction to which the beneficiary was entitled in a specific year could not (fully) take place in that year because of an insufficient positive tax base, and if the amount not effectively deducted was carried forward to a subsequent tax year, then the aid shall be deemed attributed in the subsequent year(s) when the amounts of excess profit could effectively be deducted from a positive tax base.[37]

The tax which would have been due without the benefit exemption scheme must be calculated on the basis of the general scheme applicable in Belgium at the time of the granting of aid and taking into account the actual factual and legal situation of the beneficiary - and not with hypothetical alternative situations based on different operational and legal circumstances that the beneficiary could have chosen in the absence of the excess profit exemption.[38]

[3] Timeline

The Commission's Decision clearly states that the recovery of the aid granted must take place immediately and effectively.[39] In particular, Belgium had to ensure that the decision was fully implemented within four months from the date of its notification.[40]

31. Decision, number 206 and the case law cited there.
32. Commission notice on the application of the State aid rules to measures relating to direct business taxation, *OJ C* 384/3, 10 December 1998 (hereafter: 'Communication'), point 35.
33. Decision, number 207.
34. Decision, Arts 2, 3.
35. Decision, number 208.
36. Decision, number 207, *in fine.*
37. Decision, number 210.
38. Decision, number 211.
39. Decision, Arts 3, 1.
40. Decision, Arts 3, 2.

Within two months of the notification of the decision, Belgium was also required to provide the Commission with information on the identity of the beneficiaries and the aid amounts they had received, as well as the measures already taken and planned to comply with the decision, and finally also documents showing that the beneficiaries were required to repay the aid.[41]

§9.05 PROGRAMME ACT 25 DECEMBER 2016: LEGAL BASIS FOR RECOVERY OF STATE AID

[A] Background

As there is no general legal framework in Belgium concerning procedures for the recovery of unlawful State aid, the Belgian state has created ad hoc legislation in order to meet its obligations as set out in the Decision. In the course of that process, the Belgian government has consulted with the European Commission. A timetable was also agreed.[42]

On 29 December 2016, the Programme Act of 25 December 2016 was published in the Belgian Official Gazette (hereinafter: the Programme Act). Title 4, Chapter 5 of this Programme Act (Articles 100–119) regulates the system for the recovery of the State aid granted through the so-called excess profit rulings. This arrangement was subsequently modified[43] in consultation with the relevant services of the European Commission[44] with retroactive effect to remedy certain shortcomings of the initial recovery arrangement.

Although the tax administration is able to provide itself with an enforceable title (the so-called *privilege du préalable*),[45] the aforementioned legislation aims to provide more legal certainty about the way in which the State aid to be recovered must be calculated and regarding the applicable procedural rules. This legislation is therefore primarily intended to create an enforceable title allowing the various administrations of the Federal Public Service Finance to establish and recover the amount of aid to be recovered.[46]

[B] Beneficiaries of Unlawful State Aid

The Commission, in an annex, refers to its decision to specific rulings[47] and to companies that have made use of the surplus scheme. According to the Commission,

41. Decision, Art. 4.
42. Report of the Finance Commission on the Programme Act draft, *Parl. St.* Kamer 2016–17, N° 54-2208/008, p. 6.
43. Act of 17 December 2017 on various tax provisions (II) (Arts 15–22, amending or supplementing the aforementioned Arts 101, 103, 104, 106, 111, 112 and 118 of the aforementioned Programme Act) *Belgisch Staatsblad* (Belgian Official Gazette), 22 December 2017.
44. Explanatory Memorandum, *Parl. St.* Kamer, 2017–2018, N° 54-2764/001, p. 22.
45. Luik, 19 mei 1994, *FJF* 1995, 367.
46. Explanatory Memorandum, *Parl. St.* Kamer 2016–2017, N° 54-2208/001, p. 50.
47. The annex of the Decision is indeed called: 'List of rulings granted under the contested scheme'.

this list is merely illustrative.[48] Indeed, all beneficiaries of an excess profit ruling having obtained unlawful State aid that has to be recovered, are targeted including the entities that are not mentioned in the Appendix.[49] Moreover, not only Belgian entities which are part of a multinational group are meant. The administration can also claim back the aid even if the recipient of the aid no longer exists as such. It is for instance also possible to claim the aid to be recovered from a company which has taken over the original recipient of the aid or in case the beneficiary company is split into several entities (see *infra* §9.05[C]).

[C] Reimbursement of Unlawful Aid

[1] Limitation Period

In accordance with Article 17 of Regulation 2015/1589,[50] the power of the Commission to recover aid shall lapse after a period of ten years from the date on which the aid was granted. This article does not regulate the competence of a Member State which needs to implement a decision by the European Commission to recover the State aid.[51]

As already mentioned, the European Commission has instructed the Belgian State to recover the State aid immediately and effectively within a period of four months from the notification of the Decision.[52] In accordance with Article 288 TFEU, a decision is binding in its entirety. It was therefore not necessary to determine a limitation scheme for the recovery of the aid.[53]

However, in order to avoid any confusion, the Programme Act of 25 December 2016 explicitly stipulates that the general rules regarding limitation, interruption and suspension of the ITC do not apply (article 116). In this respect, the aid to be recovered is therefore not equated with corporation tax or non-resident tax.

[2] Determination of the Amount of Aid to Be Recovered

The recovery rules aim to eliminate the beneficiary's market advantage and restore the situation to that of the time before the State aid was granted.[54] In the context of State aid in the form of tax advantages, account must be taken not only of the tax saved but also of the cumulative interest on that amount (Article 100 Programme Act).[55]

48. Decision, footnote 133 sub number 207.
49. Advice of the Legislation Section of the Council of State, *Parl. St.* Kamer 2016–2017, N° 54-2208/001, p. 163.
50. Council Regulation (EU) 2015/1589 of 13 July 2015 laying down detailed rules for the application of Art. 108 of the Treaty on the Functioning of the European Union (codification), *OJ. L.* 24 September 2015, vol. 248, 9.
51. *See also* Advice of Legislation Section of the Council of State, *Parl. St.* Kamer 2016–17, N° 54-2208/001, p. 165.
52. Decision, Art. 3
53. The Legislation Section of the Council of State came to the same conclusion in her advice N° 60.482/1-2-3-4 of 23 November 2015, *Parl. St.* Kamer 2016–17, N° 54-2208/001, p. 165.
54. *See supra* §9.02[C].
55. *See supra* §9.02[D].

The calculation of the amount of support to be recovered is further elaborated in articles 101 up to and including 103 of the Programme Act.

[a] Annual Recalculation

The calculation of the tax must be carried out again for each taxable period concerned by applying the general rules of corporation tax or tax on non-residents, as these provisions existed for the tax year related to the relevant taxable period and where no allowance is made for the exempted surplus as calculated in accordance with the excess profit ruling granted.[56]

[b] Correction If Corrected Abroad

However, account can be taken of (parts of) the exempted surplus that were actually added to their tax base at the level of other foreign companies within the group. If the exempt surplus is taxed abroad, it is not regarded as unlawful State aid and the tax saved must therefore not be reimbursed.[57]

[c] Balance of Unpaid Tax: Excluding Tax Increase in Case of Insufficient Advance Payments

The recovery rules serve to restore the market advantage due to the State aid granted. In this way, the unpaid tax due to the application of the excess profit ruling must be recovered and the balance of tax deductions must also be adjusted. The amount of tax saved in a given year by the excess profit ruling is, according to the rules, equal to the profit actually deducted from a positive taxable base, multiplied by the corporate tax rate that applied in the fiscal year concerned.

According to Article 218 ITC 92 (corporation tax) and Article 246 ITC 92 (non-resident tax), the tax is increased by a certain percentage unless advance payments have been made at specific times. This increase may also apply if the taxable base of a specific tax year is increased as a result of a subsequent inspection.[58] However, the increase in case of no or insufficient advance payments is not applicable under this scheme for the recovery of the State aid. No justification is given for this in the explanatory memorandum. The legislature seems to assume that the companies involved - if the excess profit ruling had not been applicable - had paid their taxes on time in advance.

---

56. Art. 101, 2, Programme Act.
57. Art. 101, 3, Programme Act. *See also supra* at 3, in which are mentioned the excess profit rulings in order to avoid double taxation. *See also* Explanatory Memorandum, *Parl. St.* Kamer 2016-2017, N° 54-2208/001, p. 55.
58. Cass. 4 May 2000, *Fisc. Koer.* 2000/10, 320; Gent 17 January 2006, *www.monkey.be.*

[d] *Interest Calculated According to European Rules*

Article 16(2) of Regulation (EU) 2015/1589[59] stipulates that the aid to be recovered shall include interest from the date on which the unlawful aid was available to the beneficiary until the date of effective recovery of the aid. Since the interest forms an integral part of the aid to be recovered, the Belgian legislator has clarified the date of granting the aid and from when onwards the calculation of the compound interest starts to run and this till the actual repayment.[60]

For the tax years 2016 and following, which are linked to taxable periods that are concluded as of 12 January 2016, interest shall be calculated from the first day of the second month following the date of dispatch of the first assessment notice for the relevant tax year.[61]

The Programme Act also confirms that the interest that is due is calculated in accordance with the relevant European rules.[62]

[e] *Tax Deductions That Have Not Been Formally Claimed*

Certain tax deductions (such as the deduction of dividend income, the deduction of innovation income and of transferable losses) or deductible withholding taxes that were not claimed in the relevant tax years can still be applied in accordance with Article 102 of the Program Act, to the extent that all required conditions have been met. According to the Explanatory Memorandum, this provision allows the receivers who were not in a position to claim the deduction of these items or to take these sums into consideration by reducing the tax base that they have claimed, are not disadvantaged in comparison with the situation in which they would have been entitled to this reduction, and this notwithstanding the fact that these reductions and deductions have not been formally claimed in the declarations relating to taxable periods for which the aforementioned exemption was requested.[63]

According to the Programme Act, the facts can be taken into account as they were. However, it is not allowed to take into account hypothetical policy decisions. For example, a company cannot invoke that if the fiscal result had been higher due to non-application of the excess profit ruling, additional investments would probably have been made which could have given rise to an additional tax investment deduction. If, on the other hand, a company in a certain tax year, as a result of the application of the excess profit ruling, retained too low a taxable base to still (fully) obtain a deduction for risk capital, it can still enjoy a tax deduction for risk capital also called, notional interest deduction (NID).

59. Council Regulation (EU) 2015/1589 of 13 July 2015 laying down detailed rules for the application of Art. 108 of the Treaty on the Functioning of the European Union (codification), *OJ. L.* 24 September 2015, vol. 248, 9.
60. Art. 101, 6 Programme Act. Explanatory Memorandum, *Parl. St.* Kamer 2016–17, N° 54-2208/001, p. 56.
61. Art. 101, last section, Programme Act.
62. *See* Art. 100, 2 (5) j, Art. 104 *in fine* and Art. 111 Programme Act.
63. Explanatory Memorandum, *Parl. St.* Kamer 2016–17, N° 54-2208/001, p. 57.

[f] Impact Reimbursement for Tax Year 2016 and Following

Since the repayment of the State aid also has consequences for the calculation of the taxable profit of the following tax years, Article 103 of the Programme Act stipulates that these repaid amounts are in principle equated with corporation tax or with tax on non-residents. Given that the provisions of the Programme Act regulate a specific and previously unseen situation, namely the repayment of State aid obtained in the form of a reduction of the paid tax, it was necessary to clarify the content, the limits and the consequences of the equivalence of the reimbursed State aid with corporation tax or non-resident tax.

Article 103 of the Programme Act explicitly stipulates that the amounts reimbursed are not tax deductible professional expenses, in any case with regard to the part of reimbursed tax savings (thus excluding interest). According to the Explanatory Memorandum, it was useful to make this non-deductibility explicit in the Programme Act in order to prevent the creation of a new unjustified aid, which would be derived from the initial support.[64]

Article 103, last paragraph of the Programme Act, stipulates that the aid to be recovered is also equated with corporation tax or tax on non-residents for the national accounts.

Finally, it follows from Article 103, second paragraph of the Programme Act that transferred tax deductible items (transfer regarding finally taxed dividend income, previous losses, the transferred deduction for risk capital and the investment deduction) that could not be deducted from the taxable profit due to insufficient taxable profit, must also be adjusted for the determination of the taxable profit of the following taxable periods, as if the aid had never been obtained.[65]

[3] Establishment and Recovery of the Aid to Be Recovered

In order to be able to create an enforceable title and in view of the establishment and recovery of the sums, the aid to be recovered is also treated as corporation tax.[66] For example, the amount of aid to be recovered is recorded by Belgian tax authorities and a tax bill will also be drawn up and sent.

However, a complete equalization is also out of the question: after receipt of the assessment notice, the amount of aid must be paid immediately, in deviation of the terms that apply in corporation tax or tax of non-residents.[67]

In the event that a company is acquired or split in the context of a merger, scission or a similar restructuring operation, the assessment of the repayable aid that was received by the acquired or split company up to and including the aforementioned transaction will be imposed on the acquiring or split companies, even when the

64. Explanatory Memorandum, *Parl. St.* Kamer 2016–17, N° 54-2208/001, p. 60. Note that the Memorandum indicates that the deductibility of the interest part as professional costs has been explicitly allowed by the European Commission.
65. Explanatory Memorandum, *Parl. St.* Kamer 2016–17, N° 54-2208/001, p. 61.
66. Arts 104 and 107 Programme Act.
67. Art. 110 Programme Act.

acquired or split company no longer exists as a legal entity.[68] The administration can thus effectively claim back the aid even if the recipient of the aid no longer exists as such. It is possible to claim the aid to be recovered from a company which has taken over the original recipient of the aid or in case the beneficiary company is split into several entities.[69]

[4] Calculation of the Interest: Deposit Scheme

In order to avoid the scenario wherein companies would pay interest for the period when the legislation for the recovery of the State aid did not yet exist, the Belgian State provided for a deposit scheme. For example, in the course of 2016 an amount could already be transferred to the Deposit and Consignment Office, as a result of which no interest was due anymore from the time of the deposit. Companies were informed of this possibility by letter, and a calculation had already been added in the appendix. This administrative concession (which had no legal basis at the time of the deposit scheme) was also legally anchored in the Programme Act.[70]

[5] Remedies

If a company does not agree with the assessment notice that was sent for the recovery of the state support, the general rules concerning the objection procedure as included in the ITC 92 apply in principle.[71] For example, the calculation method can be disputed with a view to the application of a tax deduction that was not automatically taken into account by the FPS Finance.[72] Although, in the case of direct taxes, the rule is normally that only the undisputed part has to be paid in case of an objection, yet it is explicitly stipulated that this rule does not apply to the reimbursement of State aid.[73] The total amount must be repaid immediately.[74] Moreover, in accordance with Article 16.3 of Regulation (EU) 2015/1589,[75] when a national procedural rule prevents immediate and/or effective recovery, the provision should be excluded.[76]

68. Art. 105 Programme Act.
69. Explanatory Memorandum, *Parl. St.* Kamer 2016–17, N° 54-2208/001, pp. 67–68.
70. Art. 104 Programme Act. In practice, however, it has been found that sometimes insufficient amounts have been allocated as a result of the deposit scheme, whether or not as a result of an incorrect calculation by the Belgian State of the aid to be recovered. In this case, interest is still due on the balance for the period after the deposit.
71. Art. 106 Programme Act: exception is made for Art. 373 ITC 92, that is specifically related to the right to object to tax supplements (Explanatory Memorandum, *Parl. St.* Kamer 2016–17, N° 54-2208/001, p. 68).
72. *See* discussion Art. 102 Programme Act under s. 5.3.4.5. and Explanatory Memorandum, *Parl. St.* Kamer 2016–17, N° 54-2208/001, p. 57.
73. Art. 109 Programme Act.
74. Art. 110 Programme Act.
75. Council Regulation (EU) 2015/1589 of 13 July 2015 laying down detailed rules for the application of Art. 108 of the Treaty on the Functioning of the European Union, *OJ. L.* 24 September 2015, vol. 248, 9.
76. Explanatory Memorandum, *Parl. St.* Kamer 2016–17, N° 54-2208/001, p. 69.

[6] Pending Appeals

As mentioned above, there are appeal procedures before the Court against the Commission Decision. In two cases the General Court has in its judgment of 14 February 2019 annulled the Commission Decision (EU) 2016/1699. The Commission may decide to bring an appeal before the Court of Justice against the judgement of the General Court. Such an appeal would then have to be lodged within two months and ten days of the notification of the judgement and should be limited to points of law (Article 56 Statute of the Court of Justice of the European Union (CJEU) and Article 51 of its Rules of Procedure). At the time this contribution was finalized it was unclear whether the Commission will accept the Court's judgement or whether it will appeal it before the Court of Justice.

In the meantime, the Belgian tax authorities may retain the alleged aid that has been reimbursed by the relevant taxpayers until the judgement of the General Court cannot longer be appealed, and in the case of an appeal, until the Court of Justice renders a final (favourable) decision.

In the case of reimbursement of the recovered aid in execution of a judgment of the General Court or of the CJEU, the Programme Act provides for the granting of a moratorium interest calculated on the amount paid from the date of repayment of the aid to the effective return of it by the government.[77] Notwithstanding the provisions of the ITC 92, this interest - in accordance with the relevant European rules - is equal to the rate determined in accordance with Chapter V of Regulation (EC) No 794/2004.[78] The award of a moratorium interest is, in the case of a reimbursement of returned aid, the counterpart of the recovery of interest due to the temporary undue advantage in case of reimbursement of the aid by the transferee.[79]

If a decision of the General Court or the Court of Justice is indeed issued, the assessed amounts of the State aid to be recovered, which are recovered between the date of entry into force of the aforementioned Programme Act and the date of judgment, will automatically be the subject of an ex officio exemption. The amounts effectively recovered and paid are fully reimbursed within twelve months of the decision.[80] The repaid amounts - the part relating to taxes, excluding the part relating to interest - are not taxable profits in corporation tax or tax on non-residents, to the extent that, in view of the reimbursement of the aid, the amounts payable were also not considered as deductible business expenses in the corporation tax or the tax on non-residents.[81] The Legislation Section of the Council of State noted in this regard that it is more legally certain to provide that a refund after the judgment of the Court can only be made if no timely appeal has been lodged against it and the judgment of the

77. Art. 112 Programme Act.
78. Commission Regulation (EC) No 794/2004 of 21 April 2004 implementing Council Regulation (EC) No 659/1999 laying down detailed rules for the application of Art. 93 of the EC Treaty, *OJ. L* 30 April 2004, vol. 140, 1.
79. Explanatory Memorandum, *Parl. St.* Kamer 2016-17, N° 54-2208/001, p. 71.
80. Art. 118, 2 Programme Act.
81. Art. 118, 4 Programme Act.

Court has the force of res judicata.[82] The legislator has taken this remark into account while editing Article 118 of the Programme Act.

[7] International Cooperation

Article 117 of the Programme Act states that the aid to be recovered is also treated as equivalent to corporation tax or tax on non-residents for the application of the international instruments that provide mutual assistance for recovery. The Belgian State has concluded a large number of bilateral double taxation treaties and multilateral agreements that provide for recovery assistance. These agreements aim to deal with tax claims and each State draws up a list of them. The agreements also apply to all identical or similar taxes that would be established after the date of signature of the agreement and that would be added to current taxes or that would replace them.

[8] International Effect

The question arises as to whether the foreign headquarters of the Belgian establishment that has to repay the State aid can include this reimbursement into its own tax arrangements. An answer to this question is not considered by this contribution.[83] This must be assessed on the basis of the respective foreign tax law and the relevant double taxation treaties. It is striking that the Programme Act equates the recovered support in many respects with corporation tax or with tax on non-residents; no judgment is made in the context of the avoidance of double taxation. For example, it is not explicitly confirmed that the aid is equated with taxation in the context of the article on the avoidance of double taxation contained in the double taxation treaties concluded by Belgium.

§9.06 CONCLUSION

On 11 January 2016, the European Commission decided that the excessive profit rulings are incompatible with the European State aid rules. As a result, the aid granted had to be immediately recovered by the Belgian State. In the absence of a general legal

82. Advice Council of State, *Parl. St.* Kamer 2016–17, N° 54-2208/001, p. 167.
83. Make notice that in the Apple Case (C-12/18) the United States of America has already argued that its economic situation would be affected by the result of that case to the extent that the recovery ordered by the decision at issue could result in an increase in the amount of tax credits or deductions which the parent company of Apple Sales International ('ASI') and Apple Operations Europe ('AOE') could claim from the tax authorities in that country, at the time where that company decides to repatriate profits obtained by its off-shore subsidiaries. Such repatriation could be chosen by the parent company of ASI and AOE or those profits could be regarded as having been repatriated following a possible tax reform in the United States of America, *see*: Order of the Vice-President of the Court, 17th May 2018: http://curia.europa.eu /juris/document/document.jsf?text = %2522state%2Baid%2522&docid = 202081&pageIndex = 0&doclang = en&mode = req&dir = &occ = first&part = 1&cid = 1152226#ctx1. (assessed 25 March 2019).

framework to enable this recovery, the Belgian legislator has developed an ad hoc arrangement. Chapter 5 of the Programme Act of 25 December 2016, as amended by Article 15 of the Act on various tax provisions II of 17 December 2017, provides the required legal framework to the tax authorities to (i) determine the amount of State aid to be recovered as a result of the Commission Decision and (ii) to legally recover this amount via an additional assessment.

In elaborating this specific legislation, the Belgian legislator has met fairly faithfully the obligations imposed by the European Commission in its decision of 11 January 2016. In any case this arrangement has led to more legal certainty for the companies involved.

CHAPTER 10

Recovery of Fiscal State Aid in the Netherlands and the Role of the National Judge

Julie Leroy

§10.01 INTRODUCTION

Judges in the Netherlands (used to) struggle with their obligations under Article 108(3) of the Treaty on the Functioning of the European Union (TFEU). More precisely, the Dutch legal order was not fully adapted to the requirements of the European Union (EU) for the recovery of unlawful (fiscal) State aid. The Dutch legislator tackled these problems through the creation of specific legislation for the national recovery procedure. After a first attempt failed in 2008, the legislator succeeded ten years later in its plans. The 'State aid Recovery Act' *(Wet terugvordering staatssteun)* was adopted by the Dutch Parliament on 21 February 2018.

This Chapter provides a general overview of this evolution, with a particular focus on the role of the national judge. In the first place, the tensions that existed between national law and the EU requirements for the recovery of unlawful (fiscal) State aid are discussed (§10.02). This is followed by a short discussion of the 2008 proposal (§10.03). Afterwards, the focus shifts to a more extensive discussion of the 'State aid Recovery Act'. This Act makes a distinction between the recovery of fiscal and non-fiscal State aid. Attention is mainly given to the procedures for the recovery of unlawful fiscal State aid (§10.04). In the last part of this Chapter, an evaluation is made of the 2018 'State aid Recovery Act'. Next to some general remarks, the position of the national judge under the new legislation is evaluated (§10.05). Throughout this Chapter, some recommendations are made to improve the 'State aid Recovery Act'.

§10.02 LESSONS FROM THE PAST: STRUGGLES OF NATIONAL JUDGES CONFRONTED WITH THE RECOVERY OF UNLAWFUL (FISCAL) STATE AID

[A] Setting the Scene: The National Judge and the Recovery of Unlawful State Aid

When an EU Member State grants State aid without respecting the notification- and/or standstill-obligation of Article 108(3) TFEU, this State aid is *unlawful*. If the European Commission (EC) decides – after a formal investigation – that the unlawful State aid is not compatible with the internal market, it issues a negative decision. In this case, the EC orders the *recovery* of the unlawful State aid, in accordance with Article 16(1) of Regulation 2015/1589 (the Procedural Regulation).[1] It is left to the Member States to decide how they will execute this recovery. However, the EU requires that the unlawful State aid is recovered immediately and effectively.[2]

The EC is not exclusively competent to order the recovery of unlawful State aid. The national judge also plays an important role in the supervision of the EU State aid rules. More precisely, the national judge must safeguard the rights that individuals derive from Article 108(3) TFEU.[3] He must grant legal protection, and attach 'all necessary consequences' to the violation of the notification- and/or standstill-obligation.[4]

The European Court of Justice (ECJ) further clarified the role of the national judge in the recovery of State aid. In *Deutsche Lufthansa*, the ECJ stressed that the national judge must react when a Member State violates the standstill-obligation, even if the EC's formal investigation is still pending.[5] The national judge can order a suspension, or even the recovery of the unlawful State aid that has already been paid.[6] To the contrary, the ECJ clarified in *CELF I* that if the unlawful State aid has in the meantime been approved by the EC, EU law does not oblige the national judge to order the recovery.[7] Nevertheless, in this situation, EU law does oblige the national judge to

1. Council Regulation (EU) 2015/1589 laying down detailed rules for the application of Article 108 of the Treaty on the Functioning of the European Union, (13 July 2015), OJ L 248/9.
2. Notice from the Commission Towards an effective implementation of Commission decisions ordering Member States to recover unlawful and incompatible State aid, nr. 22 (2007), OJ C 272/4.
3. ECJ 11 Dec. 1973, C-120/73, *Lorenz GmbH/Germany* [1973], ECLI:EU:C:1973:152, para. 8; ECJ 21 Nov. 1991, C-354/90, *FNCE/France* [1991], ECLI:EU:C:1991:440, para. 12; Commission notice on the enforcement of State aid law by national courts, nr. 21a (2009), OJ C 85/1.
4. ECJ 12 Feb. 2008, C-199/06, *CELF/SIDE* [2008], ECLI:EU:C:2008:79, paras 40–41.
5. ECJ 21 Nov. [2013], C-284/12, *Deutsche Lufthansa* 2013, ECLI:EU:C:2013:755, para. 42; A.V. Sohet, *Nationale rechter moet niet-aangemelde maatregelen opschorten bij opening formele onderzoeksprocedure door Europese Commissie*, 1 Tijdschrift voor Staatssteun 10, 15 (2014).
6. ECJ 21 Nov. [2013], C-284/12, *Deutsche Lufthansa* 2013, ECLI:EU:C:2013:755, para. 43; D. Jouve, *Recovering Unlawful and Incompatible Aids by National Courts: CELF and Scott/Kimberly Clark Cases*, 3 EStAL 367, 370 (2017); A.V. Sohet, *Nationale rechter moet niet-aangemelde maatregelen opschorten bij opening formele onderzoeksprocedure door Europese Commissie*, 1 Tijdschrift voor Staatssteun 10, 12 (2014).
7. ECJ 12 Feb. [2008], C-199/06, *CELF/SIDE* [2008], ECLI:EU:C:2008:79, para. 46; Commission notice on the enforcement of State aid law by national courts, nr. 35 and 40(b) (2009), OJ C 85/1.

order an interest payment for the period during which the aid beneficiary enjoyed the unlawful State aid.[8]

[B] Practice: The Recovery of Unlawful (Fiscal) State Aid and the Dutch Judge

Three main areas of law can come into play when the Netherlands must recover unlawful State aid: administrative law, civil law and tax law.[9] In all three areas, legislative interventions were required in order to fit the Dutch legal order to the EU requirements for the recovery. This contribution mainly focuses on the recovery of fiscal State aid. However, in order to set the scene, it is interesting to also pay attention to (some of[10]) the problems that existed for the recovery of non-fiscal State aid in the Netherlands.

[1] The Recovery of Non-fiscal State Aid

The EU framework requires that interest is added on the State aid that must be recovered.[11] This requirement conflicted with the Dutch legal order, both in the fields of civil and administrative law. On the one hand, in order to make an interest payment run, the Civil Code (CC) *(Burgerlijk Wetboek)* requires that negligence is established (Article 6:119(1) CC). Consequently, the CC does not *ipso facto* calculate the interest from the day that the unlawful State aid was available to the aid beneficiary, as required by the EU in recovery proceedings.[12] Furthermore, the rates applicable to interest payments based upon Articles 6:119 and 6:120 CC, diverge from the interest

Although the national judge can still rely upon national law to order the recovery of the unlawful State aid: ECJ 12 Feb. 2008, C-199/06, *CELF/SIDE* 2008, ECLI:EU:C:2008:79, para. 53; Commission notice on the enforcement of State aid law by national courts, nr. 35 (2009), OJ C 85/1.

8. ECJ 12 Feb. 2008, C-199/06, *CELF/SIDE* [2008], ECLI:EU:C:2008:79, paras 50–52; J. Derenne, *The Powers and Obligations of National Courts with Regard to State Aid Control: Lessons Learned from CELF I and CELF II*, 343 (C. Buts and J.L. Buendía Sierra, Milestones in State Aid Case Law: EStAL's First 15 Years in Perspective (Lexxion Publisher 2017)).
9. P. Adriaanse, *Terugvordering van onrechtmatige staatssteun: Knelpunten en oplossingen in het Nederlandse recht*, 201 (T. Barkhuysen, W. den Ouden and E. Steyger, Europees recht effectueren: algemeen bestuursrecht als instrument voor de effectieve uitvoering van EG-recht (Kluwer 2007)).
10. The cases *Residex* and *Spaansen Holding* are not discussed in this article. These cases deal with the annulment of the legal act that granted the unlawful State aid. See for a comprehensive discussion of these cases: A.J. Metselaar, *Drie rechters en één norm: Handhaving van de Europese staatssteunregels voor de Nederlandse rechter en de grenzen van de nationale procedurele autonomie*, 460–468 (Kluwer 2016).
11. Art. 16(2) Council Regulation (EU) 2015/1589 laying down detailed rules for the application of Article 108 of the Treaty on the Functioning of the European Union, (13 July 2015), OJ L 248/9.
12. Art. 16(2) Council Regulation (EU) 2015/1589 laying down detailed rules for the application of Article 108 of the Treaty on the Functioning of the European Union, (13 July 2015), OJ L 248/9; P. Adriaanse, *Terugvordering van onrechtmatige staatssteun: Knelpunten en oplossingen in het Nederlandse recht*, 217–218 and 230 (T. Barkhuysen, W. den Ouden and E. Steyger, Europees recht effectueren: algemeen bestuursrecht als instrument voor de effectieve uitvoering van EG-recht (Kluwer 2007)).

rate imposed by the EC through Regulation 794/2004.[13] On the other hand, the cases *BPM*, *Fleuren Compost* and *Zorg en Zekerheid* illustrate the tension between the EU interest requirement and national administrative law.

In the *BPM* case, the EC ordered the Netherlands to recover agricultural subsidies that constituted unlawful State aid. The aid beneficiary, Fleuren Compost, launched before the Council of State an appeal against the decision by which the Dutch Minister of Agriculture withdrew and recovered the subsidies.[14]

The Council of State first considered that the principle of legality demands a national legal basis for the withdrawal and recovery of the subsidies. The competence to withdraw cannot be derived directly from EU law.[15] However, the Council of State emphasised that the EU principle of *effet utile* and the principle of loyalty obliged the Minister to withdraw the subsidy decision. As this implies that the subsidy payment was undue, the principle of undue payment allowed the Minister to recover the payments that were already made. A national legal basis for the withdrawal of the decision and the following recovery could thus be found in the general principles of law.[16]

Secondly, the Council of State remarked that the principle of legality also requires a specific legal basis for the interest payment. However, this legal basis could not be found in EU law: neither the Procedural Regulation nor Article 107 TFEU or the negative decision of the EC grant a direct competence to the Minister for the recovery of interest on the subsidies that were unduly paid. This competence could furthermore not be found in national administrative law. The claim for the interest payment could only be based upon civil law.[17]

After the judgment in *BPM*, the Dutch State sent a letter to Fleuren Compost in which they were requested to repay the subsidies with an additional interest. However, as Fleuren Compost still refused to comply with these recovery measures, the Dutch State sued the undertaking before the Civil Court of Rotterdam.[18]

---

13. Commission Regulation (EC) 794/2004 implementing Council Regulation (EC) 659/1999 laying down detailed rules for the application of Article 93 of the EC Treaty, (21 April 2004), OJ L 140/1; A.J. Metselaar, *Een vogel in de hand: nieuwe regels voor de terugvordering van staatssteun*, 3–4 Tijdschrift voor Staatssteun 110, 112 (2016).
14. Council of State 11 Jan. 2006, nr. 200503463/1, *BPM* [2006], ECLI:NL:RVS:2006:AU9415, para. 1; Council of State 11 Jan. 2006, nr. 200410578/1, *BPM* [2006], ECLI:NL:RVS:2006:AU9416, para. 1.
15. Council of State 11 Jan. 2006, nr. 200503463/1, *BPM* [2006], ECLI:NL:RVS:2006:AU9415, para. 2.3; Council of State 11 Jan. 2006, nr. 200410578/1, *BPM* [2006], ECLI:NL:RVS:2006:AU9416, para. 2.3.
16. Council of State 11 Jan. 2006, nr. 200503463/1, *BPM* [2006], ECLI:NL:RVS:2006:AU9415, para. 2.6; Council of State 11 Jan. 2006, nr. 200410578/1, *BPM* [2006], ECLI:NL:RVS:2006:AU9416, para. 2.7; A.J. Metselaar, *Drie rechters en één norm: Handhaving van de Europese staatssteunregels voor de Nederlandse rechter en de grenzen van de nationale procedurele autonomie*, 425–426 (Kluwer 2016).
17. Council of State 11 Jan. 2006, nr. 200503463/1, *BPM* [2006], ECLI:NL:RVS:2006:AU9415, para. 2.8.1 and 2.9; Council of State 11 Jan. 2006, nr. 200410578/1, *BPM* [2006], ECLI:NL:RVS:2006:AU9416, para. 2.10; A.J. Metselaar, *Drie rechters en één norm: Handhaving van de Europese staatssteunregels voor de Nederlandse rechter en de grenzen van de nationale procedurele autonomie*, 431–432 (Kluwer 2016).
18. Civil Court Rotterdam 4 July 2007, nr. 264564 / HA ZA 06-1854, *Fleuren Compost* [2007], ECLI:NL:RBROT:2007:BB0270, para. 3.

In the *Fleuren Compost* judgment, the judge first considered that the subsidy payments to Fleuren Compost were undue due to the negative decision of the EC. Therefore, the principle of undue payment of Article 6:203 CC obliged Fleuren Compost to repay the subsidies to the Netherlands.[19] Secondly, the judge turned to the problem of the interest payment. He considered that the Council of State left the possibility open in *BPM* to use civil law as a legal basis for the interest payment.[20] However, according to the Civil Court, civil law only provides a legal basis for the payment of a statutory interest as defined and calculated in Article 6:119 CC. Following the principle of legality, the Dutch State was thus not competent to order the payment of interest calculated in accordance with the EU rules.[21]

The case *Zorg en Zekerheid* dealt with the recovery of overpaid contributions. The Dutch *Zorginstituut* grants a yearly contribution to health insurers who fulfil certain obligations. The *Zorginstituut* made a miscalculation in the contribution that was paid to health insurer *Zorg en Zekerheid* for the year 2007. The *Zorginstituut* thus revised its decision, lowered the contribution and asked the repayment of the overpaid contributions. *Zorg en Zekerheid* appealed this decision before the Council of State.

In its advice to the Council of State, the EC clarified that it approved the contribution system, but that overpaid contributions fall outside this approval and constitute unlawful State aid.[22] Consequently, the Council of State decided that Article 108(3) TFEU, due to its direct effect, granted the *Zorginstituut* the competence to review its decision and to recover the overly paid compensation. This competence had to be exercised in accordance with national law.[23] In line with *BPM*, the Council of State decided that a legal basis for the recovery was provided by the the general principles of law, more precisely the principle of undue payment.[24] As the *Zorginstituut* did not add interest on the sums it recovered, the Council of State did not express its views on this. However, it is doubtful that the Council of State would have deviated from *BPM* and would have found a legal basis in administrative law for the interest payment.[25]

19. Civil Court Rotterdam 4 July 2007, nr. 264564 / HA ZA 06-1854, *Fleuren Compost* [2007], ECLI:NL:RBROT:2007:BB0270, para. 5.6
20. Civil Court Rotterdam 4 July 2007, nr. 264564 / HA ZA 06-1854, *Fleuren Compost* [2007], ECLI:NL:RBROT:2007:BB0270, para. 5.9; A.J. Metselaar, *Drie rechters en één norm: Handhaving van de Europese staatssteunregels voor de Nederlandse rechter en de grenzen van de nationale procedurele autonomie*, 459–460 (Kluwer 2016).
21. Civil Court Rotterdam 4 July 2007, nr. 264564 / HA ZA 06-1854, *Fleuren Compost* [2007], ECLI:NL:RBROT:2007:BB0270, para. 5.21.
22. Council of State 15 Apr. 2015, nr. 201309575/1/A2, *Zorg en Zekerheid* [2015], ECLI:NL: RVS:2015:1152, para. 4.
23. Council of State 15 Apr. 2015, nr. 201309575/1/A2, *Zorg en Zekerheid* [2015], ECLI:NL: RVS:2015:1152, para. 5.3; A.J. Metselaar, *Drie rechters en één norm: Handhaving van de Europese staatssteunregels voor de Nederlandse rechter en de grenzen van de nationale procedurele autonomie*, 426–427 (Kluwer 2016); J. Van den Brink and W. den Ouden, *noot onder RvS 15 april 2015*, 28 AB Rechtspraak Bestuursrecht 1440, 1447 (nr. 7) (2015).
24. Council of State 15 Apr. 2015, nr. 201309575/1/A2, *Zorg en Zekerheid* [2015], ECLI:NL: RVS:2015:1152, para. 5.3.
25. *See* A.J. Metselaar, *Drie rechters en één norm: Handhaving van de Europese staatssteunregels voor de Nederlandse rechter en de grenzen van de nationale procedurele autonomie*, 432–433 (Kluwer 2016); J. Van den Brink and W. den Ouden, *noot onder RvS 15 april 2015*, 28 AB Rechtspraak Bestuursrecht 1440, 1448 (nr. 10) (2015).

Following den Brink and den Ouden, it can thus be said that this judgment showed (once again) the need for legislation for the recovery of unlawful State aid in the Netherlands.[26]

The cases in *BPM*, *Fleuren Compost* and *Zorg en Zekerheid* illustrate that Dutch national law conflicted with the EU requirement to recover State aid - with interest - immediately and effectively. In fact, the administrative judge passed the responsibility to deal with the interest payment to the civil judge. This made the recovery proceedings complex and time-consuming.[27]

The EC shared this view. Following the judgment of the Council of State in *BPM*, the EC opened an infringement proceeding for non-compliance with its negative decision against the Netherlands before the ECJ. The EC found it particularly troubling that the aid itself had to be recovered through an administrative procedure, while the interest payment had to be recovered through a civil procedure.[28] However, the EC withdrew its claim after the Netherlands announced that it would create legislation for the recovery of State aid in which the problem of the interest payment would be solved.[29] This commitment of the Netherlands resulted in the 2008 Proposal (*see infra* §10.03).[30]

[2] The Recovery of Fiscal State Aid

Tensions with the national legal order also popped-up when the Netherlands had to recover unlawful fiscal State aid. These tensions have been signalled in legal doctrine.[31] They were also addressed in a 2005 comparative study on the recovery of State aid, ordered by the Dutch Ministry of Justice.[32]

A first set of tensions related to direct taxation. Article 16 of the Dutch General Tax Act (GTA) (*Algemene wet inzake rijksbelastingen*) empowers the tax administration to issue a supplementary tax assessment in a number of cases (*navordering*). For

26. J. Van den Brink and W. den Ouden, *noot onder RvS 15 april 2015*, 28 AB Rechtspraak Bestuursrecht 1440, 1448 (nr. 10) (2015).
27. A.J. Metselaar, *Drie rechters en één norm: Handhaving van de Europese staatssteunregels voor de Nederlandse rechter en de grenzen van de nationale procedurele autonomie*, 434 (Kluwer 2016).
28. ECJ, C-401/07, *Commission/Netherlands*, application of the EC.
29. ECJ 5 June 2008, C-401/07, *Commission/Netherlands* [2008], ECLI:EU:C:2008:326; A.J. Metselaar, *Drie rechters en één norm: Handhaving van de Europese staatssteunregels voor de Nederlandse rechter en de grenzen van de nationale procedurele autonomie*, 434 (Kluwer 2016).
30. A.J. Metselaar, *Een vogel in de hand: nieuwe regels voor de terugvordering van staatssteun*, 3-4 Tijdschrift voor Staatssteun 110, 110 (2016).
31. *See, e.g.* T. Jestaedt, J. Derenne and T. Ottervanger, *Study on the enforcement of State aid law at national level* (European Communities 2006); P. Adriaanse, *Terugvordering van onrechtmatige staatssteun: Knelpunten en oplossingen in het Nederlandse recht*, 212–214 (T. Barkhuysen, W. den Ouden and E. Steyger, Europees recht effectueren: algemeen bestuursrecht als instrument voor de effectieve uitvoering van EG-recht (Kluwer 2007)).
32. B.W.N. de Waard, A.J.C. de Moor-van Vugt, A.A.L. Beers, J.C.A. de Poorter and G.J. van Slooten, *Terugvordering van staatssteun: Een rechtsvergelijkend onderzoek* (Ministerie van Justitie 2005).

instance if the company did not declare certain revenues which implied that it did not pay enough taxes. A supplementary tax assessment can only be issued when there is a 'new fact'. This is a fact of which the tax inspector neither was nor could have reasonably become aware of (Article 16(1) GTA). It was however not clear if the declaration that State aid is unlawful and must be recovered, constituted such a 'new fact'.[33] Besides, Article 16 GTA only applies towards the initial taxpayer. It does not allow the imposition of a supplementary tax assessment on a third party.[34] Also, a supplementary tax assessment can only be issued in the five years following the creation of the tax liability (Article 16(3) GTA). This could conflict with the longer EU limitation period (of ten years) for the recovery of unlawful State aid.[35] Finally, Article 52(4) GTA obliges taxpayers to store all information that is relevant for their taxation. This information must in principle be stored during seven years. This can possibly conflict with the longer EU limitation period for the recovery, when a recovery is ordered more than seven years after the receipt of the unlawful fiscal State aid.[36]

Tensions also arose in the field of indirect taxation. Also in this case, the tax inspector can issue a supplementary tax assessment (*naheffing*) (Article 20 GTA). There is no requirement of a 'new fact' here, but the limitation period is also five years (Article 20 (3) GTA). Furthermore, the retention period for information of seven years also applies to indirect taxes (Article 52 (4) GTA). As is the case with direct taxes, both periods can conflict with the longer EU limitation period for recovery.[37]

33. Memorie van Toelichting Regels voor de terugvordering van staatssteun (Wet terugvordering staatssteun), 9 (2017), Kamerstukken II 2016-17, nr. 34 753/3 (Explanatory Memorandum); B.W.N. de Waard, A.J.C. de Moor-van Vugt, A.A.L. Beers, J.C.A. de Poorter and G.J. van Slooten, *Terugvordering van staatssteun: Een rechtsvergelijkend onderzoek*, 39 (Ministerie van Justitie 2005); T. Jestaedt, J. Derenne and T. Ottervanger, *Study on the enforcement of State aid law at national level*, 370 (European Communities 2006); P. Adriaanse, *Terugvordering van onrechtmatige staatssteun: Knelpunten en oplossingen in het Nederlandse recht*, 212–213 (T. Barkhuysen, W. den Ouden and E. Steyger, Europees recht effectueren: algemeen bestuursrecht als instrument voor de effectieve uitvoering van EG-recht (Kluwer 2007)).
34. P. Adriaanse, *Terugvordering van onrechtmatige staatssteun: Knelpunten en oplossingen in het Nederlandse recht*, 223–224 (T. Barkhuysen, W. den Ouden and E. Steyger, Europees recht effectueren: algemeen bestuursrecht als instrument voor de effectieve uitvoering van EG-recht (Kluwer 2007)).
35. Council Regulation (EU) 2015/1589 laying down detailed rules for the application of Article 108 of the Treaty on the Functioning of the European Union, Art. 17(1)–(2) (13 July 2015), OJ L 248/9.
36. B.W.N. de Waard, A.J.C. de Moor-van Vugt, A.A.L. Beers, J.C.A. de Poorter and G.J. van Slooten, *Terugvordering van staatssteun: Een rechtsvergelijkend onderzoek*, 40 (Ministerie van Justitie 2005); T. Jestaedt, J. Derenne and T. Ottervanger, *Study on the enforcement of State aid law at national level*, 370 (European Communities 2006); P. Adriaanse, *Terugvordering van onrechtmatige staatssteun: Knelpunten en oplossingen in het Nederlandse recht*, 212–213 (T. Barkhuysen, W. den Ouden and E. Steyger, Europees recht effectueren: algemeen bestuursrecht als instrument voor de effectieve uitvoering van EG-recht (Kluwer 2007)).
37. B.W.N. de Waard, A.J.C. de Moor-van Vugt, A.A.L. Beers, J.C.A. de Poorter and G.J. van Slooten, *Terugvordering van staatssteun: Een rechtsvergelijkend onderzoek*, 41 (Ministerie van Justitie 2005); P. Adriaanse, *Terugvordering van onrechtmatige staatssteun: Knelpunten en*

§10.03 FAILURE OF THE PAST: THE 2008 PROPOSAL

As mentioned previously, the Netherlands promised the EC after *BPM/Fleuren Compost* to deal with the national hurdles for the recovery of unlawful (fiscal) State aid. This resulted in 2008 in a first legislative proposal.[38] The proposal was never adopted, as the members of Parliament found it too far-going.[39] In November 2017, the proposal was eventually formally repealed.[40] It is not the aim of this Chapter to discuss the content of the 2008 proposal extensively. Nevertheless, a selective discussion of certain features is relevant in order to allow a comparison with and an evaluation of the 'State aid Recovery Act' adopted in 2018.

National recovery procedures can be designed in several ways.[41] One option is to directly rely upon the decision of the EC as a legal basis for the national recovery actions. However, as shown in *BPM*, *Fleuren Compost* and *Zorg en Zekerheid*, the Dutch principle of legality requires that the recovery actions are based on national law.

Another option, which is more in line with the Dutch principle of legality, is to rely upon national law for the national recovery actions. Several approaches can be taken when using this option. In the first place, the recovery can be executed through existing legislation. Due to the primacy of EU law, national rules that prevent an immediate and effective recovery must however be set aside. This approach was used by the Netherlands prior to the adoption of the 'State aid Recovery Act' in 2018. The

---

oplossingen in het Nederlandse recht, 213 (T. Barkhuysen, W. den Ouden and E. Steyger, Europees recht effectueren: algemeen bestuursrecht als instrument voor de effectieve uitvoering van EG-recht (Kluwer 2007)).

38. Voorstel van wet Wijziging van het Burgerlijk Wetboek, de Algemene wet bestuursrecht en de Algemene wet inzake rijksbelastingen in verband met de tenuitvoerlegging van een beschikking van de Commissie van de Europese Gemeenschappen of een rechterlijke uitspraak inzake staatssteun, alsmede wijziging van het Burgerlijk Wetboek om de procedure voor het vaststellen van de wettelijke rente aan te passen (terugvordering staatssteun), (2008), Kamerstukken II 2007-2008, nr. 31 418/2 (Legislative proposal).

    See for an extended discussion of the 2008 proposal i.a. P.C. Adriaanse and W. den Ouden, *Effectuering van staatssteunrecht in Nederland: Een bestuursrechtelijke blik op de uitvoeringspraktijk en het wetsvoorstel terugvordering staatssteun*, 40 Nederlands Tijdschrift voor Bestuursrecht, ss. 4-5 (2008); G.J. van Slooten, *Het wetsvoorstel terugvordering staatssteun: een te kleine pleister op een veel te grote wonde?*, 6-7 Tijdschrift voor Formeel Belastingrecht (2008).

39. Verslag Wijziging van het Burgerlijk Wetboek, de Algemene wet bestuursrecht en de Algemene wet inzake rijksbelastingen in verband met de tenuitvoerlegging van een beschikking van de Commissie van de Europese Gemeenschappen of een rechterlijke uitspraak inzake staatssteun, alsmede wijziging van het Burgerlijk Wetboek om de procedure voor het vaststellen van de wettelijke rente aan te passen (terugvordering staatssteun) (2008), Kamerstukken II 2007-2008, nr. 31 418/5 (Report).

40. Brief van de minister van Justitie en Veiligheid Wijziging van het Burgerlijk Wetboek, de Algemene wet bestuursrecht en de Algemene wet inzake rijksbelastingen in verband met de tenuitvoerlegging van een beschikking van de Commissie van de Europese Gemeenschappen of een rechterlijke uitspraak inzake staatssteun, alsmede wijziging van het Burgerlijk Wetboek om de procedure voor het vaststellen van de wettelijke rente aan te passen (terugvordering staatssteun) (2008), Kamerstukken II 2007–2008, nr. 31 418/6 (Letter of the Minister of Security and Justice).

41. The following overview does not intend to be exhaustive, but merely addresses certain options.

struggles that national judges experienced when trying to fit the EU requirements for recovery in the Dutch legal order show that this approach was not perfect. A second approach is to modify existing legislation, in order to adapt these rules to the requirements imposed by the EU for the recovery of unlawful State aid. This approach was used in the 2008 proposal and is also applied by the 'State aid Recovery Act' for the recovery of fiscal State aid. A third approach is to adopt new legislation, which creates a (possibly exclusive) legal basis and procedure for national recovery actions. This approach was chosen by the Dutch legislator in the 'State aid Recovery Act' for the recovery of non-fiscal State aid. The 'State aid Recovery Act' of 2018 will be discussed in §10.04.

The proposal of 2008 followed the second approach. It modified existing legislation, in order to create specific legal bases for the recovery of unlawful (fiscal) State aid. There was thus no enactment of a separate national recovery regime. The proposal of 2008 wanted to modify the Dutch CC, the General Administrative Law Act (GALA) (*Algemene wet bestuursrecht*), and the GTA, in order to ensure an immediate and effective recovery of unlawful (fiscal) State aid.[42]

Through this approach, the legislator wanted to preserve the connection with the legal relationship in which the State aid was granted. The choice to modify existing legislation also avoided a fragmentation of legislation.[43] The legislator furthermore found that this approach fitted best into the existing legal framework, specifically taking into account the separation of powers between judges.[44] A disadvantage of this approach is however that several judges are possibly competent for a single State aid case. This could have the undesired outcome that several judges have to express their - possibly differing - views on the recovery procedure in a particular case.[45]

An important feature of the 2008 proposal was its broad scope of application. The procedure would have been applicable to the recovery of unlawful State aid based upon (i) a decision of the EC; (ii) a judgment of the General Court (GC)/the ECJ or (iii) a judgment of a national Court.[46] However, the initial legislative proposal only referred

---

42. Memorie van Toelichting Wijziging van het Burgerlijk Wetboek, de Algemene wet bestuursrecht en de Algemene wet inzake rijksbelastingen in verband met de tenuitvoerlegging van een beschikking van de Commissie van de Europese Gemeenschappen of een rechterlijke uitspraak inzake staatssteun, alsmede wijziging van het Burgerlijk Wetboek om de procedure voor het vaststellen van de wettelijke rente aan te passen (terugvordering staatssteun), 1 (2008), Kamerstukken II 2007-2008, nr. 31 418/3 (Explanatory Memorandum); A.J. Metselaar, *Drie rechters en één norm: Handhaving van de Europese staatssteunregels voor de Nederlandse rechter en de grenzen van de nationale procedurele autonomie*, 511-512 en 529 (Kluwer 2016).
43. A.J. Metselaar, *Drie rechters en één norm: Handhaving van de Europese staatssteunregels voor de Nederlandse rechter en de grenzen van de nationale procedurele autonomie*, 528 (Kluwer 2016).
44. Memorie van Toelichting Wijziging van het Burgerlijk Wetboek, de Algemene wet bestuursrecht en de Algemene wet inzake rijksbelastingen in verband met de tenuitvoerlegging van een beschikking van de Commissie van de Europese Gemeenschappen of een rechterlijke uitspraak inzake staatssteun, alsmede wijziging van het Burgerlijk Wetboek om de procedure voor het vaststellen van de wettelijke rente aan te passen (terugvordering staatssteun), 7 (2008), Kamerstukken II 2007-2008, nr. 31 418/3 (Explanatory Memorandum).
45. A.J. Metselaar, *Drie rechters en één norm: Handhaving van de Europese staatssteunregels voor de Nederlandse rechter en de grenzen van de nationale procedurele autonomie*, 533 (Kluwer 2016).
46. Voorstel van wet Wijziging van het Burgerlijk Wetboek, de Algemene wet bestuursrecht en de Algemene wet inzake rijksbelastingen in verband met de tenuitvoerlegging van een beschikking

to recovery proceedings ordered by the EC or the EU judge. This was addressed by the Council of State in its advice on the proposal. The Council of State stressed that the national judge has the duty to order the recovery of unlawful State aid when the standstill-obligation of Article 108(3) TFEU has been violated (*see supra* §10.02[A]). Consequently, the Council of State advised to extend the scope of the proposal in order to also cover a recovery ordered by the national judge.[47]

Although the legislator followed the advice of the Council of State, the result of this was rather unsatisfactory. The proposed Article 4:80b (1) GALA mentioned that a recovery would take place, when ordered by the EC or in an *irrevocable* Court ruling.[48] Through a cross-reference in the proposed Article 5a GTA, this would also have been applicable in fiscal recovery procedures. The Explanatory Memorandum did not mention any justification for this requirement of irrevocability.

Adriaanse and den Ouden signal that this requirement would have impeded an effective application of the State aid rules, for instance when an undertaking opposes a decision that grants unlawful State aid to his competitor. The EU framework requires that the national judge immediately couples the necessary consequences upon a violation of Article 108 (3) TFEU. What if the Court would have decided that unlawful State aid was indeed granted, and the recovery of this aid was ordered? If the aid beneficiary would appeal this judgment, the competent administrative body would not have been able to recover the unlawful aid as long as the appeal would be pending. This would conflict with the need to recover unlawful State aid immediately and

---

van de Commissie van de Europese Gemeenschappen of een rechterlijke uitspraak inzake staatssteun, alsmede wijziging van het Burgerlijk Wetboek om de procedure voor het vaststellen van de wettelijke rente aan te passen (terugvordering staatssteun), Art. I s. C (2008), Kamerstukken II 2007–2008, nr. 31 418/2 (Legislative proposal); Memorie van Toelichting Wijziging van het Burgerlijk Wetboek, de Algemene wet bestuursrecht en de Algemene wet inzake rijksbelastingen in verband met de tenuitvoerlegging van een beschikking van de Commissie van de Europese Gemeenschappen of een rechterlijke uitspraak inzake staatssteun, alsmede wijziging van het Burgerlijk Wetboek om de procedure voor het vaststellen van de wettelijke rente aan te passen (terugvordering staatssteun), 7 (2008), Kamerstukken II 2007–2008, nr. 31 418/3 (Explanatory Memorandum). *See also* P.C. Adriaanse and W. den Ouden, *Effectuering van staatssteunrecht in Nederland: Een bestuursrechtelijke blik op de uitvoeringspraktijk en het wetsvoorstel terugvordering staatssteun*, 40 Nederlands Tijdschrift voor Bestuursrecht, s. 4-2 (2008).

47. Advies Raad van State en nader rapport Wijziging van het Burgerlijk Wetboek, de Algemene wet bestuursrecht en de Algemene wet inzake rijksbelastingen in verband met de tenuitvoerlegging van een beschikking van de Commissie van de Europese Gemeenschappen of een rechterlijke uitspraak inzake staatssteun, alsmede wijziging van het Burgerlijk Wetboek om de procedure voor het vaststellen van de wettelijke rente aan te passen (terugvordering staatssteun), 2 (2008), Kamerstukken II 2007–2008, nr. 31 418/4 (Advice Council of State).
48. The Explanatory Memorandum clarifies that this refers to decisions of national judges: Memorie van Toelichting Wijziging van het Burgerlijk Wetboek, de Algemene wet bestuursrecht en de Algemene wet inzake rijksbelastingen in verband met de tenuitvoerlegging van een beschikking van de Commissie van de Europese Gemeenschappen of een rechterlijke uitspraak inzake staatssteun, alsmede wijziging van het Burgerlijk Wetboek om de procedure voor het vaststellen van de wettelijke rente aan te passen (terugvordering staatssteun), 8–9 (2008), Kamerstukken II 2007–2008, nr. 31 418/3 (Explanatory Memorandum). Questions were also raised on the interpretation of this requirement, when can a Court ruling be considered 'irrevocable'? *See* A.J. Metselaar and P.C. Adriaanse, *Nut en noodzaak van het wetsvoorstel terugvordering staatssteun: Verslag van het LEGA Symposium op 19 januari 2011*, 2 Tijdschrift voor Staatssteun 57, 60 (2011).

effectively. The rights that the complaining undertaking derives from the violation of Article 108(3) TFEU would have been reduced to a rather empty box, as the competition in the internal market would have remained disrupted.[49] The requirement of an irrevocable judgment - in the way that it was designed in the 2008 proposal - would have significantly reduced the role that national Courts are intended to play in the supervision of Article 108(3) TFEU.

In another part of its advice, the Council of State touched upon the recovery of unlawful fiscal State aid. In its initial draft, the Explanatory Memorandum of the 2008 proposal mentioned that the administrative body would decide how the recovery would be executed. For the recovery of fiscal State aid, this meant that a choice could be made between applying the tax procedures of the GTA or the administrative procedures of the GALA.

The Council of State did not agree with this room for choice and advised to mention explicitly that fiscal State aid would be recovered through tax procedures. As such, the Council of State wanted to ensure a transparent recovery, to allow the application of fiscal corrections and to safeguard that appeals against the national recovery measures would fall under the competence of the tax judge. The legislator followed this advice, and modified the Explanatory Memorandum. Also, the legislator added a provision (proposed Article 4:80b (5) GALA) that mentions explicitly that fiscal State aid must be recovered through the procedures provided in the GTA and the Tax Collection Act 1990 (TCA 1990) (*Invorderingswet 1990*).[50]

In order to ensure an immediate and effective recovery of unlawful fiscal State aid, the 2008 proposal modified certain articles of the GTA (Article II proposal). First, the requirement of a 'new fact' and the five-year limitation period for a supplementary tax assessment were set aside in recovery procedures. Finally, explicit reference was made to the EU rules for the calculation of the interest.[51]

49. P.C. Adriaanse and W. den Ouden, *Effectuering van staatssteunrecht in Nederland: Een bestuursrechtelijke blik op de uitvoeringspraktijk en het wetsvoorstel terugvordering staatssteun*, 40 Nederlands Tijdschrift voor Bestuursrecht, nr. 5.2 (2008). *See also* A.J. Metselaar, *Drie rechters en één norm: Handhaving van de Europese staatssteunregels voor de Nederlandse rechter en de grenzen van de nationale procedurele autonomie*, 518-519 (Kluwer 2016).
50. Advies Raad van State en nader rapport Wijziging van het Burgerlijk Wetboek, de Algemene wet bestuursrecht en de Algemene wet inzake rijksbelastingen in verband met de tenuitvoerlegging van een beschikking van de Commissie van de Europese Gemeenschappen of een rechterlijke uitspraak inzake staatssteun, alsmede wijziging van het Burgerlijk Wetboek om de procedure voor het vaststellen van de wettelijke rente aan te passen (terugvordering staatssteun), 3 (2008), Kamerstukken II 2007-2008, nr. 31 418/4 (Advice Council of State).
51. Voorstel van wet Wijziging van het Burgerlijk Wetboek, de Algemene wet bestuursrecht en de Algemene wet inzake rijksbelastingen in verband met de tenuitvoerlegging van een beschikking van de Commissie van de Europese Gemeenschappen of een rechterlijke uitspraak inzake staatssteun, alsmede wijziging van het Burgerlijk Wetboek om de procedure voor het vaststellen van de wettelijke rente aan te passen (terugvordering staatssteun), Art. II (2008), Kamerstukken II 2007-2008, nr. 31 418/2 (Legislative proposal); Memorie van Toelichting Wijziging van het Burgerlijk Wetboek, de Algemene wet bestuursrecht en de Algemene wet inzake rijksbelastingen in verband met de tenuitvoerlegging van een beschikking van de Commissie van de Europese Gemeenschappen of een rechterlijke uitspraak inzake staatssteun, alsmede wijziging

However, the proposal left some important questions open. It did not explicitly address the impact of the recovery procedure on taxation in other years, prior to or after the years in which the unlawful State aid was granted.[52] There was also a lack of provisions on the recovery of State aid from indirect beneficiaries. The legislator tried to tackle these problems in the 'State aid Recovery Act' of 2018 (*see infra* §10.04[B][3]-[4]).

The 2008 proposal would not have led to a 'legislative revolution', as the legislator chose to stick to existing legislation as a basis for the national recovery procedures. Furthermore, the proposal did not give new tools to national judges dealing with the recovery of unlawful (fiscal) State aid.[53] Experts also stressed that the proposal had almost no added value for private enforcement claims, nor did it facilitate the cooperation between the EC and the national judges.[54]

§10.04 THE ACHIEVEMENT OF 2018: 'WET TERUGVORDERING STAATSSTEUN'[55]

After the cold welcome of the 2008 proposal, several years passed by without any legislative action on the recovery of unlawful (fiscal) State aid. This ended in 2016,

van het Burgerlijk Wetboek om de procedure voor het vaststellen van de wettelijke rente aan te passen (terugvordering staatssteun), 21 (2008), Kamerstukken II 2007-2008, nr. 31 418/3 (Explanatory Memorandum).

The proposal of 2008 created not only the necessary legal basis for the interest payment in tax law, but also in administrative and civil law. However, the proposal linked this interest payment to the recovery of the State aid itself. Since the proposal was launched before the *CELF I* judgment, it did not provide a legal basis for a sole recovery of interest ordered by the national judge: *See* A.J. Metselaar, *Drie rechters en één norm: Handhaving van de Europese staatssteunregels voor de Nederlandse rechter en de grenzen van de nationale procedurele autonomie*, 517 (Kluwer 2016).

52. Commissie Wetsvoorstellen van de Nederlandse Orde van Belastingadviseurs (Dutch Order of Tax Advisors), *Commentaar op het wetsvoorstel Wijziging van het Burgerlijk Wetboek, de Algemene wet bestuursrecht en de Algemene wet inzake rijksbelastingen in verband met de tenuitvoerlegging van een beschikking van de Commissie van de Europese Gemeenschappen of een rechterlijke uitspraak inzake staatssteun, alsmede wijziging van het Burgerlijk Wetboek om de procedure voor het vaststellen van de wettelijke rente aan te passen (nr. 31 418)*, 2-3, https://www.nob.net/system/files/content/article/uploads/Commentaar%20wetsvoorstel%20staatssteun%20aan%20kamercommissie%20justitie.pdf (accessed 6 Mar. 2019).
53. A.J. Metselaar and P.C. Adriaanse, *Nut en noodzaak van het wetsvoorstel terugvordering staatssteun: Verslag van het LEGA Symposium op 19 januari 2011*, 2 Tijdschrift voor Staatssteun 57, 60 (2011); A.J. Metselaar, *Drie rechters en één norm: Handhaving van de Europese staatssteunregels voor de Nederlandse rechter en de grenzen van de nationale procedurele autonomie*, 548 (Kluwer 2016).
54. A.J. Metselaar and P.C. Adriaanse, *Nut en noodzaak van het wetsvoorstel terugvordering staatssteun: Verslag van het LEGA Symposium op 19 januari 2011*, 2 Tijdschrift voor Staatssteun 57, 62-63 (2011).
55. The discussion of the 2018 'State aid Recovery Act' is based upon a previous discussion of this Act by the author: *see* J.C.J. Leroy, *Terugvordering van fiscale staatssteun: Een confrontatie tusssen de 'Wet terugvordering staatssteun' en de Belgische Programmawet van 25 december 2016*, 9 Maandblad Belasting Beschouwingen 335-345, (2018).

when an internet consultation on a new proposal was launched.[56] This resulted in July 2017 in a proposal for a 'State aid Recovery Act' (*Wet terugvordering staatssteun*).[57] This proposal was adopted by Parliament on 21 February 2018 and the 'State aid Recovery Act' entered into force on 1 July 2018.[58]

This section focuses on the provisions of the 'State aid Recovery Act' dealing with the recovery of unlawful fiscal State aid. The framework designed for the recovery of non-fiscal State aid is only discussed to the extent necessary to evaluate the procedures provided by and the role of the national judge under the 'State aid Recovery Act'.

[A] Design and Scope of Application of the Procedure

The 'State aid Recovery Act' creates a legal framework for the recovery of both fiscal and non-fiscal State aid. Compared to the 2008 proposal, the legislator changed its mind on the design of the framework. Instead of modifying the existing legislation, the legislator preferred a recovery using - as far as possible - a new, uniform and specific procedure. As such, the legislator wanted to guarantee an efficient recovery, regardless of the legal nature of the State aid. The 'State aid Recovery Act' thus creates an autonomous and separate legal regime for recovery procedures in the Dutch legal order.[59] Unlawful State aid must be recovered through an - in principle - exclusive and mandatory procedure.[60] However, as will be discussed below, an important exception to this exclusivity principle is made for fiscal aid measures.

The 2008 proposal had a broad scope of application, as it covered the recovery of unlawful State aid based upon a decision of the EC, a judgment of the GC/ECJ or an (irrevocable) judgment of a national Court (*see supra* §10.03). Compared to this, the 'State aid Recovery Act' has a restricted scope of application. Article 2 limits its application to recovery procedures ordered by *a decision of the EC*. According to Article 1 this covers a recovery injunction,[61] a recovery decision[62] or a decision based directly

56. Concept voorstel van wet Regels voor de terugvordering van staatssteun (Wet terugvordering staatssteun), (3 June 2016), https://www.internetconsultatie.nl/wetterugvorderingstaatssteun /details (accessed 6 March 2019).
57. Voorstel van wet Regels voor de terugvordering van staatssteun (Wet terugvordering staatssteun) (2017), Kamerstukken II 2016-17, nr. 34 753/2 (Legislative proposal).
58. Wet houdende regels voor de terugvordering van staatssteun (Wet terugvordering staatssteun) (21 februari 2018), Staatsblad 2018 75 ('State aid Recovery Act'); Besluit tot vaststelling van het tijdstip van inwerkingtreding van de wet van 21 februari 2018 houdende regels voor de terugvordering van staatssteun (Wet terugvordering staatssteun), (26 maart 2018), Staatsblad 2018 99.
59. Memorie van Toelichting Regels voor de terugvordering van staatssteun (Wet terugvordering staatssteun), 3 (2017), Kamerstukken II 2016-2017, nr. 34 753/3 (Explanatory Memorandum); Nota naar aanleiding van het verslag Regels voor de terugvordering van staatssteun (Wet terugvordering staatssteun), 5 (2017), Kamerstukken II 2017-2018, nr. 34 753/6 (Note).
60. Memorie van Toelichting Regels voor de terugvordering van staatssteun (Wet terugvordering staatssteun), 2/Art. 2(1) (2017), Kamerstukken II 2016-2017, nr. 34 753/3 (Explanatory Memorandum).
61. Council Regulation (EU) 2015/1589 laying down detailed rules for the application of Article 108 of the Treaty on the Functioning of the European Union, Art. 13(1) (13 July 2015), OJ L 248/9.
62. Council Regulation (EU) 2015/1589 laying down detailed rules for the application of Article 108 of the Treaty on the Functioning of the European Union, Art. 16(1) (13 July 2015), OJ L 248/9.

upon Article 108(3) TFEU that contains a recovery obligation. The Explanatory Memorandum clarifies that the legislator only wanted to create a legal basis and framework for the recovery in cases where the recovery obligation constitutes an 'undeniable fact'.[63] Consequently, the 'State aid Recovery Act' does not apply to a recovery of unlawful State aid ordered by the national judge, when there is no decision of the EC (yet). The impact of this finding for the role of the national judge under the 'State aid Recovery Act' is discussed further on (*see infra* §10.05).

[B] Recovery of Unlawful Fiscal State Aid

[1] Recovery Through Existing Tax Law Instruments ...

The procedure for the recovery of *fiscal* State aid deviates from the general idea of the 'State aid Recovery Act' that unlawful State aid must be recovered through an exclusive and mandatory procedure (*see supra* §10.04[A]). More precisely, for the recovery of fiscal State aid, the legislator chose to modify existing tax legislation instead of creating a new procedure. As such, the 'State aid Recovery Act' refers to the existing instruments contained in the GTA and TCA 1990. The new Article 20a GTA clarifies that unlawful fiscal State aid will be recovered through a supplementary tax assessment (*navorderingsaanslag/naheffingsaanslag*).[64]

The Explanatory Memorandum underpins the choice to recover fiscal State aid through existing tax law instruments. In the first place, the legislator wanted to avoid any doubt - on the international level - regarding the qualification of the amounts recovered as a 'tax' (*see infra* §10.04[B][2]).[65] Secondly, the control of supplementary tax assessments falls under the competence of the tax judge. According to the legislator, the tax judge is particularly suited to verify the quantification of the amounts of unlawful State aid to be recovered. This choice is furthermore in line with the advice of the Council of State on the 2008 proposal (*see supra* §10.03).[66] The use of tax procedures also offers other advantages. It is for instance more convenient to take into account fiscal corrections (e.g., tax deductions) when the aid that must be recovered is quantified. The tax administration can also use its already existing tax collection procedures. Furthermore, the aid beneficiary will receive the same legal protection as 'ordinary' taxpayers (*see infra* §10.04[B][5]).

---

63. Memorie van Toelichting Regels voor de terugvordering van staatssteun (Wet terugvordering staatssteun), 3 (2017), Kamerstukken II 2016-2017, nr. 34 753/3 (Explanatory Memorandum).
64. Also, if the aid beneficiary agrees, Art. 64 GTA allows the tax inspector to aggregate several fiscal years into a single tax assessment: Memorie van Toelichting Regels voor de terugvordering van staatssteun (Wet terugvordering staatssteun), 33 (2017), Kamerstukken II 2016-2017, nr. 34 753/3 (Explanatory Memorandum).
65. Memorie van Toelichting Regels voor de terugvordering van staatssteun (Wet terugvordering staatssteun), 2 (2017), Kamerstukken II 2016-2017, nr. 34 753/3 (Explanatory Memorandum).
66. Memorie van Toelichting Regels voor de terugvordering van staatssteun (Wet terugvordering staatssteun), 2 (2017), Kamerstukken II 2016-2017, nr. 34 753/3 (Explanatory Memorandum). *See also* E.A.G. van der Ouderaa, *Staatssteun en de rol van de Nederlandse belastingrechter*, s. 4.2 (L.J.A. Pieterse and R. Van Scharrenburg, Springende punten (Kluwer 2017)).

[2] ... With Some Modifications

Nevertheless, the 'State aid Recovery Act' modifies the existing tax procedures on certain points, through the addition of new provisions in the GTA and TCA 1990.[67] This is necessary to ensure that the recovery procedure complies with all requirements of the EU framework. As has been pointed out previously, some tensions existed between these EU requirements and the existing tax procedures in the Netherlands (*see supra* §10.02[B][2]).

In the new Articles 20a (1) GTA and 63aa (1) TCA 1990, the amounts to be recovered are explicitly qualified as a 'tax'. This qualification is important in the international context as it allows the aid beneficiary to claim a foreign tax credit for the amounts recovered.[68] As such, the Dutch legislator wanted to prevent double taxation of the amounts recovered. Whether double taxation is effectively avoided depends however on the other country. Namely if the other country recognises the qualification of the sums recovered as a tax in its own legal order.[69]

The 'State aid Recovery Act' furthermore excludes the application of the 'new fact' requirement.[70] As discussed previously, Article 16(1) GTA only allows a supplementary tax assessment of direct taxes when there is a 'new fact' (*see supra* §10.02[B][2]). This requirement is set aside in procedures for the recovery of unlawful fiscal State aid through the new Article 20a(2) GTA.[71] Also, the new Article 63ab(1) TCA 1990 forbids the tax collector to grant a deferment of payment or a (partial) waiver of the sums to be recovered.[72] Through this restriction of the tax collector's discretion, the legislator probably wanted to ensure an immediate and effective recovery.

The new Article 20a(2) GTA also excludes the application of limitation periods for the issuing of supplementary tax assessments.[73] The new Article 63aa(2)(a) TCA 1990

67. Wet houdende regels voor de terugvordering van staatssteun (Wet terugvordering staatssteun), Arts 10 and 11 (21 februari 2018), Staatsblad 2018 75.
68. This was also stressed by the 'Nederlandse Orde van Belastingadviseurs' (Dutch Order of Tax Consultants): Commissie Wetsvoorstellen van de Nederlandse Orde van Belastingadviseurs, *Commentaar op het wetsvoorstel Regels voor de terugvordering van staatssteun (34 753)*, speerpunt 1, https://www.nob.net/system/files/content/article/uploads/nob_commentaar_terugvordering_staatssteun.pdf (accessed 6 Mar. 2019).
69. *See also* A.F. Gunn, *Wet Terugvordering Staatssteun: nieuwe regels per 1 juli 2018*, 4 Tijdschrift voor Formeel Belastingrecht 22, 25 (2018).
70. According to the study of de Waard e.o., there were no obstacles to set aside the requirement of a 'new fact': B.W.N. de Waard, A.J.C. de Moor-van Vugt, A.A.L. Beers, J.C.A. de Poorter and G.J. van Slooten, *Terugvordering van staatssteun: Een rechtsvergelijkend onderzoek*, 43–44 (Ministerie van Justitie 2005).
71. It is clear that Art. 20a(2) GTA refers i.a. to the 'new fact', although it does not explicitly mention this requirement: R. Luja, *Het conceptwetsvoorstel Terugvordering staatssteun: navorderen, naheffen of niets doen?*, 171 Weekblad Fiscaal Recht, s. 2.2 (2016); A.F. Gunn, *Wet Terugvordering Staatssteun: nieuwe regels per 1 juli 2018*, 4 Tijdschrift voor Formeel Belastingrecht 22, 25 (2018).
72. Memorie van Toelichting Regels voor de terugvordering van staatssteun (Wet terugvordering staatssteun), 36 (2017), Kamerstukken II 2016–2017, nr. 34 753/3 (Explanatory Memorandum).
73. Memorie van Toelichting Regels voor de terugvordering van staatssteun (Wet terugvordering staatssteun), 33 (2017), Kamerstukken II 2016–2017, nr. 34 753/3 (Explanatory Memorandum).

does the same for limitation periods applicable to tax collection (*invorderingen*).[74] From the point of view of legal certainty, it is rather remarkable that the 'State aid Recovery Act' sets aside limitation periods applicable in tax procedures. The ECJ made however clear in its case law that EU Member States must set aside national limitation periods who prevent an immediate and effective recovery.[75] As such, through the new Articles 20a(2) GTA and 63aa(2)(a) TCA 1990, the Dutch legislator prevents a conflict between the national limitation periods and the (mostly) longer EU limitation period for the recovery of unlawful State aid. This nevertheless raised some concern of interest groups and in Parliament. The State Secretary of Economic Affairs even had to clarify that the limitation periods of the GTA continue to apply in situations other than the recovery of unlawful fiscal State aid.[76]

The 'State aid Recovery Act' also implicitly sets aside national retention periods for the information on unlawful State aid.[77] Article 4 namely clarifies that during the EU limitation period for the recovery, the aid beneficiary cannot rely upon these (mostly shorter) national retention periods. This applies to both fiscal and non-fiscal State aid.[78] Following Article 52(4) GTA the retention period in tax matters is in principle seven years. It is thus recommended for undertakings to take into account the longer EU limitation period when storing information on (potential) State aid.[79]

A last important modification of the GTA and TCA 1990 relates to the interest payment. As national judges struggled to find a legal basis for the interest payment (*see supra* §10.02[B][1]), this basis is created by the 'State aid Recovery Act' for both fiscal and non-fiscal recovery procedures.[80] For the recovery of fiscal State aid in particular, the new Article 20b GTA and Articles 63aa(2)(b) and 63ab(2) TCA 1990 set aside the normally applicable interests *(belastingrente/invorderingsrente)*. These articles refer instead to Article 16(2) of the Procedural Regulation and Article 9 of Regulation 794/2004. As such, the 'State aid Recovery Act' grants the tax administration the

74. Memorie van Toelichting Regels voor de terugvordering van staatssteun (Wet terugvordering staatssteun), 35-36 (2017), Kamerstukken II 2016-2017, nr. 34 753/3 (Explanatory Memorandum).
75. *See, e.g.* ECJ 20 Mar. 1997, C-24/95, *Land Rheinland-Pfalz/Alcan Deutschland* [1997], ECLI:EU:C:1997:163, para. 38; ECJ 17 Nov. 2011, C-496/09, *Commission/Italy* [2011], ECLI:EU:C:2011:740, para. 78.
76. Nota naar aanleiding van het verslag Regels voor de terugvordering van staatssteun (Wet terugvordering staatssteun), 14 (2017), Kamerstukken II 2017-2018, nr. 34 753/6 (Note); X, *Terugvordering staatssteun: Nota naar aanleiding van het verslag*, 17 Vakstudie Nieuws 4, 20-21 (2018).
77. De Waard e.a. however remarked in their study that the EU Procedural Regulation does not oblige the EU Member States to set aside retention periods, taking into account their procedural autonomy: B.W.N. de Waard, A.J.C. de Moor-van Vugt, A.A.L. Beers, J.C.A. de Poorter and G.J. van Slooten, *Terugvordering van staatssteun: Een rechtsvergelijkend onderzoek*, 46-47 (Ministerie van Justitie 2005).
78. New Art. 20a (3) GTA and new Art. 63aa (2) (b) TCA 1990.
79. Memorie van Toelichting Regels voor de terugvordering van staatssteun (Wet terugvordering staatssteun), 16 and 28 (2017), Kamerstukken II 2016-2017, nr. 34 753/3 (Explanatory Memorandum).
80. Wet houdende regels voor de terugvordering van staatssteun (Wet terugvordering staatssteun), Arts 3(2), 10 and 11 (21 februari 2018), Staatsblad 2018 75.

competence to calculate the interest in accordance with the EU rules and ensures that EU law is respected.

[3] Restoring the Status Quo Ante *and Tax Corrections*

The recovery of unlawful State aid aims at restoring the *status quo ante* on the internal market.[81] The Explanatory Memorandum of the 'State aid Recovery Act' stresses that the aid beneficiary must be put back in the (financial and fiscal) position in which he would have been if he had not received the unlawful aid.[82] The tax inspector must thus perform all necessary actions in order to achieve this restoration of the *status quo ante*. This implies that the tax inspector can correct the effects of the recovery on other taxable years (*fiscale doorwerking*).[83] Examples of such a correction are a revision of loss compensations, or the revival of the right to deduct costs that the aid beneficiary could not (fully) deduct while receiving the unlawful fiscal State aid.[84]

The legislator also paid attention to the effects of the recovery at the international level. Double taxation of the amounts that are recovered must be prevented. The possibility to claim a foreign tax credit has already been discussed (*see supra* §10.04[B][2]). However, this problem also plays the other way around: what if a tax credit is claimed in a recovery procedure in the Netherlands? The Explanatory Memorandum discusses the example of a recovery leading to a higher amount of taxes to be paid in the Netherlands. Consequently, it must be possible to deduct a higher amount of foreign withholding tax from the tax debt in the Netherlands.[85]

[4] Recovery from Indirect Beneficiaries

The legislator made a distinction between fiscal and non-fiscal State aid in the design of the recovery procedure. The first is recovered through existing legislation, while the latter is recovered through a newly created legal regime. However, contrary to what may be thought at first glance, the 'State aid Recovery Act' does not make an absolute distinction between both procedures. This becomes clear in the considerations of the Explanatory Memorandum on the recovery of unlawful fiscal State aid from indirect

81. Settled case law, *see, e.g.* ECJ 14 Sep. 1994, C-278/92, *Spain v. Commission* [1994], ECLI: EU:C:1994:325, para. 75.
82. Memorie van Toelichting Regels voor de terugvordering van staatssteun (Wet terugvordering staatssteun), 33 (2017), Kamerstukken II 2016-2017, nr. 34 753/3 (Explanatory Memorandum).
83. Memorie van Toelichting Regels voor de terugvordering van staatssteun (Wet terugvordering staatssteun), 33 (2017), Kamerstukken II 2016-2017, nr. 34 753/3 (Explanatory Memorandum). Consequently, depending on the facts of the case, these tax corrections can be applied both in a beneficial or in a disadvantageous way for the aid beneficiary: A.F. Gunn, *Wet Terugvordering Staatssteun: nieuwe regels per 1 juli 2018*, 4 Tijdschrift voor Formeel Belastingrecht 22, 24 (2018). This is an important improvement compared to the 2008 proposal (*see supra* §10.03).
84. Memorie van Toelichting Regels voor de terugvordering van staatssteun (Wet terugvordering staatssteun), 33–34 (2017), Kamerstukken II 2016-2017, nr. 34 753/3 (Explanatory Memorandum); A.F. Gunn, *Wet Terugvordering Staatssteun: nieuwe regels per 1 juli 2018*, 4 Tijdschrift voor Formeel Belastingrecht 22, 24 (2018).
85. Memorie van Toelichting Regels voor de terugvordering van staatssteun (Wet terugvordering staatssteun), 34 (2017), Kamerstukken II 2016–2017, nr. 34 753/3 (Explanatory Memorandum).

beneficiaries. It is stated that if the EC orders to recover unlawful fiscal State aid from a third-party beneficiary, but the liability rules of the TCA 1990 do not allow this, the recovery must be executed following the general (non-fiscal) recovery regime.[86]

Let's imagine that the EC decides that the Netherlands granted unlawful fiscal State aid to an undertaking that is part of a large group. In its decision, the EC designates both the undertaking itself and the group as aid beneficiaries.[87] If the tax administration determines that the liability rules of the TCA 1990 do not enable a recovery from the group, it must fall back upon the non-fiscal recovery procedure of the 'State aid Recovery Act'.[88] Through this 'fall-back', the legislator aims to ensure that unlawful fiscal State aid can be recovered from an indirect beneficiary, even if the tax instruments do not allow this. It is however a pity that this 'fall-back' blurs the distinction between the recovery procedures for fiscal and non-fiscal State aid. Beneficiaries of unlawful fiscal State aid can thus still be confronted with a confusing mix of procedures.[89]

[5] Legal Protection of the Aid Beneficiary

To the contrary, the distinction between the fiscal and non-fiscal recovery procedures is clearly present regarding the legal protection of the aid beneficiary. In the non-fiscal recovery procedure, the responsible administrative body issues an order for payment.[90] Article 9(c) of the 'State aid Recovery Act' forsees that this order for payment can be appealed in first (and only) instance at the 'College van Beroep voor het bedrijfsleven (CBb)'. This is the highest Court in the field of economic administrative law in the Netherlands.[91] A separate regime of legal protection is thus provided.[92]

This approach is not followed *in fiscalibus*. In line with the idea to recover fiscal State aid through existing tax instruments, legal protection to the aid beneficiary is also granted through these instruments. The tax administration will issue a supplementary tax assessment in order to execute the recovery (*see supra* §10.04[B][1]). This supplementary tax assessment can be challenged through a complaint, a (higher)

86. Memorie van Toelichting Regels voor de terugvordering van staatssteun (Wet terugvordering staatssteun), 36 (2017), Kamerstukken II 2016–2017, nr. 34 753/3 (Explanatory Memorandum).
87. *See, e.g.* Commission decision on State aid SA.38374 (2014/C ex 2014/NN) implemented by the Netherlands to Starbucks, Art. 2(1–2) (21 Oct. 2015), OJ L 83/38.
88. See the wording 'to the extent possible' *(voor zover mogelijk)* in Wet houdende regels voor de terugvordering van staatssteun (Wet terugvordering staatssteun), Art. 2(2) (21 februari 2018), Staatsblad 2018 75. *See also* Memorie van Toelichting Regels voor de terugvordering van staatssteun (Wet terugvordering staatssteun), 23 (2017), Kamerstukken II 2016–2017, nr. 34 753/3 (Explanatory Memorandum).
89. R. Luja, *Het wetsvoorstel Terugvordering staatssteun: het wordt navorderen en naheffen*, 160 Weekblad Fiscaal Recht, s. 2 (2017).
90. Wet houdende regels voor de terugvordering van staatssteun (Wet terugvordering staatssteun), Art. 3(1) (21 februari 2018), Staatsblad 2018 75.
91. De Rechtspraak, *College van Beroep voor het bedrijfsleven*, https://www.rechtspraak.nl/Organisatie-en-contact/Organisatie/College-van-Beroep-voor-het-bedrijfsleven (accessed 6 Mar. 2019).
92. Memorie van Toelichting Regels voor de terugvordering van staatssteun (Wet terugvordering staatssteun), 32 (2017), Kamerstukken II 2016–2017, nr. 34 753/3 (Explanatory Memorandum).

appeal and an appeal in cassation.[93] As the amounts to be recovered are qualified as a tax (*see supra* §10.04[B][2]), it seems correct to grant the aid beneficiary the same legal protection as 'ordinary taxpayers'. Furthermore, taking into account the limited number of fiscal recovery procedures, it is probably little meaningful to create specific legal remedies for these procedures.

[6] Refund after Recovery

The obligation to recover unlawful (fiscal) State aid elapses when the negative decision of the EC is annulled by the EU judge.[94] In this case, the Netherlands must thus repay to the 'aid beneficiaries' the amounts of 'aid' that it previously recovered. The 'State aid Recovery Act' does not contain any provision on this 'refund after recovery' (or 'reversed recovery'). This is an important shortage. Following Dutch administrative law, the annulment of the EC's decision does not directly affect the legal force of the national administrative decisions taken in the recovery process.[95] The legislator is thus not entirely correct when he claims that national law already contains sufficient possibilities for an (ex officio) refund or a refund based upon the principle of undue payment in case a 'refund after recovery' is required.[96]

The same applies to the recovery of unlawful fiscal State aid. The legal force of the supplementary tax assessments issued during the recovery process is not affected by the annulment of the EC's decision. Through the 'State aid Recovery Act', the tax collector or inspector is merely granted the competence to repay the previously collected sums.[97] Luja points out that the GTA had to be further modified, in order to also oblige the tax collector or inspector to revise (ex officio or upon request) the supplementary tax assessments once it is clear that the EC will not take a new decision

93. Memorie van Toelichting Regels voor de terugvordering van staatssteun (Wet terugvordering staatssteun), 19 (2017), Kamerstukken II 2016–2017, nr. 34 753/3 (Explanatory Memorandum). This passage in the Explanatory Memorandum possibly follows-up the request of the 'Dutch Order of Tax Advisors' to clarify the applicable appeal procedures against the supplementary tax assessment: Commissie Wetsvoorstellen van de Nederlandse Orde van Belastingadviseurs, *Commentaar op de internetconsultatie Regels voor de terugvordering van staatssteun (Wet terugvordering staatssteun)*, nr. 3.2, https://www.nob.net/sites/default/files/content/article/uploads/nob_commentaar_internetconsultatie_terugvordering_staatssteun.pdf (accessed 6 Mar. 2019).
94. Art. 264 TFEU. This Chapter does not discuss which steps the EC can or must take after the annulment of a negative decision (Art. 266(1) TFEU).
95. R. Luja, *Reactie op internetconsultatie wetsvoorstel Terugvordering staatssteun*, https://www.internetconsultatie.nl/wetterugvorderingstaatssteun/reactie/d9512d6d-f124-4a7e-bf790b259f7a175a (accessed 20 Mar. 2019).
96. Memorie van Toelichting Regels voor de terugvordering van staatssteun (Wet terugvordering staatssteun), 11 (2017), Kamerstukken II 2016–2017, nr. 34 753/3 (Explanatory Memorandum).
97. Memorie van Toelichting Regels voor de terugvordering van staatssteun (Wet terugvordering staatssteun), 11 (2017), Kamerstukken II 2016–2017, nr. 34 753/3 (Explanatory Memorandum). In order to grant this competence, the 'State aid Recovery Act' supplements the 'Decision on Fiscal Administrative Law' (*Besluit Fiscaal Bestuursrecht*).

in which it obliges the Netherlands to recover the 'State aid'.[98] Furthermore, the 'State aid Recovery Act' does not arrange the modalities of the refund, such as the delay for the refund and the eventual interest rate. Is the tax administration obliged to add an interest on the sums that it refunds, running from the period of the recovery until the refund? Would the refund be governed by the general rules for ex officio reductions or restitutions of taxes? Finally, the 'State aid Recovery Act' could have created an obligation for the tax administration to put the amounts recovered on a blocked bank account, while an appeal against the EC's negative decision is pending before the EU judge.[99]

§10.05 A BRIGHT FUTURE? AN EVALUATION OF THE 2018 'STATE AID RECOVERY ACT'

[A] General Remarks

National procedures for the recovery of unlawful (fiscal) State aid can be designed in several ways (*see supra* §10.03). With the 'State aid Recovery Act', the Dutch legislator chose to create a general and exclusively applicable procedure for the recovery of non-fiscal State aid. For fiscal State aid, the choice was made to stick to the already existing tax procedures and modify these where necessary.

The 'State aid Recovery Act' can grant legal certainty to aid beneficiaries, as they know upfront - to a large extent - the procedure that will be applied to recover the unlawful State aid they received. Nonetheless, the procedures must be suitable to ensure an immediate and effective recovery in a large variety of cases. There is namely little point in creating general recovery procedures if these procedures still have to be substantially adapted to the needs of a specific recovery case. The concrete application of the procedures created by the 'State aid Recovery Act' must prove if this is actually the case. This prerequisite is however not easy to fulfil as the interpretation of Article 107 TFEU is continuously evolving and widening. This is especially the case for the fiscal sphere.

98. R. Luja, *Reactie op internetconsultatie wetsvoorstel Terugvordering staatssteun*, Art. 3, https://www.internetconsultatie.nl/wetterugvorderingstaatssteun/reactie/d9512d6d-f124-4a7e-bf790b259f7a175a (accessed 20 Mar. 2019); R. Luja, *Het conceptwetsvoorstel Terugvordering staatssteun: navorderen, naheffen of niets doen?*, 171 Weekblad Fiscaal Recht, s. 3.1 (2016); R. Luja, *Het wetsvoorstel Terugvordering staatssteun: het wordt navorderen en naheffen*, 160 Weekblad Fiscaal Recht, s. 3 (2017).

99. Commissie Wetsvoorstellen van de Nederlandse Orde van Belastingadviseurs, *Commentaar op het wetsvoorstel Regels voor de terugvordering van staatssteun (34 753)*, speerpunt 2, https://www.nob.net/system/files/content/article/uploads/nob_commentaar_terugvordering_staatssteun.pdf (accessed 6 Mar. 2019). The EC also acknowledges the advantages of using a blocked bank account: Notice from the Commission Towards an effective implementation of Commission decisions ordering Member States to recover unlawful and incompatible State aid, nr. 70 (2007), OJ C 272/4; Communication from the Commission - Draft Commission Notice on the recovery of unlawful and incompatible State aid, nr. 115–117 (2019).

The number of (fiscal) recovery procedures is currently rather limited.[100] It cannot be ruled out, however, that these numbers will rise in the future. There can be an increase in the number of negative decisions in which the EC orders the recovery of unlawful State aid. The 'State aid Recovery Act' can also lead to an increased awareness of national judges on State aid issues, possibly leading to a stricter control of Article 108(3) TFEU and a rise in the number of recoveries ordered.

The 'State aid Recovery Act' seems thus to be a step in the right direction. The legislator provides solutions to the struggles of national judges in proceedings dealing with the recovery of unlawful (fiscal) State aid. At the moment of writing, one recovery procedure that involves the Netherlands is pending in the EC's files: the notorious *Starbucks* case.[101] However, the recovery in *Starbucks* took place before the entry into force of the 'State aid Recovery Act'. It remains therefore to be seen in practice if the 'State aid Recovery Act' will turn out to ensure an immediate and effective recovery of (fiscal) State aid.

[B] The Role of the National Judge

[1] The 'State Aid Recovery Act' in Court Proceedings

Although the 'State aid Recovery Act' is not directly applicable to a recovery of unlawful State aid ordered by the national judge, reference is made – either by the judge, or by one of the parties – to this legislation in a handful of judgments. Taking into account the fact that the 'State aid Recovery Act' entered into force on 1 July 2018, the number of judgments that can be discussed in this Chapter is very restricted.[102]

The Court of 's-Hertogenbosch for instance considered that the 'State aid Recovery Act', due to Article 7 (*see infra* §10.05[B][2]), can also be relevant for cases in which the EC did not (yet) issue a negative decision. As the parties did not yet pay attention to the possible relevance of the 'State aid Recovery Act' for their case, the Court would give them the chance – if necessary – to do this at a later stage in the proceedings.[103] The Court was thus well aware of its role to supervise Article 108(3) TFEU, and of the possible impact of the new legislation on the case pending before him.

In the proceedings before the CBb on the production rights of phosphates for farmers, the Minister of Agriculture relied upon the 'State aid Recovery Act' in its

100. Statistics of the EC show that it adopted 10 recovery decisions involving the Netherlands since 1999: European Commission, *Information on recovery of unlawful aid*, http://ec.europa.eu/competition/state_aid/studies_reports/recovery.html (Excel sheet) (accessed 6 Mar. 2019).
101. European Commission, *Information on recovery of unlawful aid*, http://ec.europa.eu/competition/state_aid/studies_reports/recovery.html (Excel sheet) (accessed 6 Mar. 2019); Commission decision on State aid SA.38374 (2014/C ex 2014/NN) implemented by the Netherlands to Starbucks, (21 Oct. 2015), OJ L 83/38. See for a discussion of the *Starbucks* case: e.g., J. Leroy, *Tax rulings in evolutie: staatssteun en transparantie*, 1 Algemeen Fiscaal Tijdschrift 5, 17–18 (2019).
102. The discussion in this Chapter is restricted to case law that has been published until April 2019.
103. Appeal Court 's-Hertogenbosch 18 Dec. 2018, nr. 200.203.683_01, [2018], ECLI:NL:GHSHE:2018:5278, para. 3.4.8.

defence. According to the Minister, the competence to grant the production rights also implies the competence to revise them. The Minister reinforces this claim through stating that Article 7(1) 'State aid Recovery Act' even obliges him to revise the rights, as these have been granted in violation of Article 108(3) TFEU.[104] However, as will be discussed below, Article 7(1) only plays when it is 'clear' that unlawful State aid was granted. Article 7(1) 'State aid Recovery Act' should not be used as an 'escape route' for administrative bodies that want to revise their decisions, but do not find a suitable legal basis for these revisions. This would undermine the principles of legality and legal certainty, and violate the *rationale* of the EU State aid rules. Unfortunately, the CBb did not comment on the argument raised by the Minister, as it rejected the requested provisional measures.

[2] The Limited Scope of Application of the 'State Aid Recovery Act'

The scope of application of the 'State aid Recovery Act' is limited to the recovery of unlawful State aid ordered by a decision of the EC (*see supra* §10.04[A]). The legislator wanted however to prevent that, in case no decision of the EC is available, hurdles in the recovery of unlawful (fiscal) State aid would continue to exist. Two situations must be distinguished. On the one hand, there can be a problem if an administrative body finds out that its decision grants unlawful State aid and it wants to revise this decision. This was e.g., the case in *Zorg en Zekerheid* (*see supra* §10.02[B][1]). On the other hand, a national judge can order the recovery of unlawful State aid.[105]

The legislator addressed the first situation through Article 7 'State aid Recovery Act'. When there there is no decision of the EC (yet), Article 7(1) grants the competence and even obliges[106] the administrative body to revise its decision that violates Article 108(3) TFEU. Following Article 7(3), this applies to both fiscal State aid and State aid granted through administrative law.[107] Fiscal State aid can be recovered through the fiscal recovery procedure provided by the 'State aid Recovery Act'.[108] Article 7(2) also

104. CBb 12 Nov. 2018, nrs. 18/2172-2132-2108-1998, [2018], ECLI:NL:CBB:2018:589-592, para. 3.3.
105. Nota naar aanleiding van het verslag Regels voor de terugvordering van staatssteun (Wet terugvordering staatssteun), 10 (2017), Kamerstukken II 2017–2018, nr. 34 753/6 (Note).
106. The Explanatory Memorandum clarifies that the administrative body is obliged to use this competence: Memorie van Toelichting Regels voor de terugvordering van staatssteun (Wet terugvordering staatssteun), 31 (2017), Kamerstukken II 2016–2017, nr. 34 753/3.
107. Memorie van Toelichting Regels voor de terugvordering van staatssteun (Wet terugvordering staatssteun), 31 (2017), Kamerstukken II 2016–2017, nr. 34 753/3 (Explanatory Memorandum). The tax assessment must in this case be seen as the administrative decision: X, *Terugvordering staatssteun: Nota naar aanleiding van het verslag*, 17 Vakstudie Nieuws 4, 17 (2018).
108. Wet houdende regels voor de terugvordering van staatssteun (Wet terugvordering staatssteun), Art. 7(3) (21 februari 2018), Staatsblad 2018 75; Memorie van Toelichting Regels voor de terugvordering van staatssteun (Wet terugvordering staatssteun), 31 (2017), Kamerstukken II 2016-2017, nr. 34 753/3 (Explanatory Memorandum).

creates a legal basis for the interest payment when a recovery based upon Article 7(1) takes place.[109]

Although Article 7 'State aid Recovery Act' can grant legal certainty in situations like *Zorg en Zekerheid*,[110] this provision contains some pitfalls. In the first place, Article 7(1) does not apply to unlawful State aid granted through civil law.[111] Secondly, no solution is provided when the unlawful State aid also indirectly benefits certain undertakings that are not covered by the decision of the administrative body.[112] Furthermore, Metselaar points out that interested parties will argue before the administrative body that its decision violates Article 108(3) TFEU and request it to use its competence under Article 7. This can seriously affect the legal certainty of the beneficiaries of these - alleged - unlawful State aid decisions.[113] However, the obligation to revise the decision only applies when it is 'clear' that unlawful State aid was granted. The Explanatory Memorandum clarifies that this is on the one hand the case if the EC made clear in an advice that a decision granted unlawful State aid. On the other hand, EU or national case law can trigger the application of Article 7(1).[114] It remains nevertheless to be seen how flexible the administrative bodies will be in their interpretation of their requirement of clarity.

The legislator did not address the second situation, namely when a recovery of unlawful State aid is ordered by the national judge (and there is no decision of the EC in the meaning of Article 1 'State aid Recovery Act'). As has been said, this situation falls outside the scope of application of the 'State aid Recovery Act' (*see supra* §10.04[A]). In response to questions raised by members of Parliament, the State Secretary of Economic Affairs clarified that there are no problems in the enforcement and execution of judgments which order the recovery of unlawful State aid.[115] According to the State Secretary, the recovery constitutes an 'enforceable fact' in this case, using as its legal basis the principle that what is unduly paid can be recovered.[116] Consequently, no framework for these recovery procedures had to be created. It is

109. *See also* Memorie van Toelichting Regels voor de terugvordering van staatssteun (Wet terugvordering staatssteun), 12 (2017), Kamerstukken II 2016–2017, nr. 34 753/3 (Explanatory Memorandum).
110. A.J. Metselaar, *Een vogel in de hand: nieuwe regels voor de terugvordering van staatssteun*, 3–4 Tijdschrift voor Staatssteun 110, 116 (2016).
111. A.J. Metselaar, *Een vogel in de hand: nieuwe regels voor de terugvordering van staatssteun*, 3–4 Tijdschrift voor Staatssteun 110, 116 (2016). Art. 7(4) only grants a legal basis for the interest payment when State aid granted through an agreement is annulled due to a violation of Art. 108(3) TFEU: Memorie van Toelichting Regels voor de terugvordering van staatssteun (Wet terugvordering staatssteun), 31 (2017), Kamerstukken II 2016–2017, nr. 34 753/3 (Explanatory Memorandum).
112. A.J. Metselaar, *Een vogel in de hand: nieuwe regels voor de terugvordering van staatssteun*, 3–4 Tijdschrift voor Staatssteun 110, 116 (2016).
113. A.J. Metselaar, *Een vogel in de hand: nieuwe regels voor de terugvordering van staatssteun*, 3–4 Tijdschrift voor Staatssteun 110, 116–117 (2016).
114. Memorie van Toelichting Regels voor de terugvordering van staatssteun (Wet terugvordering staatssteun), 31 (2017), Kamerstukken II 2016–2017, nr. 34 753/3 (Explanatory Memorandum).
115. Nota naar aanleiding van het verslag Regels voor de terugvordering van staatssteun (Wet terugvordering staatssteun), 10 (2017), Kamerstukken II 2017–2018, nr. 34 753/6 (Note).
116. Nota naar aanleiding van het verslag Regels voor de terugvordering van staatssteun (Wet terugvordering staatssteun), 11 (2017), Kamerstukken II 2017–2018, nr. 34 753/6 (Note).

notable that the State Secretary asserts that the principle of undue payment serves as a legal basis for the execution of a recovery ordered by the national judge. This is in fact a return to the case law in *BPM*, *Fleuren Compost* and *Zorg en Zekerheid* (*see supra* §10.02[B][1]). Furthermore, the State Secretary does not distinguish between the recovery of fiscal and non-fiscal State aid. A civil law concept, the principle of undue payment, must thus be used as a legal basis for the recovery of fiscal State aid.

The procedure that must be followed for the execution of a recovery of unlawful fiscal State aid ordered by the national judge in this case is also not clear. Is a procedure in accordance with civil law applicable, since the principle of undue payment must – apparently – be relied upon? Or must the idea proclaimed by the 'State aid Recovery Act' that the recovery of fiscal and non-fiscal State aid requires a different approach also be followed in this situation? Meaning that the unlawful fiscal State aid must be recovered through a fiscal procedure? Will the instruments provided by the GTA and TCA 1990 be used, although without taking into account the modifications introduced by the 'State aid Recovery Act'? In any case, due to the primacy of EU law, provisions of the GTA and TCA 1990 who hinder an immediate and effective recovery must be set aside. Nonetheless these questions show that the legislator should have given more attention to the role of the national judge in the supervision of Article 108(3) TFEU.[117] The national judge did not receive any new tools to execute its task, and a lot of ambiguities surround the execution of a recovery ordered by the national judge.

117. *See also* – although cautious – A.J. Metselaar, *Drie rechters en één norm: Handhaving van de Europese staatssteunregels voor de Nederlandse rechter en de grenzen van de nationale procedurele autonomie*, 548 (Kluwer 2016).

CHAPTER 11

Conclusions: Legitimacy and Effectiveness of Fiscal State Aid Control – Some Reflections on New Perspectives on Fiscal State Aid

Carla De Pietro

National (tax) judges have a fundamental role within the framework of (fiscal) State aid control as they are requested to protect the rights of individuals in case of unlawful (fiscal) State aid, regardless of the existence of a decision of the European Commission. In fact, the Commission cannot adopt a decision ordering recovery exclusively on the basis of the unlawfulness of the national measure, but it must conclude the assessment and evaluate the possible compatibility/incompatibility.[1,2] In practice, therefore, national (tax) judges are also requested to indirectly evaluate the existence of (fiscal) State aid under Article 107(1) of the Treaty on the Functioning of the European Union (TFEU). Furthermore, national (tax) judges have competence within the framework of the recovery of (fiscal) State aid that has been ordered by the Commission.

It is clear that an effective exercise of these multifaceted powers necessarily presupposes a certain level of autonomy for national (tax) judges. However, as shown throughout the development of the entire book, the role of national (tax) judges is characterized by many uncertainties and a profound interference of the Court of Justice, which has – in fact – made national (tax) judges substantially dependent on its preliminary rulings. As emphasised by Advocate General Cosmas in the context of

1. *See*, European Commission, Commission Notice on the Enforcement of State Aid Law by National Courts, (2009/C 85/01), 2009, para. 25.
2. The powers of the Commission to issue preliminary recovery injunctions are very limited. *See*, Art. 13(2) of the Procedural Regulation (Council Regulation (EU) 2015/1589 of 13 July 2015 laying down detailed rules for the application of Article 108 of the Treaty on the Functioning of the European Union).

legitimate expectations, 'precisely because of the particular nature of State aid and the need to safeguard the imperative Community interest in rectifying the conditions of competition, the Court has the tendency to restrict the legal autonomy of the national legal orders, by laying down itself the substantive requirements for recognizing that legitimate expectations are entertained'.[3]

This passage is particularly significant also because it highlights that the powers of national judges have been shaped in light of a certain conception of Internal Market almost exclusively aimed at protecting economic factors. In general, the development of the book has made it clear that – within the field of State aid law – the principle of procedural autonomy has been strongly undermined.

The result is a very EU-centralized system of State aid control, characterized by a rather uncertain role of national (tax) judges and in which – as shown in Chapter 6 – the protection of individuals' rights like legitimate expectations is subordinated to the protection of economic factors.

To what extent can this outcome be considered legitimate? This question has become central in the reasoning underlying the development of the book.

Chapter 2 has grounded the foundations of the legitimacy problems of (fiscal) State aid control in the absence of a normative agreement about the goals and functions of (fiscal) State aid control. Thus, from a combined legal and political science approach, it follows that there are competing visions about the objectives that this part of EU law should be establishing. This uncertainty is reflected in the difficulties with the interpretation of Article 107(1) TFEU.

In more practical terms, as shown in Chapter 3, the problem appears clear in the case law of the Court of Justice, in which many uncertainties, mainly concerning the identification of selectivity, substantially affect the interpretation of the notion of State aid.

These uncertainties characterizing the case law of the Court of Justice are – indeed – at the origin of the debate affecting the most recent decisions of the European Commission concerning tax rulings and in which the notion of selectivity is identified with a principle of equality on the basis of a very broad reference system including the entire national corporate income tax system.

How to identify the criteria that define the legitimacy of (fiscal) State aid control and, therefore, justify certain interpretative choices? The development of this book has shown the need of answering this question by combining the notions of legitimacy and effectiveness. Indeed, the synthesis between these two concepts is represented by a certain conception of Internal Market. In other words, the adoption of a certain approach in terms of legitimacy justifies a certain interpretation of the notion of (fiscal) State aid. By guaranteeing certainty on the interpretation of this notion, legitimacy guarantees the effectiveness of (fiscal) State aid control. Consequently, legitimacy and effectiveness eventually shape the Internal Market. Therefore, it is the most desirable conception of Internal Market that should represent the matrix for legitimacy and, consequently, for effectiveness.

3. Opinion of Advocate General Cosmas, delivered on 23 November 1999 in case C-83/98 P, *France v. Ladbroke Racing and Commission*, para. 58.

The question is, therefore, what kind of Internal Market we want in the European Union. In the light of the significantly social and political crisis that is affecting the EU, according to this author, a renewed approach to the conception of Internal Market based on the strengthening of non-market values has become necessary. Thus, according to this author, a better balance between the protection of competition and the protection of non-market values within the Internal Market is required. More specifically, this renewed balance would probably be reached at best by further integrating non-market values within the Internal Market through the justifications to the prima facie selectivity of national measures. In this case, the integration of non-market values would be determined at the EU level, by granting solutions common to the different EU Member States. Indeed, in this case the identification of the justifications to selective measures could not be left to the Court of Justice, which has no political competence.

These conclusions significantly affect the role of national (tax) judges. More in particular, as it is clear from the above, guaranteeing certainty on the legitimacy of (fiscal) State aid control will lead (mainly through the case law of the Court of Justice) to clarify the scope of (fiscal) State aid law and, in particular, of Article 107(1) TFEU. This clarification will, in turn, guarantee more autonomy to national (tax) judges and, therefore, a more effective State aid control at national level.

Bibliography

Adams, C. and R. Coombes. *Global Transfer Pricing: Principles and Practice*, LexisNexis, 2003.

Adriaanse, P. Appropriate Measures to Remedy the Consequences of Unlawful State Aid, 2 REALaw 73, 80 (2009).

Adriaanse, P. Terugvordering van onrechtmatige staatssteun: Knelpunten en oplossingen in het Nederlandse recht, in *Europees recht effectueren: algemeen bestuursrecht als instrument voor de effectieve uitvoering van EG-recht*, edited by T. Barkhuysen, W. den Ouden & E. Steyger, Kluwer 2007, 212-213.

Adriaanse, P.C. and W. den Ouden. *Effectuering van staatssteunrecht in Nederland: Een bestuursrechtelijke blik op de uitvoeringspraktijk en het wetsvoorstel terugvordering staatssteun*, 40 Nederlands Tijdschrift voor Bestuursrecht, sec. 4-5 (2008)

Aldestam, M. *EC State Aid Rules Applied to Taxes: An Analysis of the Selectivity Criterion*, Iustus Förlag, Uppsala, 2005.

Ashenden, S. Legality, Legitimacy, and the Circumstances of Sociology, in *Legality and Legitimacy: Normative and Sociological Approaches*, edited by C. Thornhill and S. Ashenden, Nomos, Baden-Baden, 2010.

Augenstein, D. and M. Dawson, What Law for What Polity? 'Integration Through Law' in the European Union Revisited, in *Integration Through Law' Revisited: The Making of the European Polity*, edited by D. Augenstein, Ashgate, Farnham, 2012, p. 1.

Bacon, K. State Aids and General Measures, 17(1) Yearbook of European Law 270-271 (1997).

Beetham, D. *The Legitimation of Power*, 2nd ed., Palgrave Macmillan, Basingstoke, 2013, p. 4.

Biondi, A. and E. Righini. An Evolutionary Theory of State Aid Control, in *The Oxford Handbook of European Union Law*, edited by A. Arnull and D. Chalmers, Oxford University Press, Oxford, 2015, pp. 670-690.

Biondi, A. *The Rationale of State Aid Control: A Return to Orthodoxy*, Cambridge Yearbook of European Legal Studies, volume 12, 2010, p. 42.

Birnstiel, A. 'Recovery of Unlawful State Aid: The Role of Member State Courts in State Aid Recovery Scenarios' 3 European State Aid Law Quarterly 645-650 (2012).

Blauberger, M. State Aid Control from a Political Science Perspective, in *Research Handbook on European State Aid Law*, edited by E. Szyszczak, Edward Elgar Publishing Limited, Cheltenham, 2011, pp. 28, 33.

Bonnici, M. The European Commission's Arm's Length Standard: Relationship and Compatibility with the Arm's Length Principle under Transfer Pricing, ITPJ 2019, published online on 29 November 2018.

Brandtner, B., T. Beranger and C. Lessenich. Private State Aid Enforcement, 1 European State Aid Law Quarterly 23, 25 (2010).

Buendia Sierra, J.L. and B. Smulders. The Limited Role of the 'Refined Economic Approach' in Achieving the Objectives of State Aid Control: Time for Some Realism, in *Liber Amicorum Francisco Santaolalla Gadea, EC State Aid Law*, Kluwer Law International, Alpen aan den Rijn, 2008, p. 9.

Buendia Sierra, J.L. and M.A. Bolsa Ferruz, State Aid Assessment: What National Courts Can Do and What They Must Do, 3 European State Aid Law Quarterly 408-417 (2017).

Burley, A.-M. and W. Mattli. Europe Before the Court: A Political Theory of Legal Integration, 47(1) International Organization 44.

Burton, M. and K. Sadiq, *Tax Expenditure Management: A Critical Assessment*, Cambridge University Press, Cambridge, 2013, p. 150.

Cheynel, B. and A. Giraud. New Paradigm for Recovery of Unlawful Aid in the EU – National Judges and the 'Exception of Compatibility', 31 World Competition 557, 564 at 559 (2008).

Christensen, R. The Rise of the EU in International Tax Policy, in *Global Networks and European Actors: Navigating and Managing Complexity*, edited by G. Christou and J. Hasselbalch, Routledge, 2019, forthcoming.

Collier, R.S. and J.L. Andrus, Transfer Pricing and the Arm's Length Principle after BEPS, Oxford University Press, Oxford, 2017.

Kyriazis, D. From Soft Law to Soft Law Through Hard Law: The Commission's Approach to the State Aid Assessment of Tax Rulings, 15(3) European State Aid Law Quarterly 436 (2016).

da Cruz Vilaça, J. Material and Geographic Selectivity in State Aid – Recent Developments, 4(4) European State Aid Law Quarterly 443-451 (2009).

Dagan, T. *International Tax Policy: Between Competition and Cooperation*, Cambridge University Press, Cambridge, 2018.

De Broe, L. The State Aid Selectivity-Test in Corporate Tax Matters: CJEU Applies Common Sense in Its Judgments on the German 'Sanierungs'-clause, but Do We Have All Pieces of the Puzzle Now?, 6 EC Tax Review (2018).

De Brue, L. Editorial XL. Can Tax Treaties Confer State Aid?, EC Tax Review 232 (2017).

De Cecco, F. State Aid and the European Economic Constitution, Hart Publishing, Oxford and Portland, 2013, pp. 31-55.

De Vos, A. 'De Rol van het Europese en het Belgische vertrouwensbeginsel bij terugvordering van Europese subsidies en staatssteun' (2012-2013). Rechtskundig Weekblad 4, 122-135.

de Waard, B.W.N., A.J.C. de Moor-van Vugt, A.A.L. Beers, J.C.A. de Poorter and G.J. van Slooten. Terugvordering van staatssteun: Een rechtsvergelijkend onderzoek (Ministerie van Justitie 2005).

Dellmuth, L., J. Scholte and J. Tallberg. Institutional Sources of Legitimacy for International Organisations: Beyond Procedure Versus Performance, Review of International Studies (2019), pp. 1-20, doi:10.1017/S026021051900007X.

Derenne, J. The Powers and Obligations of National Courts with Regard to State Aid Control: Lessons Learned from CELF I and CELF II, *Milestones in State Aid Case Law: European State Aid Law Quarterly's First 15 Years in Perspective*, edited by C. Buts & J.L. Buendía Sierra, Lexxion Publisher, 2017, 343.

Doleys, T. Managing the Dilemma of Discretion: The European Commission and the Development of EU State Aid Policy, 13(1) Journal of Industry, Competition and Trade 23-38 (2013).

Douma, S.C.W. Staatssteunpraatjes vullen geen gaatjes!, NTFR 2018/2105

Ecker-Ehrhardt, M. Self-Legitimation in the Face of Politicization: Why International Organizations Centralized Public Communication, 13(4) The Review of International Organizations 519-546 (2018).

Engelen, F. and A. Gunn. State Aid: Towards a Theoretical Assessment Framework, in *State Aid and Tax Law*, edited by C. Micheau and A. Rust, Wolters Kluwer, Alphen aan den Rijn, 2013, pp. 140-141.

Fantozzi, A. The Applicability of State Aid Rules to Tax Competition Measures: A Process of 'De Facto' Harmonization in the Tax Field?, in *Tax Competition in Europe*, edited by W. Schön, IBFD Publications BV, Amsterdam, 2003, pp. 121, 131.

Fink, E. The Possibility of Protection of Legitimate Expectations in Recovery of Unlawful State Aid, 20 Juridica Intrenational 133, (2013);

Forrester, E. Is the State Aid Regime a Suitable Instrument to Be Used in the Fight Against Harmful Tax Competition?, 27(1) EC Tax Review 30-31 (2018).

Genschel, P. One Trap, Many Exits, but No Free Lunch: How the Joint-Decision Trap Shapes EU Tax Policy, in *The EU's Decision Traps: Comparing Policies*, edited by G. Falkner, Oxford University Press, Oxford, 2011, pp. 54-72.

Giraud, A. & S. Petit. Tax Rulings and State Aid Qualification: Should Reality Matter?, European State Aid Law Quarterly 233 (2/2017).

Giraud, A. A Study of the Notion of Legitimate Expectations in State Aid Recovery Proceedings: 'Abandon All Hope, Ye Who Enter Here'?, 45 CML Rev. 1405-1406 (2008).

Gormsen, L.L. *European State Aid and Tax Rulings*, Edward Elgar Publishing, 2019, pp. 32 et seq.

Goudswaard, K. and H. Vording., De analyse van belastinguitgaven, in *Gielebundel*, edited by C. van Raad and G. Frank, Kluwer, Deventer, 1990, p. 232.

Gronau, J. and H. Schmidtke. The Quest for Legitimacy in World Politics – International Institutions' Legitimation Strategies, 42(3) Review of International Studies 535-557 (2016)

Guerrero, V.H. Defining the Balance Between Free Competition and Tax Sovereignty in EC and WTO Law: The 'Due Respect' to the General Tax System, 5(1) German Law Journal 95 (2004).

Gunn, A.F. *Wet Terugvordering Staatssteun: nieuwe regels per 1 juli 2018*, 4 Tijdschrift voor Formeel Belastingrecht 22, 25 (2018).

Habermas, J. *Between Facts and Norms: Contributions to a Discourse Theory of Law and Democracy*, Polity Press, 1997, p. 56 (translation of Faktizität und Geltung. Beiträge zur Diskurstheorie des Rechts und des demokratischen Rechtsstaats, Suhrkamp Verlag, Frankfurt, 1992; translated by William Rehg).

Habermas, J. *The Lure of Technocracy*, Polity Press, Cambridge, 2015.

Hancher, L. State Aid Recovery: A New Public Order?, 1 European State Aid Law Quarterly 1-4 (2013).

Hofmann, H. State Aid Review in a Multi-level System: Motivations for Aid, Why Control It, and the Evolution of State Aid Law in the EU, in *State Aid Law of the European Union*, edited by H. Hofmann and C. Micheau, Oxford University Press, Oxford, 2016, pp. 3-11.

Ismer, R. and S. Piotrowski. The Selectivity of Tax Measures: A Tale of Two Consistencies, 43(10) Intertax 559-570 (2015).

Jaeger, T. Tax Incentives under State Aid Law: A Competition Law Perspective, in *State Aid Law and Business Taxation*, edited by I. Richelle, W. Schön and E. Traversa, Springer, 2016, p. 51.

Jaeger, T. The CELF-Judgement: A Precarious Conception of the Standstill Obligation (in SIDE v. CELF Case Law and Notes), 2 European State Aid Law Quarterly 259, 285-286 (2008).

Jaros, K. and N. Ritter, Pleading Legitimate Expectations in the Procedure for the Recovery of State Aid, 4 European State Aid Law Quarterly 573 (2004).

Jestaedt, T., J. Derenne and T. Ottervanger. *Study on the Enforcement of State Aid Law at National Level*, European Communities, 2006.

Jouve, D. Recovering Unlawful and Incompatible Aids by National Courts: CELF and Scott/Kimberly Clark Cases, 3 European State Aid Law Quarterly 367, 370 (2017)

Kleiner, T. Modernization of State Aid Policy, in *Research Handbook on European State Aid Law*, edited by E. Szyszczak, Edward Elgar Publishing Limited, Cheltenham, 2011.

Kokott, J. *Das Steuerrecht der Europäischen Union*, C.H. Beck, 2018, § 2 para. 196.

Lang, M. Selectivity as a Criterion to Determine Whether a Tax Measure Constitutes State Aid, in *Legal Remedies in European Tax Law*, edited by P. Pistone 270, IBFD Publications, Amsterdam, 2009.

Lang, M. State Aid and Taxation: Selectivity and Comparability Analysis, in *State Aid Law and Business Taxation*, edited by I. Richelle, W. Schön and E. Traversa, Springer, Berlin and Heidelberg, 2016, p. 36.

Leroy, J. Tax Rulings in Evolutie: Staatssteun en Transparantie, 1 Algemeen Fiscaal Tijdschrift 5, 17-18 (2019).

Leroy, J.C.J. Terugvordering van fiscale staatssteun: Een confrontatie tusssen de 'Wet terugvordering staatssteun' en de Belgische Programmawet van 25 december 2016, 9 Maandblad Belasting Beschouwingen 335-345 (2018).

López López, H. General Though on Selectivity and Consequences of a Broad Concept of State Aid in Tax Matters, 9(4) European State Aid Law Quarterly 807 (2010).

López, J. *The Concept of State Aid under EU Law: From Internal Market to Competition and Beyond*, Oxford University Press, Oxford, 2015.

Luja, R. Assessment and Recovery of Tax Incentives in the EC and the WTO. A View on State Aids, Trade Subsidies and Direct Taxation. Doctoral thesis 29-30 and 53, University of Maastricht, Maastricht, 2003.

Luja, R. Fictional Interest Payments and Abuse of European Tax Law: New State Aid Challenges?, Blog entry of 12 March 2019, accessible under https://www.maastrichtuniversity.nl/blog/2019/03/fictional-interest-payments-and-abuse-european-tax-law-new-state-aid-challenges.

Luja, R. *Het wetsvoorstel Terugvordering staatssteun: het wordt navorderen en naheffen*, 160 Weekblad Fiscaal Recht, sec. 3 (2017).

Luja, R. *Reactie op internetconsultatie wetsvoorstel Terugvordering staatssteun*, art. 3, https://www.internetconsultatie.nl/wetterugvorderingstaatssteun/reactie/d9512d6d-f124-4a7e-bf790b259f7a175a (accessed 20 March 2019).

Luja, R. State Aid Benchmarking and Tax Rulings: Can We Keep It Simple?, in *State Aid Law and Business Taxation*, edited by I. Richelle, W. Schön and E. Traversa, Springer, 2016, p. 118.

Luja, R. Tax Treaties and State Aid: Some Thoughts, European Taxation 234-238 (2004).

Luja, R.H.C. Will the EU's State Aid Regime Survive BEPS?, 3 British Tax Review 379-390 (2015).

Lyal, R. Transfer Pricing Rules and State Aid, 38 Fordham International Law Journal 1017 (2015).

Maitrot de la Motte, A. 'The Recovery of the Illegal Fiscal State Aids: Tax Less to Tax More', 2 EC Tax Review 75-88 (2017).

Majone, G. Europe's 'Democratic Deficit': The Question of Standards, 4(1) European Law Journal 5-28 (1998).

Majone, G. Regulatory Legitimacy, in *Regulating Europe*, edited by G. Majone, Routledge, London and New York, 1996, pp. 284-301.

Martin, S. and P. Valbonesi. State Aid to Business, in *International Handbook on Industrial Policy*, edited by P. Bianchi and S. Labory, Edward Elgar, Cheltenham/Northampton, 2006, p. 134.

McDaniel, P. and S. Surrey (eds), *International Aspects of Tax Expenditures: A Comparative Study*, Kluwer Law and Taxation Publishers, Deventer, 1985, p. 9.

Merola, M. The Rebus of Selectivity in Fiscal Aid: A Nonconformist View on and Beyond Case Law, 39(4) World Competition 539 (2016).

Metselaar, A.J. and P.C. Adriaanse. Nut en noodzaak van het wetsvoorstel terugvordering staatssteun: Verslag van het LEGA Symposium op 19 januari 2011, 2 Tijdschrift voor Staatssteun 57, 60 (2011)

Metselaar, A.J. *Drie rechters en één norm: Handhaving van de Europese staatssteunregels voor de Nederlandse rechter en de grenzen van de nationale procedurele autonomie* (Kluwer 2016).

Metselaar, A.J. *Een vogel in de hand: nieuwe regels voor de terugvordering van staatssteun*, 3-4 Tijdschrift voor Staatssteun 110, 112 (2016).

Meyer, L. and P. Sanklecha. Introduction: Legitimacy, Justice and Public International Law. Three Perspectives on the Debate, in *Legitimacy, Justice and Public International Law*, edited by L. Meyer, Cambridge University Press, Cambridge, 2009, p. 2.

Micheau, C. *State Aid, Subsidy, and Tax Incentives under EU and WTO Law*, Alphen Aan Den Rijn, Kluwer Law International, 2014, pp. 38-40.

Micheau, C. Tax Selectivity in European Law of State Aid: Legal Assessment and Alternative Approaches, 40(3) European Law Review 323-348 (2015).

Mihayl, A. and H. Kirilov. *Bulgaria*, 189 (J.L. da Cruz Vilaça, C. Botelho Moniz, R. Leandro Vasconcelos and A. Saavedra, Taxation, State Aid and Distortions of Competition - XXVIII FIDE CONGRESS Congress Proceedings vol. 2, Almedina 2018).

Nanetti, F. and G. Mameli. The Creeping Normative Role of the EC Commission in the Twin-Track Struggle Against State Aids and Harmful Tax Competition, 11(4) EC Tax Review 185-191 (2002).

Netelenbos, B. *Political Legitimacy Beyond Weber: An Analytical Framework*, Palgrave Macmillan, London, 2016, pp. 82-83.

Nicolaides, P. Are National Courts Becoming an Extension of the Commission, 3 European State Aid Law Quarterly 409-413 (2014).

Ordonez-Solis, D. Waiting for National Judges in Infringement Proceedings on State Aid, 3 European State Aid Law Quarterly 377-394 (2017).

Ortino, F. *Basic Legal Instruments for the Liberalisation of Trade: A Comparative Analysis of EC and WTO Law*, Hart Publishing, Oxford and Portland Oregon, 2004, pp. 17-24.

Panayi, C. Limitations on Benefits and State Aid, European Taxation 91-93 (2004).

Peters, C. *On the Legitimacy of International Tax Law*, IBFD, Amsterdam, 2014.

Peters, C. Tax Policy Convergence and EU Fiscal State Aid Control: In Search of Rationality, 28(1) EC Tax Review 6-17 (2019).

Pistone, P. Smart Tax Competition and the Geographical Boundaries of Taxing Jurisdictions: Countering Selective Advantages Amidst Disparities, 40(2) Intertax 85-91 (2012).

Romariz, C. Revisiting Material Selectivity in EU State Aid Law - Or 'the Ghost of Yet-to-Come', 13(1) European State Aid Law Quarterly 46 (2014).

Rossi-Maccanico, P. Fiscal Aid, Tax Competition, and BEPS, Tax Notes International 857 et seq. (2014).

Rzotkiewicz, M. The General Principles of EU Law and Their Role in the Review of State Aid Put into Effect by Member States, 3 European State Aid Law Quarterly 464, 467-470 (2013)

Scharpf, F. *Community and Autonomy: Institutions, Policies, and Legitimacy in Multi-level Europe*, Campus Verlag, Frankfurt / New York, 2010.

Scharpf, F. Economic Integration, Democracy and the Welfare State, 4(1) Journal of European Public Policy 18-36 (1997).

Scharpf, F. The JDT Model: Context and Extensions, in *The EU's Decision Traps: Comparing Policies*, edited by G. Falkner, Oxford University Press, Oxford, 2011, pp. 217-236.

Scharpf, F. The Joint-Decision Trap Revisited, 44(4) Journal of Common Market Studies 845-864 (2006).

Schön, W. State Aid in the Area of Taxation, in *EU State Aids*, edited by L. Hancher, T. Ottervanger and P. Slot, Fourth Edition, Sweet & Maxwell, London, 2012.

Schön, W. Tax Competition in Europe - General Report, in *Tax Competition in Europe*, edited by W. Schön, IBFD Publications BV, Amsterdam, 2003.

Schön, W. Tax Legislation and the Notion of Fiscal Aid: A Review of 5 Years of European Jurisprudence, in *State Aid Law and Business Taxation*, edited by I. Richelle, W. Schön and E. Traversa, Springer Verlag Berlin and Heidelberg, 2016.

Schön, W. Taxation and State Aid Law in the European Union, 36 Common Market Law Review, 1999.

Scott, A. Cooperation and Good Faith: State Aid Rules and National Courts - Procedural and Interpretive Consequences, 3 European State Aid Law Quarterly 354-366 (2017).

Shuibhne, N. Introduction, in *Regulating the Internal Market*, edited by N. Shuibne, Edward Elgar Publishing, Cheltenham and Northampton, 2006, p. 1.

Snell, J. The Internal Market and the Philosophies of Market Integration, in *European Union Law*, edited by C. Barnard and S. Peers, Oxford University Press, Oxford, 2014, pp. 300-324.

Sohet, A.V. Nationale rechter moet niet-aangemelde maatregelen opschorten bij opening formele onderzoeksprocedure door Europese Commissie, 1 Tijdschrift voor Staatssteun 10, 12 (2014).

Spaak, P.-H. Intergovernmental Committee on European Integration. The Brussels Report on the General Common Market (abridged, English translation of document commonly called the Spaak Report) (June 1956).

Spector, D. The Economic Analysis of State Aid Control, in *Economic Analysis of State Aid Rules - Contributions and Limits*, edited by M. Merola and J. Derenne, Lexxicon, Berlin, 2007, pp. 7-27.

Staatssteun en economische activiteiten van de kerk - Marc Fierstra Nederlands Tijdschrift voor Europees Recht (NtER), 2017, p. 181-189

Steffek, J. The Legitimation of International Governance: A Discourse Approach, 9(2) European Journal of International Relations 253 (2003).

Struys, M.L. and H. Abbott. The Role of National Courts in State Aid Litigation, 28 E.L. Rev. 172 (2003).

Surrey, S. *Pathways to Tax Reform: The Concept of Tax Expenditures*, Harvard University Press, Cambridge, MA, 1973.
Szotek, P. Is the Council about to Confirm the Existence of an EU at Arm's Length Principle?, July 2017, Kluwer International Tax Blog.
Szudoczky, R. and J.L. van de Streek. Revisiting the Dutch Interest Box under the EU State Aid Rules and the Code of Conduct: When a 'Disparity' Is Selective and Harmful, 38 Intertax 272 (2010).
Szudoczky, R. Convergence of the Analysis of National Tax Measures under the EU State Aid Rules and the Fundamental Freedoms, (3) European State Aid Law Quarterly 370 (2016).
Szudoczky, R. Selectivity, Derogation, Comparison: How to Put Together the Pieces of the Puzzle in the State Aid Review of National Tax Measures?, in *EU Income Tax Law: Issues for the Years Ahead*, edited by D. Weber, IBFD, 2013, pp. 184-188.
Szyszcak, E. National Judges and Training in EU State Aid Law, 3 European State Aid Law Quarterly 470-475 (2017).
Tallberg, J. and M. Zürn. The Legitimacy and Legitimation of International Organizations: Introduction and Framework, The Review of International Organizations (https://doi.org/10.1007/s11558-018-9330-7).
Traversa, E. and A. Flamini. Fighting Harmful Tax Competition Through EU State Aid Law: Will the Hardening of Soft Law Suffice?, 14(3) European State Aid Law Quarterly 323-331 (2015)
Van den Brink, J. and W. den Ouden, noot onder RvS 15 april 2015, 28 AB Rechtspraak Bestuursrecht 1440, 1448 (nr. 10) (2015).
van der Ouderaa, E.A.G. *Staatssteun en de rol van de Nederlandse belastingrechter*, sec. 4.2 (L.J.A. Pieterse and R. Van Scharrenburg, Springende punten, Kluwer 2017).
van Slooten, G.J. *Het wetsvoorstel terugvordering staatssteun: een te kleine pleister op een veel te grote wonde?*, 6-7 Tijdschrift voor Formeel Belastingrecht, (2008).
Vanistendael, F. Fiscal Support Measures and Harmful Tax Competition, 9(3) EC Tax Review 156 (2000).
Verouden, V. and P. Werner. Introduction – The Law and Economics of EU State Aid Control, in *EU State Aid Control. Law and Economics*, edited by P. Werner and V. Verouden, Wolters Kluwer International B.V., Alphen aan den Rijn, 2017.
Wattel, P. Comparing Criteria: State Aid, Free Movement, Harmful Tax Competition and Market Distorting Disparities, in *State Aid Law and Business Taxation*, edited by I. Richelle, W. Schön and E. Traversa, Springer, Berlin and Heidelberg, 2016, pp. 59-71.
Wattel, P. Forum: Interaction of State Aid, Free Movement, Policy Competition and Abuse Control in Direct Tax Matters, 5(1) World Tax Journal 128-144 (2013).
Wattel, P. General EU Law Concepts and Tax Law, in *European Tax Law. Volume I – General Topics and Direct Taxation*, edited by P. Wattel, O. Marres and H. Vermeulen, Wolters Kluwer, Deventer, 2018, Chapter 3, p. 24.
Wattel, P. Introduction, in *European Tax Law. Volume I – General Topics and Direct Taxation*, edited by P.J. Wattel, O. Marres and H. Vermeulen, Student Edition, Wolters Kluwer, Deventer, 2018, p. 4.

Wattel, P. The Cat and the Pigeons: Some General Comments on (TP) Tax Rulings and State Aid after the Starbucks and Fiat Decisions, in State Aid Law and Business Taxation, edited by I. Richelle, W. Schön and E. Traversa, Springer, Berlin and Heidelberg, 2016, p. 34.

Weber, D.M. *Tax Avoidance and the EC Treaty Freedoms*, Kluwer Law International, Alphen aan den Rijn, 2005.

Weisbrot, M. Application of the Principle of Protection of Legitimate Expectations in Recovery of Unduly Paid Subsidies in the Context of Judicial Coherence in the European Union, 8 REALaw 347, 368-373 (2015);

Wittendorff, J. *Transfer Pricing and the Arm's Length Principle in International Tax Law*, Kluwer, 2010.

X, *Terugvordering staatssteun: Nota naar aanleiding van het verslag*, 17 Vakstudie Nieuws 4 (2018).

Zürn, M. A *Theory of Global Governance: Authority, Legitimacy, and Contestation*, Oxford University Press, Oxford, 2018, p. 69.

Table of Cases

European Commission

Decisions

Notices

Commission notice on the enforcement of State aid law by national courts, nr. 21a (2009), OJ C 85/1, 160
Commission notice on the enforcement of State aid law by national courts, nr. 35 and 40 (b) (2009), OJ C 85/1, 160
Commission notice on the enforcement of State aid law by national courts, nr. 35 (2009), OJ C 85/1, 161
Commission Notice on the notion of State aid as referred to in Art 107(1) of the Treaty on the Functioning of the European Union, C/2016/2946, OJ C 262, 19.7.2016, p. 1–50 [hereinafter: Notion of Aid Notice], para. 169, 55
Commission Notice on the notion of State aid as referred to in Article 107(1) of the Treaty on the Functioning of the European Union, C/2016/2946, OJ C 262, 19.7.2016, p. 1 et seq., para. 183, 90
Commission of the European Communities, First survey on state aids in the European Commission, section 72 and section 10.5 of the Technical Annex (Luxembourg: Office for Official Publications of the European Communities 1989), 17
Notice from the Commission Towards an effective implementation of Commission decisions ordering Member States to recover unlawful and incompatible State aid (2007/C 272/05), 131
Notice from the Commission Towards an effective implementation of Commission decisions ordering Member States to recover unlawful and incompatible State aid, nr. 22 (2007), OJ C 272/4, 160
Notice from the Commission Towards an effective implementation of Commission decisions ordering Member States to recover unlawful and incompatible State aid, nr. 70 (2007), OJ C 272/4, 178
Notice on the notion of the State aid as referred to in Article 107(1) of the Treaty on the Functioning of the European Union, OJ 2016 C 262, 117

Regulations

Commission Regulation (EC) 794/2004 implementing Council Regulation (EC) 659/1999 laying down detailed rules for the application of Article 93 of the EC Treaty, (21 April 2004), OJ L 140/1, 162
Art. 16 (2) Council Regulation (EU) 2015/1589 laying down detailed rules for the application of Article 108 of the Treaty on the Functioning of the European Union, (13 July 2015), OJ L 248/9, 161
Council Regulation (EC) 1/2003 of 16 December 2002 ont he implementation of the rules on competition laid down in Articles 81 and 82 of the Treaty, OJ 2003 L1.
Council Regulation (EU) 2015/1589 laying down detailed rules for the application of Article 108 of the Treaty on the Functioning of the European Union, (13 July 2015), OJ L 248/9, 160, 161
Council Regulation (EU) 2015/1589 laying down detailed rules for the application of Article 108 of the Treaty on the Functioning of the European Union, art. 17 (1)-(2) (13 July 2015), OJ L 248/9, 165

Communications

Directives

Other

WTO

Other reports

Advice Council of State, Parl.St. Kamer 2016-17, N° 54-2208/001, p. 167, 156

Advice of Legislation Section of the Council of State, Parl.St. Kamer 2016-17, N° 54-2208/001, p. 165, 150

Advice of the Legislation Section of the Council of State, Parl.St. Kamer 2016-17, N° 54-2208/001, p. 163, 150

Advies Raad van State en nader rapport Wijziging van het Burgerlijk Wetboek, de Algemene wet bestuursrecht en de Algemene wet inzake rijksbelastingen in verband met de tenuitvoerlegging van een beschikking van de Commissie van de Europese Gemeenschappen of een rechterlijke uitspraak inzake staatssteun, alsmede wijziging van het Burgerlijk Wetboek om de procedure voor het vaststellen van de wettelijke rente aan te passen (terugvordering staatssteun), 2 (2008), Kamerstukken II 2007-2008, nr. 31 418/4 (Advice Council of State), 168, 169

Advies Raad van State en nader rapport Wijziging van het Burgerlijk Wetboek, de Algemene wet bestuursrecht en de Algemene wet inzake rijksbelastingen in verband met de tenuitvoerlegging van eenbeschikking van de Commissie van de Europese Gemeenschappen of een rechterlijke uitspraak inzake staatssteun, alsmede wijziging van het Burgerlijk Wetboek om de procedure voor het vaststellen van de wettelijke rente aan te passen (terugvordering staatssteun), 3 (2008), Kamerstukken II 2007-2008, nr. 31 418/4 (Advice Council of State), 169

Besluit tot vaststelling van het tijdstip van inwerkingtreding van de wet van 21 februari 2018 houdende regels voor de terugvordering van staatssteun (Wet terugvordering staatssteun), (26 maart 2018), Staatsblad 2018 99, 171

Brief van de minister van Justitie en Veiligheid Wijziging van het Burgerlijk Wetboek, de Algemene wet bestuursrecht en de Algemene wet inzake rijksbelastingen in verband met de tenuitvoerlegging van een beschikking van de Commissie van de Europese Gemeenschappen of een rechterlijke uitspraak inzake staatssteun, alsmede wijziging van het Burgerlijk Wetboek om de procedure voor het vaststellen van de wettelijke rente aan te passen (terugvordering staatssteun), (2008), Kamerstukken II 2007-2008, nr. 31 418/6 (Letter of the Minister of Security and Justice), 166

Commissie Wetsvoorstellen van de Nederlandse Orde van Belastingadviseurs, *Commentaar op de internetconsultatie Regels voor de terugvordering van staatssteun (Wet terugvordering staatssteun)*, nr. 3.2, https://www.nob.net/sites/default/files/content/article/uploads/nob_commentaar_internetconsultatie_terugvordering_staatssteun.pdf (accessed 6 March 2019), 177

Commissie Wetsvoorstellen van de Nederlandse Orde van Belastingadviseurs, *Commentaar op het wetsvoorstel Regels voor de terugvordering van staatssteun (34 753)*, speerpunt 2, https://www.nob.net/system/files/content/article/uploads/nob_commentaar_terugvordering_staatssteun.pdf (accessed 6 March 2019), 173

Other

Press releases

EUCOTAX Series on European Taxation

(1) Peter HJ Essers, Guido JME de Bont & Eric CCM Kemmeren (eds), *The Compatibility of Anti-Abuse Provisions in Tax Treaties with EC Law*, 1998 (ISBN 90-411-9678-1).
(2) Gerard TK Meussen (ed.), *The Principle of Equality in European Taxation*, 1999 (ISBN 90-411-9693-5).
(3) Michael Lang (ed.), *Tax Treaty Interpretation*, 2001 (ISBN 90-411-9857-1).
(4) Pasquale Pistone, *The Impact of Community Law on Tax Treaties: Issues and Solutions*, 2002 (ISBN 90-411-9860-1).
(5) René Offermanns, *The Entrepreneurship Concept in a European Comparative Tax Law Perspective*, 2002 (ISBN 90-411-9887-3).
(6) Michael Lang & Mario Züger, *Settlement of Disputes in Tax Treaty Law*, 2002 (ISBN 90-411-9904-7).
(7) Carlo Pinto, *Tax Competition and EU Law*, 2003 (ISBN 90-411-9913-6).
(8) Michael Lang, Hans-Jörgen Aigner, Ulrich Scheuerle & Markus *Stefaner, CFC Legislation, Tax Treaties and EC Law*, 2004 (ISBN 90-411-2284-2).
(9) Mattias Dahlberg, *Direct Taxation in Relation to the Freedom of Establishment and the Free Movement of Capital*, 2005 (ISBN 90-411-2363-6).
(10) Michael Lang, Judith Herdin & Ines Hofbauer, *WTO and Direct Taxation*, 2005 (ISBN 90-411-2371-7).
(11) Dennis Weber, *Tax Avoidance and the EC Tray Freedoms: A Study of the Limitations under European Law for the Prevention of Tax Avoidance*, 2005 (ISBN 90-411-2402-0).
(12) Félix Alberto Vega Borrego, *Limitations on Benefits Clauses on Double Taxation Conventions*, 2005 (ISBN 90-411-2370-9).
(13) Michael Lang, Josef Schuch & Claus Staringer, *ECJ-Recent Developments in Direct Taxation*, 2006 (ISBN 90-411-2509-4).
(14) Reuven S. Avi-Yonah, James R. Hines Jr. & Michael Lang, *Comparative Fiscal Federalism. Comparing the European Court of Justice and the US Supreme Court's Tax Jurisprudence*, 2007 (ISBN 978-90-411-2552-1).
(15) Christiana HJI Panayi, *Double Taxation, Tax Treaties, Treaty-Shopping and the European Community*, 2007 (ISBN 978-90-411-2658-0).
(16) Dennis Weber, *The Influence of European Law on Direct Taxation: Recent and Future Developments*, 2007 (ISBN 978-90-411-2667-2).
(17) Michael Lang & Pasquale Pistone, *The EU and Third Countries: Direct Taxation*, 2007 (ISBN 978-90-411-2665-8).
(18) Oskar Henkow, *Financial Activities in European VAT: A Theoretical and Legal Research of the European VAT System and Preferred Treatment of Financial Activities*, 2007 (ISBN 978-90-411-2703-7).
(19) Michael Lang (ed.), *Tax Compliance Costs for Companies in an Enlarged European Community*, 2008 (ISBN 978-90-411-2666-5).

(20) Michael Lang (ed.), *Source versus Residence. Problems Arising from the Allocation of Taxing Rights in Tax Treaty Law and Possible Alternatives,* 2008 (ISBN 978-90-411-2763-1).
(21) Ioanna Mitroyanni, *Integration Approaches to Group Taxation in the European Internal Market,* 2008 (ISBN 978-90-411-2779-2).
(22) Rolf Eicke, *Tax Planning with Holding Companies. Repatriation of US Profits from Europe:Concepts, Strategies, Structures,* 2008 (ISBN978-90-411-2794-5).
(23) Peter Essers et al. (ed.), *The Influence of IAS/IFRS on the CCCTB, Tax Accounting, Disclosure and Corporate Law Accounting Concepts: 'A Clash of Cultures',* 2008 (ISBN 978-90-411-2819-5).
(24) Tonny Schenk-Geers, *International Exchange of Information and the Protection of Taxpayers,* 2009 (ISBN 978-90-411-3142-3).
(25) Raymond Adema, *UCITS and Taxation: Towards Harmonization of the Taxation of UCITS,* 2009 (ISBN 978-90-411-2839-3).
(26) Michael Lang, Jianwen Liu & Gongliang Tang (eds), *Europe–China Tax Treaties,* 2010 (ISBN 978-90-411-3216-1).
(27) Michael Lang, Pasquale Pistone, Josef Schuch & Claus Staringer (eds), *Procedural Rules in Tax Law in the Context of European Union and Domestic Law,* 2010 (ISBN 978-90-411-3376-2).
(28) Sjaak J.J.M. Jansen, *Fiscal Sovereignty of the Member States in an Internal Market: Past and Future,* 2011 (ISBN 978-90-411-3403-5).
(29) Dennis Weber & Bruno da Silva, *From Marks & Spencer to X Holding: The Future of Cross-Border Group Taxation,* 2011 (ISBN 978-90-411-3399-1).
(30) Claus Bohn Jespersen, *Intermediation of Insurance and Financial Services in European VAT,* 2011 (ISBN 978-90-411-3732-6).
(31) Sabine Heidenbauer, *Charity Crossing Borders: The Fundamental Freedoms' Influence on Charity and Donor Taxation in Europe,* 2011 (ISBN 978-90-411-3813-2).
(32) Michael Lang, et al., *The Future of Indirect Taxation: Recent Trends in VAT and GST Systems around the World,* 2012 (ISBN 978-90-411-3797-5).
(33) Harm van den Broek, *Cross-Border Mergers within the EU: Proposals to Remove the Remaining Tax Obstacles,* 2012 (ISBN 978-90-411-3824-8).
(34) Michael Lang, et al. (eds), *Tax Treaty Case Law around the Globe – 2011,* 2012 (ISBN 978-90-411-3876-7).
(35) Dennis Weber (ed.), *CCCTB: Selected Issues,* 2012 (ISBN 978-90-411-3872-9).
(36) Daniël Smit, *EU Freedoms, Non-EU Countries and Company Taxation,* 2012 (ISBN 978-90-411-4041-8).
(37) Rita de la Feria, *VAT Exemptions: Consequences and Design Alternatives,* 2013 (ISBN 978-90-411-3276-5).
(38) Karin Simader, *Withholding Taxes and the Fundamental Freedoms,* 2013 (ISBN 978-90-411-4842-1).
(39) Madeleine Merkx, *Establishments in European VAT,* 2013 (ISBN 978-90-411-4554-3).
(40) Carla De Pietro, *Tax Treaty Override,* 2014 (ISBN 978-90-411-5406-4).

(41) G.K. Fibbe & A.J.A. Stevens (eds), *Hybrid Entities and the EU Direct Tax Directives*, 2015 (ISBN 978-90-411-5942-7).
(42) Gerard Staats, *Personal Pensions in the EU*, 2015 (ISBN 978-90-411-5953-3).
(43) Michael Lang & Ine Lejeune (eds), *VAT/GST in a Global Digital Economy*, 2015 (ISBN 978-90-411-5952-6).
(44) Massimo Basilavecchia, Lorenzo del Federico & Pietro Mastellone (eds), *Tax Implications of Environmental Disasters and Pollution*, 2015 (ISBN 978-90-411-5611-2).
(45) Cristina Trenta, *Rethinking EU VAT for P2P Distribution*, 2015 (ISBN 978-90-411-6137-6).
(46) Marie Lamensch, Edoardo Traversa & Servaas van Thiel (eds), *Value Added Tax and the Digital Economy: The 2015 EU Rules and Broader Issues*, 2016 (ISBN 978-90-411-6612-8).
(47) Raffaele Petruzzi, *Transfer Pricing Aspects of Intra-Group Financing*, 2016 (ISBN 978-90-411-6732-3).
(48) Mario Grandinetti (ed.), *Corporate Tax Base in the Light of the IAS/IFRS and EU Directive 2013/34: A Comparative Approach*, 2016 (ISBN 978-90-411-6745-3).
(49) Bruno da Silva, *The Impact of Tax Treaties and EU Law on Group Taxation Regimes*, 2016 (ISBN 978-90-411-6905-1).
(50) Michael Lang, Alfred Storck & Raffaele Petruzzi (eds), *Transfer Pricing in a Post-BEPS World*, 2016 (ISBN 978-90-411-6710-1).
(51) Marta Papis-Almansa, *Insurance in European VAT: Current and Preferred Treatment in the Light of the New Zealand and Australian GST Systems*, 2017 (ISBN 978-90-411-8360-6).
(52) Wolfgang Speckhahn, *Real Estate Investment Trusts In Europe: Europeanising Tax Regimes*, 2017 (ISBN 978-90-411-8360-6).
(53) Frank J.G. Nellen, *Information Asymmetries in EU VAT*, 2017 (ISBN 978-90-411-8837-3).
(54) Erik Ros, *EU Citizenship and Direct Taxation*, 2017 (ISBN 978-90-411-8584-6).
(55) Werner Haslehner, Georg Kofler & Alexander Rust (eds), *EU Tax Law and Policy in the 21st Century*, 2017 (ISBN 978-90-411-8815-1).
(56) Claudia Sanò, *National Legal Presumptions and European Tax Law*, 2018 (ISBN 978-90-411-6613-5).
(57) Christoph Marchgraber, *Double (Non-)Taxation and EU Law*, 2018 (ISBN 978-90-411-9410-7).
(58) Dennis Weber & Jan van de Streek (eds), *The EU Common Consolidated Corporate Tax Base: Critical Analysis*, 2018 (ISBN 978-90-411-9233-2).
(59) Werner Haslehner (ed.), *Investment Fund Taxation: Domestic Law, EU Law, and Double Taxation Treaties*, 2018 (ISBN 978-90-411-9669-9).
(60) Jérôme Monsenego, *Selectivity in State Aid Law and the Methods for the Allocation of the Corporate Tax Base*, 2018 (ISBN 978-90-411-9413-8).
(61) José Manuel Almudí Cid, Jorge A. Ferreras Gutiérrez & Pablo A. Hernández González-Barreda (eds), *Combating Tax Avoidance in the EU: Harmonization and Cooperation in Direct Taxation*, 2019 (ISBN 978-94-035-0154-3).

(62) Werner Haslehner, Georg Kofler & Alexander Rust (eds), *Time and Tax: Issues in International, EU, and Constitutional Law*, 2019 (ISBN 978-94-035-0354-7).
(63) Nathalie Wittock, *Sales Promotion Techniques and VAT in the EU*, 2019 (ISBN 978-94-035-0861-0).
(64) Carla De Pietro (ed.), *New Perspectives on Fiscal State Aid: Legitimacy and Effectiveness of Fiscal State Aid Control*, 2019 (ISBN 978-94-035-1415-4).

www.ingramcontent.com/pod-product-compliance
Ingram Content Group UK Ltd.
Pitfield, Milton Keynes, MK11 3LW, UK
UKHW020807290926
15470UKWH00003B/1006

9 789403 514154